WILDERNESS REGIONS

MANAGING

John Chaffey

To Ruth,
who has accompanied me on all my ventures
into the wilderness areas of the world

Much of the material for this book was gathered on visits, during the last five years, to the wilderness regions within the text. Everywhere I found people willing to supply me with materials, and very helpful with their advice. In this country I would like to extend special thanks to Dr Julian Paren and his colleagues at the British Antarctic Survey for all their assistance with materials on a wilderness that it was not possible for me to visit. Dr Geoffrey Halliday, Sue Warn and Steve Frampton supplied me with most useful materials on a range of topics, and Professor Mike Morris readily helped me with ideas and information on biosphere reserves.

Julia Morris and Joanne Osborn at Hodders were cheerful and helpful editorial colleagues. Finally my thanks, as always, go to my wife Ruth. With me she trekked in the high Himalayas, trod the unseasonable snows of Alaska's North Slope in August, scaled the magnificent peaks of Torridon, felt frustration at not being allowed to climb Uluru, and experienced the exhilaration of the magnificent wilderness flights over Denali and Aoraki. At home, in Dorset, her language skills were invaluable in reviewing early drafts of the manuscript.

John Chaffey

Acknowledgements

The author and publisher thank the following for permission to reproduce material in this book:

Abrams and Leo Le Bon, Figure 2.2.8; Allen and Unwin, Figure 4.5.9; Arctic Power, Figure 6.3.10; Australian National Parks and Wildlife Service, 1991. Kakadu National Park Plan of Management, ANPWS, Canberra, Figure 5.4.10; Australian Surveying and Land Information Group (AUSLIG), Figures 3.7.8, 3.8.1, 3.8.5, 3.8.7, 4.7.8–10, source: Explore Antartica ©; British Antarctic Survey, Figures 2.6.2, 2.6.4, 3.8.6; Cambridge University Press, Figures 3.8.6 (MJ Hambrey & Jurg Alean), 3.8.8 (CSM Doake); Central Bank of Kenya, Figure 5.6.7; Collins Educational, Figure 4.4.23; Commission on Development and Environment for Amazonia, Figure 2.4.4; CSIRO, Figure 6.4.6 from *A guide to the Management of Mimosa pigra*, K L S Harley; Filter Press, Figure 1.1.4; Fiordland National Park, Figures 5.4.14–17; The Geographical Magazine, Figures 5.5.7, 5.6.2, 6.6.1, 7.1.4, 7.3.1; Geological Survey Bulletin, Figure 3.4.5; Longman, Figure 4.6.4; Northern Territorial Geological Survey, Figures 3.7.8, 5.4.6; Ordnance Survey, Figures 3.3.8, 5.3.4; Otago Daily Times, Figures 6.8.7, 7.1.1, Sid Scales; Oxford University Press, Figures 4.5.11–12, adapted from *The Geography of the Canadian North: Issues and Challenges*, Robert M

Bone. Copyright © Robert M Bone, 1992; Reader's Digest Association, Figure 3.6.8; RSPB, Figure 4.4.23; Santree, Figures 4.4.7–8; Swiss Foundation for Alpine Research, Figure 3.6.10; The Times, extract from 25 June 1989; United Nations Development Programme, Figure 2.4.4.

The publishers would like to thank the following for giving permission to reproduce copyright photographs in this book:

J Allen Cash, Figures 3.5.2, 3.5.4; Heather Angel, Figures 1.4.6, 4.5.7, 4.7.5, 4.7.6; Brian Rogers/Biofotos, Figure 1.4.5; David Chaffey, 3.3.5; Hutchison Library, Figures 2.2.7, 2.4.2, 2.5.4, 3.8.9d, 4.2.1, 4.4.27, 4.5.1b; NHPA, Figure 4.7.3; D C Money, Figures 2.1.1, 6.8.2; Science Photo Library, Figures 3.7.9, 3.8.2; Still Pictures, Figures 6.5.6, 6.7.2; Topham, Figure 2.2.3; Zefa, Figure 3.8.9a.

All other photos belong to the author.

Every effort has been made to contact the holders of copyright material but if any have been inadvertently overlooked, the publishers will be pleased to make the necessary alterations at the first opportunity.

Contents

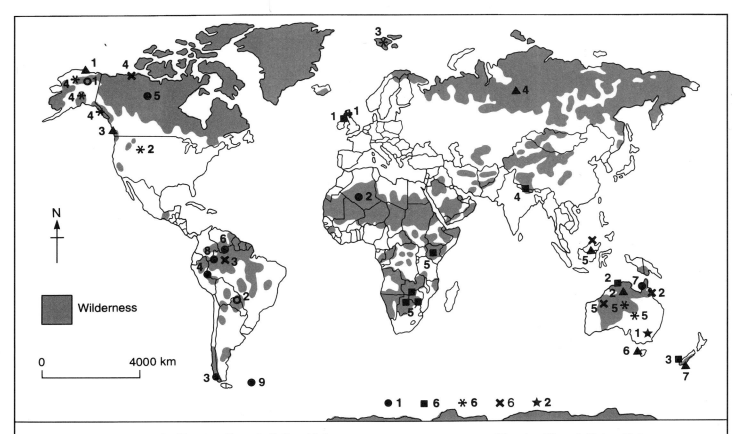

INTRODUCTION

Nearly one-third of the earth's land surface is wilderness, and it is of unique value to the world's inhabitants. Wilderness regions embrace certain qualities that need to be maintained and preserved for the future. Vast areas within the Arctic and Antarctic, the Sahara and the Australian outback, the Amazon rainforest and the empty lands of Botswana and Namibia are still relatively untouched and undeveloped. The surface of some remain unexplored, although satellite imagery now gives us a basic knowledge of even the most remote areas. Yet these wilderness areas are under increasing threat from a variety of sources. Global changes in the atmosphere and oceans may well endanger large expanses of wilderness. Pressure to develop resources of outstanding global importance in the wilderness regions will pose problems for indigenous groups, national governments and the international community. Awareness of the need for carefully planned and sensitively sustained management of these areas is emerging as an important theme at all levels. The conservation of wilderness quality, and managing these regions for a sustainable future are important goals which demand not only vision, co-operation and enlightened attitudes, but also adequate funding for research and regeneration projects.

Wilderness qualities are not easy to define. Areas that are untouched have a certain pristine quality, particularly apparent in regions such as the South Polar Plateau or the empty lands of southern Saudi Arabia. The vastness of their huge open spaces is another quality that is distinctive, yet the more confined space of the Amazonian rainforest, or the mulga scrub of Australia possess a genuine wilderness quality of different character. Lack of human settlement also distinguishes wilderness regions, and contributes towards the feeling of emptiness, although it has to be remembered that certain indigenous peoples, such as the Aborigines of the Australian Outback, and the Native Americans of the Amazon rainforest are a constituent part of the wilderness system in the areas that they live.

Wilderness regions possess clear values for people. It is often said that wilderness fulfills a basic spiritual need in people: a place to visit where tranquillity and emptiness reveal new perspectives and yield new experiences. Elements of urban-based populations increasingly seek refreshment of spirit and renewal of energy through visits to locations such as the high Himalayas or the National Parks of Alaska. Apart from the spiritual value of wilderness, these regions offer potential for research in a number of disciplines. Increasing understanding of the world's weather and ocean systems results from investigations and research in Antarctica, a '*Continent for Science*'. Research into the structure and functions of ecosystems in the rainforest of Amazonia or in the tundra lands of the Arctic yields data and understanding that has applications in many fields of science. Work on glaciology in the Antarctic, and in Greenland, on hydrology in the tropical rainforests of Brunei and in northern Lapland widens the frontiers of understanding in particular research projects. Antarctica has also been referred to as a '*laboratory for diplomacy*', where international co-operation on a range of issues, from mineral activities to seal conservation, has been seen to be effective.

The landscapes and ecosystems of wilderness areas provide the global population with a rich and varied heritage. Wilderness landscapes exist on different scales, from the relatively small-scale ice-covered plateau of the Jotunheim in Norway to the endless expanses of the Greenland ice sheet, from the remote and rocky Simpson Desert in Australia to the vast dune fields and gravel flats of the western Sahara. Wildlife and plants in wilderness ecosystems represent another aspect of heritage. The protection of endangered species and biodiversity within these systems represent challenges for management both now and in the future. It is also important that the role of indigenous communities within these systems is recognised so that the essential function of, for instance, the Aborigine fire regimes in Kakadu National Park in Australia's Northern Territory, is properly understood.

Wildernesses are, however, increasingly under threat. As known natural resources become increasingly exhausted, it is inevitable that mineral deposits, forests, lakes and rivers in wilderness regions come increasingly under close scrutiny by governments, and other national and international organisations. Exploitation of the natural resources of wilderness regions is not new: much of the spirit of the frontier in the west of the United States in the nineteenth century stemmed from the search for gold and other minerals in what was then the wilderness of the Rockies and their intermontane plateaux; the deserts of Chile and parts of the Australian outback are littered with old mining camps. Parts of the Siberian North have undergone development for minerals and timber under the former Soviet Regime, and scant attention has been paid to a sustainable future. The international tourist industry looks increasingly towards wilderness areas as zones to be exploited for new 'experiences' and 'adventures'.

Management of the resources of wilderness areas emerges as a key theme in their future development. A parallel strand in the future of wildernesses is the role played by various interest and pressure groups, such as the Sierra Club in the United States and the Wilderness Society in Australia. Indeed the latter groups have often emerged as important influences in the way that management policies have been shaped and modified. It would appear that most types of resource development in the wildernesses of the more economically developed countries (MEDCs) now operate under increasingly strict environmental controls. Protected areas, such as National Parks, and World Heritage areas, place very strict limitations on most kinds of development. In less economically developed countries (LEDCs) it seems that the idea of sustainable development is gaining ground, but has yet to be universally acknowledged.

The future of the world's wilderness regions possesses the potential for conflict. Awareness of their spiritual, ecological and environmental value has certainly reached new levels in the second half of the twentieth century. Equally the demand on wilderness resources is likely to increase. International recognition of the value of wilderness is nowhere more important than in Antarctica, and genuine co-operation has achieved much. In other wilderness regions, set within a national context, the future is less clear, but sustainable development must remain a substantive goal.

1
THE WILDERNESS CONCEPT AND WILDERNESS REGIONS

What would the world be, once bereft
Of wet and of wildness? Let them be left,
O let them be left, wildness and wet;
Long live the weeds and the wilderness yet.
Gerard Manley Hopkins

KEY IDEAS

■ Wilderness regions are remote, possess a harsh physical environment, and generally carry little or no population.
■ Wilderness regions may be seen as a part of a continuum: from areas totally dominated by natural systems to those dominated by human systems.
■ Wilderness regions have been defined in different ways. Most definitions stress their remoteness and lack of population.
■ Wilderness regions can be classified according to the biomes within which they occur.
■ Remoteness in wilderness regions is a function of accessibility, and the development of new routes and changes in transport technology can reduce remoteness.

1.1 Some images of wilderness

FIGURE 1.1.1 Mount Connor, the Australian Outback

FIGURE 1.1.2 The Assynt Wilderness, North West Scotland (*right*)

FIGURE 1.1.3 Cordillera Real, the High Andes, from Lake Titicaca (*far right*)

'Dawn broke to find the landscape had been coated with a layer of snow during the night. The scenery was magnificent: down the valley Loch na Sealga lay ringed with white mountains, whilst across the glen Beinn Dearg Mor rose majestically, its triple peaks cloaked in a garb of white. It was a scene of utter peace and beauty ...'
David Bellamy, *Painting the Northern Giants in The Wild Places of Britain*

'Gradually the Otway Massif and the peaks of the distant mountains, the Trans-Antarctic Range, floated into view. This massive bastion, that effectively dams a mile deep ocean of ice is 2000 miles long and 200 miles wide. ... The scale of rock and ice is massive, the pent-up power of Nature threatening, the jumble of gigantic tributary glaciers, contorted ice-falls and deep hidden valleys more grandiose than anywhere on earth.'
Ranulph Fiennes, *Mind over Matter*, his crossing of the Antarctic Continent

'Amazonia evokes all manner of images. Of an "endless" sea of vegetation, usually tangled. Of creatures teeming and unknown, fascinating at a distance but often fearful at close quarters. Of landscapes laden with moisture, and daily downpours as the norm. Of a giant climatic flywheel, moderating weather patterns far and wide. And finally, of a last wild region that is to be tamed by pioneering man.'
Dr Norman Myers, *Rainforests, Land use Options for Amazonia*

'When one speaks of the desert, one inevitably thinks of the Sahara. Is it because of the immensity of its empty and flat spaces? Is it because of its extreme aridity? Or is it because of its lost civilisations? These three reasons clearly identify the distinctiveness of the Sahara.'
Pierre Rognon, *Le Sahara, Biographie d'un desert*

'We were sampling a unique moment in our lives. Down and over into the brown plains of Tibet a purple shadow of Everest was projected for something like 200 miles. On these north and east sides there was a sense of wildness and remoteness, almost untouchability.'
Dougal Haston, on reaching the summit of Everest in Chris Bonington, *Everest the Hard Way*

FIGURE 1.1.4 The Great Alone

Were you ever out in the Great Alone, when the moon was awful clear,
And the icy mountains hemmed you in with a silence you could almost hear,
With only the howl of a timber wolf, and you camped there in the cold,
A half-dead thing in a stark dead world, clean mad for the muck called gold,
While high overhead, green yellow and red, the North Lights swept in bars? –
Then you've a haunch what the music meant ... hunger and night and the stars.
Robert W Service, Alaska's best known poet

'The mist lifted to show forests filled with tall beeches, poplars and a few firs ... Slowly, as we watched, the scenery changed and we entered the **taiga** for the first time, the primeval uncut virgin forest. Gloomy country sunk in swamp and shadow and very cold, where the trees are all firs ...'
Eric Newby, *The Big Red Train Ride*

Student Activity 1.1

1 The extracts from the writings of travellers, together with the photographs in Figures 1.1.1–3 · present a series of images of wilderness.
   Use a matrix similar to the one in Figure 1.1.5 to show how the extracts and photographs reveal a set of wilderness qualities. Decide on up to six wilderness qualities, after discussion with others.
2 Considering the different examples, to what extent can scale affect wilderness qualities?

WILDERNESS AUTHOR/LOCATION	WILDERNESS QUALITIES					
	1	2	3	4	5	6
David Bellamy						
Robert Service						
Eric Newby						
Ranulph Fiennes						
Norman Myers						
Pierre Rognon						
Dougal Haston						
Mount Connor						
Assynt						
Cordillera Real, Bolivia						

FIGURE 1.1.5 Wilderness quality matrix

1.2 The concept of wilderness

Wilderness regions appear to be remote, experience harsh physical conditions, and are therefore, for the most part uninhabited, except for small groups of indigenous peoples. Some would add that the very size, remoteness and forbidding nature of many wilderness regions provide an opportunity for spiritual refreshment for those that wish to experience wholly natural environments untouched by humans. Ecologists would point to wilderness areas being of inherent value for purely scientific reasons.

1 The need to maintain a **gene pool** of wild organisms to ensure the maintenance of genetic variety, particularly in regions like the tropical rainforests.

2 The need to retain wild areas so that animal communities can remain in their natural environments. Large wilderness areas such as the North Slope of Alaska enable research into migration patterns of caribou to be successfully pursued.

3 Wholly natural systems that still exist in wilderness regions can be used as control systems for comparison with managed or mismanaged systems elsewhere.

The concept of wilderness is best approached through establishing a **continuum** from areas that are totally dominated by natural systems to those that function principally as human systems. This continuum is illustrated in Figure 1.2.1, originally used in compiling a National Wilderness Inventory Handbook in Australia.

In the diagram a wilderness quality continuum and a human modification continuum are shown, together with related levels of wilderness quality, and the range of environments that result from the interaction of the two. The ideas embodied within the diagram can be interpreted on a number of different scales from regional, through national to

global. For example Dartmoor is sometimes referred to as the last natural wilderness in the south of England, although only the central remote parts of the Moor would qualify for wilderness status. A continuum such as the one shown in Figure 1.2.1 could be established between the centre of Plymouth and the remotest areas of Dartmoor (see Figure 1.2.2). Over a much larger area a similar continuum can be traced in South Australia (Figures 1.2.3–4).

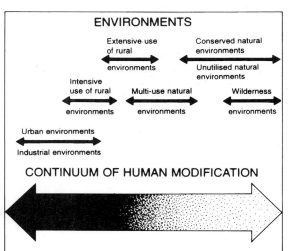
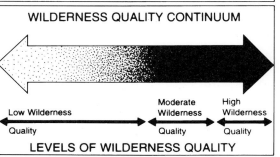

FIGURE 1.2.1 The wilderness continuum

FIGURE 1.2.2 Plymouth
Dartmoor continuum

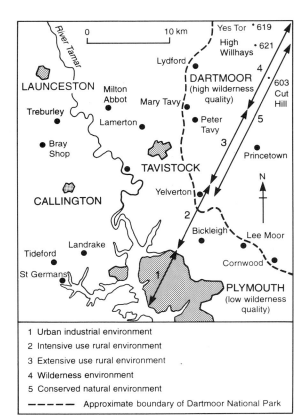

1 Urban industrial environment
2 Intensive use rural environment
3 Extensive use rural environment
4 Wilderness environment
5 Conserved natural environment
- - - - - Approximate boundary of Dartmoor National Park

FIGURE 1.2.3 (*far right*)
Wilderness south of
Coober Pedy, South
Australia

FIGURE 1.2.4 (*below*)
Wilderness continuum in
South Australia

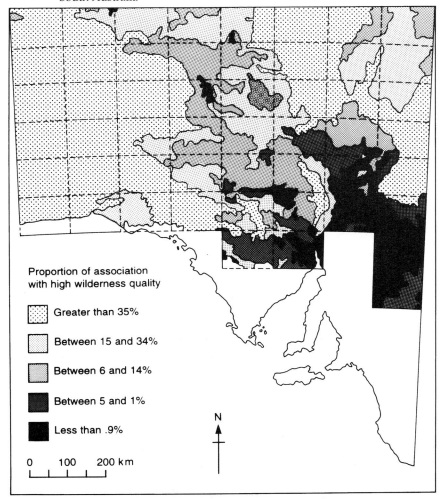

Proportion of association
with high wilderness quality

Greater than 35%

Between 15 and 34%

Between 6 and 14%

Between 5 and 1%

Less than .9%

0   100   200 km

Student Activity 1.2

1 Select any two areas, on approximately the same scales as the two examples used above, and draw maps/diagrams to illustrate the continuum between urban environment and wilderness.
2 Draw a diagram to show how a global continuum between urban/industrial environments and wilderness environments might look. Annotate your diagram with appropriate examples.

At the end of Section 1.1 (Images of Wilderness) you were required to identify wilderness qualities revealed in the comments of travellers and the photographs. It will be useful to compare your findings with the range of wilderness qualities used in mapping wildernesses in Australia. The Australian National Wilderness Inventory used four wilderness quality indicators to represent two essential characteristics of wilderness: remoteness and naturalness. The four quality indicators are:
■ 'remoteness from settlement – how remote a site is from places of permanent human occupation;
■ remoteness from access – how remote a site is from established access routes;
■ apparent naturalness – the degree to which a site is free from the permanent structures associated with modern technological society;
■ biophysical naturalness – the degree to which a site is free from biophysical disturbance caused by the influence of modern technological society.'
Source: *The National Wilderness Inventory*, Lesslie, Taylor and Maslen in *Wilderness – The Future*, Envirobook.

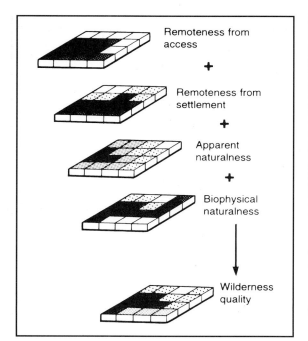

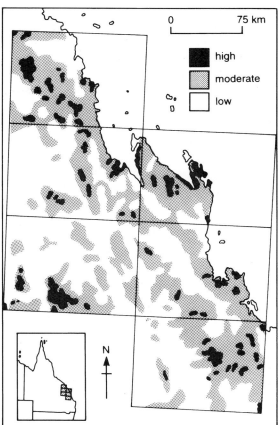

FIGURE 1.2.5 (*far left*)
Sieving technique

The level of wilderness quality is obtained by using a **sieving technique** as indicated in Figure 1.2.5. A completed map for the Shoalwater Bay area of Queensland is shown in Figure 1.2.6.

FIGURE 1.2.6 Wilderness quality: Shoalwater Bay, Australia

1.3 Defining, locating and classifying wilderness regions

FIGURE 1.3.1 Remaining wilderness areas, world-wide

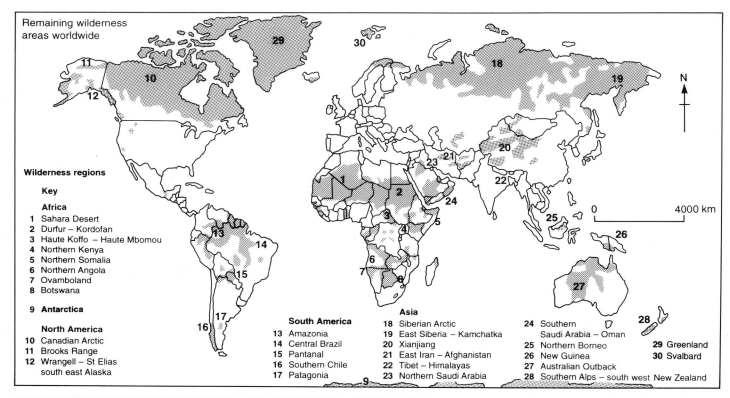

Remaining wilderness areas worldwide

Wilderness regions

Key

Africa
1 Sahara Desert
2 Durfur – Kordofan
3 Haute Koffo – Haute Mbomou
4 Northern Kenya
5 Northern Somalia
6 Northern Angola
7 Ovamboland
8 Botswana

9 **Antarctica**

North America
10 Canadian Arctic
11 Brooks Range
12 Wrangell – St Elias
    south east Alaska

South America
13 Amazonia
14 Central Brazil
15 Pantanal
16 Southern Chile
17 Patagonia

Asia
18 Siberian Arctic
19 East Siberia – Kamchatka
20 Xianjiang
21 East Iran – Afghanistan
22 Tibet – Himalayas
23 Northern Saudi Arabia

24 Southern
    Saudi Arabia – Oman
25 Northern Borneo
26 New Guinea
27 Australian Outback
28 Southern Alps – south west New Zealand

29 Greenland
30 Svalbard

FIGURE 1.3.2 Gebel
Shayib el Banat

An alternative to mapping wilderness areas by recognition of wilderness qualities is to use a definition of wilderness as the starting point. In the late 1980s a reconnaissance level inventory of all world wilderness regions was attempted. Jet Navigation Charts (JNCs) at a scale of 1:2 000 000 were used to plot and record data on wilderness units. Only blocks of more than 400 000 ha were identified (Figure 1.3.1). This area limit was imposed simply to make the project manageable and inevitably placed something of a restriction on the delimitation of smaller areas of wilderness. In producing this inventory the basic definition of wilderness used in the 1964 Wilderness Act in the USA was adopted, i.e. land that *'generally appears to have been affected primarily by the forces of nature, with the imprints of man's works substantially unnoticeable'*. (see Figure 1.3.2, the Gebel Shayib el Banat in Upper Egypt, and Figure 1.3.3, the south east Greenland Ice Cap, both parts of major wilderness areas). J Michael McCloskey, Chairman of the Sierra Club in 1990, qualified the above definition:

FIGURE 1.3.4 (*far right*)
Percentage of wilderness areas, by countries

FIGURE 1.3.3 South East
Greenland Ice Cap

'It is an area where modern man and his works do not dominate the landscape, where human influence is limited. Under this definition there is no requirement that an area be absolutely untouched; few such areas exist.

Most simply, wilderness is land without permanent human settlements or roads, and is land that is not regularly cultivated or heavily and continuously grazed. It is likely, however, that most of the land has been lightly used and occupied by indigenous peoples who practised traditional ways of life.'

Figure 1.3.1 shows the distribution of wilderness areas world-wide, using the definition above. The study found almost 4800 million ha (48 069 951 km²) of wilderness in over 1000 tracts) – approximately one-third of the world's land area. Figure 1.3.4 shows the ten countries that have the highest percentage of wilderness.

COUNTRY	% OF WILDERNESS
Greenland	99
Canada	65
Mauritania	68
Algeria	58
Sudan	32
Russia	32
Australia	30
Saudia Arabia	28
Brazil	24
China	24

Antarctica, as a continent, is not included above but clearly would have a percentage of almost 100.

Student Activity 1.3

1 The Wilderness Society of Australia has defined wilderness in the following way.

'A wilderness area is a large tract of land remote at its core from access and settlement, substantially unmodified by modern technological society or capable of being restored to the state, and of sufficient size to make practicable the long-term protection of its natural systems.'

Consider carefully this definition of wilderness. It differs substantially from the one used by the team that produced the world-wide inventory of wilderness regions. What are the important differences, and what are their principal implications for the definition of wilderness regions?

2 Discuss some of the difficulties that would be encountered in plotting wilderness regions using the definition in the USA Wilderness Act. What additional difficulties would arise in using the wilderness definition of the Wilderness Society of Australia?

3 Consider the distribution of wilderness regions shown in Figure 1.3.1. What appear to be the main reasons for the distribution of wilderness areas as shown on the map?

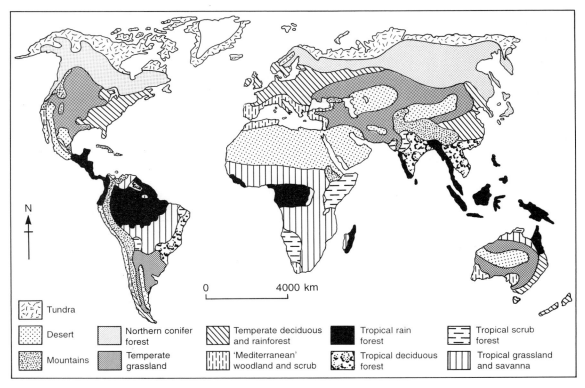

FIGURE 1.3.5 World biomes

Legend:

- Tundra
- Desert
- Mountains
- Northern conifer forest
- Temperate grassland
- Temperate deciduous and rainforest
- 'Mediterranean' woodland and scrub
- Tropical rain forest
- Tropical deciduous forest
- Tropical scrub forest
- Tropical grassland and savanna

0   4000 km

FIGURE 1.3.6 (*below*) Classification of wildernesses

BIOME \\ SCALE	TROPICAL RAINFOREST	TROPICAL GRASSLAND/ SAVANNA	DESERT	TEMPERATE GRASSLAND	NORTHERN CONIFEROUS FOREST	TUNDRA	MOUNTAIN	ICE CAP
Small scale	Belalong	Amboseli (Kenya)	Nevada (USA)	Patagonia	Vancouver Island	Denali (Alaska)	Fisherfield Forest (North West Scotland)	Vatnajokull (Iceland)
Medium scale	Gabon Congo (Brazzaville)	Pantanal (seasonal wetland)	Oman	Kazakhstan Steppes	Tongass (South East Alaska)	North Slope (Alaska)	Brooks Range (Alaska)	Svalbard (Spitzbergen)
Large scale	Amazonia	Northern Angola	Sahara	Xinjiang (China)	Eastern Siberia	Northern Arctic Fringe Siberia	Himalayas	Antarctica

Patterns on Figure 1.3.1 give some important indications of the manner in which wilderness regions might be classified according to the USA Wilderness Act (remembering that only wilderness areas in excess of 400 000 ha were included). There appears to be some latitudinal element in the distribution of wildernesses, and it is therefore useful to compare the wilderness map with one of the distribution of the major world **biomes** (Figure 1.3.5) in which latitude also plays an important part. It would appear that the most useful initial classification of wildernesses could be based on the biomes within which they appear. Such a classification, with appropriate examples is shown in Figure 1.3.6.

The world map of wilderness areas only includes wilderness areas in excess of more than 400 000 ha. Many smaller wilderness areas exist and are particularly important, since many of them are afforded some degree of protection, largely but not solely because of their size.

McCloskey makes a useful comparison between the mapped wilderness areas and existing protected areas. Protection is afforded to the different wilderness 'realms' as shown in Figure 1.3.7.

FIGURE 1.3.7 Protected wildernesses

REALM	% PROTECTED
Arctic realm	18
Afrotropical realm	20
South American	14
Australian	13

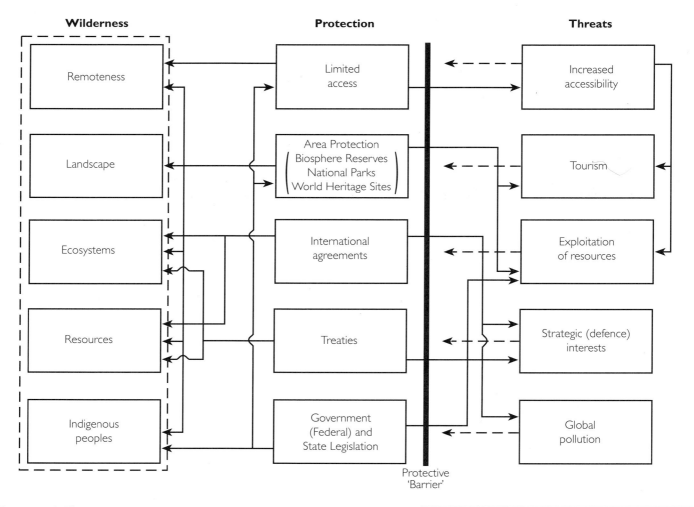

Wilderness	Protection	Threats
Remoteness	Limited access	Increased accessibility
Landscape	Area Protection (Biosphere Reserves National Parks World Heritage Sites)	Tourism
Ecosystems	International agreements	Exploitation of resources
Resources	Treaties	Strategic (defence) interests
Indigenous peoples	Government (Federal) and State Legislation	Global pollution

Protective 'Barrier'

FIGURE 1.3.8 Threats to wildernesses and possible protection

Overall, less than 20 per cent of the remaining wilderness area is protected. Wilderness areas smaller than 400 000 ha are included in the total for protected areas and, in reality, the total protected areas within the inventory may be quite small, e.g. within the African wildernesses the protected area may be as low as 7 per cent. Clearly there is opportunity to protect more land in large blocks. Figure 1.3.8 shows some of the threats to wilderness areas and their various components. Possible measures of protection are also shown.

Student Activity 1.4

1 Discuss some of the problems that might be encountered in defining wilderness areas in Britain.
2 Is protection of wilderness areas more or less difficult in small countries like Britain, compared to the large-scale wildernesses mapped in the examples in this section?

1.4 Remoteness and accessibility

It is often said that the concept of wilderness is a relative one. Since remoteness is a major feature of wilderness, then this very isolation may be challenged by improved accessibility. Many of the large remaining wilderness areas have seen considerable improvements in accessibility in the second half of the twentieth century. Amazonia is now crossed by several major highways, albeit the result of the geopolitical need for greater security within the northern states and territories of Brazil, and the stimulus they would give to economic development (see Figure 2.5.8, page 29).

Much of the Arctic has become far more accessible by air, not only through the establishment of regular flights to such locations as Prudhoe Bay on Alaska's North Slope but also through the supply of remote mining camps and survey parties by helicopter and specially adapted aircraft. Many Antarctic bases rely on supply by air from bases in the southern continents (see Figure 5.7.1, page 93). Railways have a longer history of making wilderness areas more accessible, although often they have been built for the specific purpose of developing mineral deposits. This was the case in western Australia, the Canadian and Siberian Arctic and parts of the Sahara, but exhaustion of the mineral resource often leads to closure of the railway. Waterways provided the only means of access to wilderness areas for initial exploration, and they still retain much of their importance today. Finally modern satellite communications, although not improving accessibility, have done much to remove the feeling of remoteness in wilderness regions. Two case studies illustrate the way in which new routes can improve accessibility to wilderness areas, but can cause concern over less desirable ecological effects.

The Dalton Highway: Alaska's wilderness road

Figure 1.4.1 shows the route of the Dalton Highway in northern Alaska. It runs for 666 km from Livengood, some 127 km north of Fairbanks, to Deadhorse, the supply centre for the Prudhoe Bay oil fields on the North Slope of Alaska. It crosses some of the most spectacular wilderness country in North America (see Figure 1.4.2), traversing the Brooks Range and the tundra of the North Slope before reaching Deadhorse. It was originally built in 1974 to support the construction of the Trans-Alaska Pipeline, which runs from Prudhoe Bay to the ice-free port of Valdez on the south coast of Alaska.

The Highway passes through a variety of landscapes, which illustrate different aspects of wilderness. From Livengood it passes through the Yukon lowlands, mantled with a forest of white and black spruce, willow, birch and aspen. It threads through the valleys of the Middle Fork and the Dietrich Rivers to cross the remote and forbidding Brooks Range through the Atigun Pass. As the Highway emerges from Atigun it passes between the Gates of the Arctic National Park to the west, and the Alaska National Wildlife Refuge to the east, and it then traverses the empty lands of the tundra with their distinctive landforms, flora and fauna. Deadhorse, at the northern terminus of the Highway, acts as a supply and service centre for the oil fields.

Commercial traffic supplying the oil fields operates at levels of some 15 000 trucks a year. Progressively more and more of the Highway has been opened to 'civilian' traffic. Originally, this traffic was only allowed as far as the Yukon River bridge, but was later allowed as far as Disaster Creek, with the visit to the point where the Highway crosses the Arctic Circle being a particularly popular one. Beyond Coldfoot there are no service facilities, apart from the small store at Wiseman, 20 km further on. Driving over the Atigun Pass, and through the North Slope can be extremely hazardous, with no recovery facilities or services available. Some tourist companies operate trips as far as Deadhorse, with visits to the oil field installations included. In August 1994 the Alaska Supreme Court made a unanimous ruling that the

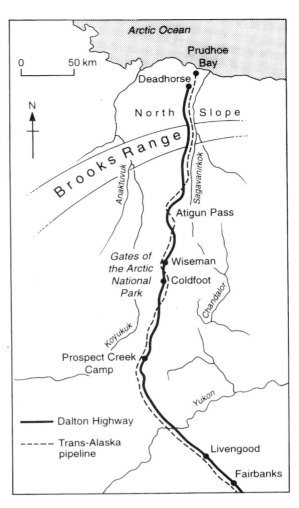

FIGURE 1.4.1 The Dalton Highway

FIGURE 1.4.2 Atigun Pass, Brooks Range

total length of the Dalton Highway could be open to the public, subject to Alaska State revealing the costs that would be involved.

Previous announcements in 1991 of a plan to open the Dalton Highway to the public brought immediate disapproval from North Slope Borough, and the Fairbanks-based Tanana Chiefs Conference. Typical of the opposition that still exists to the opening of the whole of the Dalton is the comment from Alaskan naturalist Jim Chumbley.

FIGURE 1.4.3 *Fairbanks Daily News-Miner*, 27 August 1994

Flooding washes out highway

River and creek flooding washed out the Dalton Highway in six spots Friday, stranding tourists and truckers at Coldfoot.

More than 4 inches of rain has fallen at Coldfoot since Tuesday, swelling a number of creeks feeding the Koyukuk River along the Dalton Highway.

About 60 tourists and 10 truckers were holed up Friday night at the Coldfoot Inn.

Alyeska trucker Jim Swenson, who has been driving the Dalton Highway for nearly 20 years, said he had never seen the Koyukuk so high.

"It's the worst I've ever seen it," Swenson said. "The bridges are right to the max."

On Friday night the highway was closed in four areas south of Coldfoot and two areas to the north.

Swenson, who was forced into cele-brating his 48th birthday with other truckers rather than with his wife in Fairbanks, said his was the last vehicle to cross the road near Nutirwik Creek at Mile 227 of the Dalton. The water reached well over the tires of his 18-wheeler.

"They closed the road right after we went through it," he said. "It's pretty nasty."

In Coldfoot the only way to get to the airport is with a front-end loader, said News-Miner correspondent Jan Thacker.

The Koyukuk is normally a river full of islands and sloughs, Thacker said.

"Now, it's probably as big as the Yukon," she said. "It's just a huge river right now."

Rain was still falling Friday night.

"The permafrost is so close to ground level that there's no place for the water to go. It just sits on top," Thacker said.

An area of the Dalton Highway was washed out on Aug. 19 at Rosie Creek, Mile 170, injuring a truck driver who drove his rig into a 25-foot deep washout in the highway.

State Department of Transportation workers dug a deep culvert last week at Rosie Creek, but even that looked as if it was about to be washed out Friday, Thacker said.

"The road is in incredibly bad shape," she said.

Another inch of rain was expected to fall in the area over Friday night. Rain was expected to stop as two cold fronts moved into the area early Saturday morning, said a National Weather Service forecaster.

Fairbanks Daily News-Miner,
27 August 1994

FIGURE 1.4.4 The Hidrovia Project

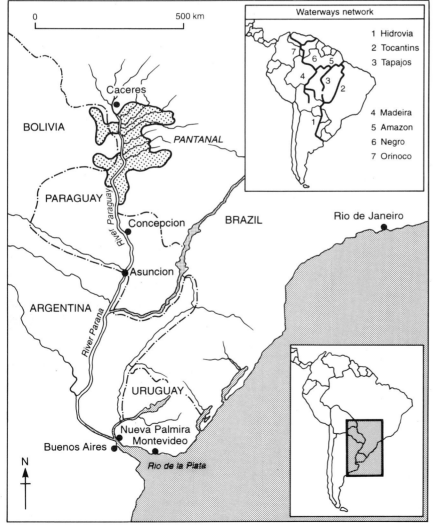

'Some say that there should be easy means of access and visitor facilities because the Gates of the Arctic National Park in the Brooks Range is taxpayer-supported. Still others think that all of this land should be thrown open to any kind of exploitation, anywhere. Since the 1980 Alaska Lands Act was passed, they have accused Washington of locking up Alaska by reclassifying 42 million hectares of federal land for conservation purposes. I think that this whole far north area is a national treasure and exploitation should be made as difficult as possible. Such wilderness has to be preserved at all costs.'

Evidence of the hazards of travelling the Dalton Highway is shown in the article from the Fairbanks Daily News-Miner in Figure 1.4.3.

Student Activity 1.5

1 Use the article in Figure 1.4.3. to articulate some of the arguments against opening the Highway for public use.

2 How far do you agree with the comments of the naturalist, Jim Chumbley?

The Hidrovia Project: opening up the Parana–Paraguay system

The aim of the Hidrovia Project is to improve navigation on the Parana–Paraguay system (3400 km in length) shown in Figure 1.4.4. Much of the present channel is unsafe for shipping or impassable, by virtue of its meandering route, and variable depth. Although much of the lower courses of both of the Rivers Parana and Paraguay run through areas that would hardly qualify as wilderness regions, it is in the upper parts of its course that the Paraguay runs through the wetlands of the Pantanal (see Figure 1.4.5). This huge wilderness, shared between Paraguay, Bolivia and Brazil, possesses one of the richest and most fragile ecosystems in the continent. Much of the Pantanal is only 100–200 m above sea level. It is surrounded by uplands and the seasonal runoff from these surrounding areas causes much flooding of the low-lying Pantanal. During the wet season animals cluster on the isolated **cordilheiras**, patches of higher ground above flood level. The floodwaters are particularly rich in fish life, which becomes increasingly concentrated in ponds as the floodwaters recede. As the lagoons and marshes dry out fresh growth of grass begins. Within its swamp forests and grasslands there are 658 species of birds in the Pantanal, including rare toucans, macaws, kingfishers and hawks, more than 1100 species of butterflies and 400 species of fish. Thirteen endangered species of mammals, including the marsh deer, the giant otter, the jaguar and the giant anteater also inhabit the region (see Figure 1.4.6).

It is likely that the Hidrovia project will disrupt the seasonal variations in the levels of water and sediment that are fundamental to the functioning of the ecosystem of the Pantanal. It is also likely that the Hidrovia scheme would disrupt the hydrology of the river system. The Pantanal acts as a huge sponge, retaining water in the rainy season and releasing it slowly throughout the year, thus reducing the possibility of flooding lower down the system.

Landward access to the Pantanal (see Figure 1.4.7) is still restricted to one track from Pocone to Porto Jofre. The track and a strip of land on either side is designated as the Transpantanal National Park. The Brazilian Environment and Natural Resources Institute (IBAMA) is hoping to extend its jurisdiction over the whole of the Pantanal. Increased landward accessibility to the Pantanal is unlikely in the near future, but attempts to preserve

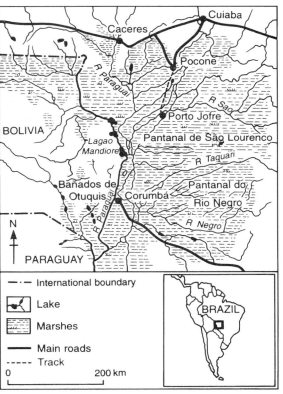

FIGURE 1.4.5 The Pantanal

FIGURE 1.4.6 (*far left*) Anteater

FIGURE 1.4.7 Landward access to Pantanal

the fragile ecology of these wetlands may be frustrated by the Hidrovia Project. Opposition to the scheme is organised by the Hidrovia Co-ordinating Committee and on World Environment Day, 5 June 1995, it called for a stop to the Hidrovia Project until impact studies of the effect on ecology, environment and the way of life of indigenous peoples had been carried out.

ESSAYS

1 Discuss some of the difficulties encountered in defining wilderness.

2 To what extent can improved accessibility change the nature of wilderness regions?

2
WILDERNESS
ENVIRONMENTS AND
PEOPLE

'The road is rust-red gravel, the sandhills are the same colour and so are the anthills which look like rotten old teeth sprouting from the ground. It is an utterly lonely place with the long straight tracks of the prospectors running through it, and soon we are lost ...'
Eric Newby, *What the Traveller Saw*

KEY IDEAS

■ Harsh physical environments are a deterrent to population.

■ Wildernesses occur where varying combinations of physical factors render permanent human settlement difficult or sometimes impossible.

■ Climate, rugged relief and high altitude are all important deterrents to permanent human settlement.

■ Indigenous peoples inhabit some of the more favoured parts of wilderness regions, and follow a way of life that is generally in equilibrium with the environment.

■ Non-indigenous groups of people seek to use wilderness regions for their resources (minerals, forests and water), and for their strategic value.

■ Improvements in survival technology (buildings, clothing and diet) have rendered wilderness exploration and exploitation less demanding.

2.1 Wilderness environments as a deterrent to population

Figure 2.1.1 Amazon rainforest

In Chapter 1 it has been seen that wilderness regions may be defined in terms of remoteness, and a lack of human influence in their environments. People have been deterred from settling in the wilderness regions largely because of the prevailing harsh physical conditions. The nature of these conditions varies considerably across the globe, from the polar wastes of the Antarctic plateau to the dense tropical rainforests of Amazonia, from the highest mountain groups of the Himalayas to the most arid and least frequented parts of the Sahara and the Australian Deserts.

It is clear that an inclement climatic environment acts as a primary deterrent in polar regions, in the deserts and in the highest mountain regions. Of itself, climate may not be a deterrent in tropical moist areas. Some of the world's densest concentrations of population are found in parts of the tropics that receive large amounts of rainfall, as in some areas of Indonesia and West Africa. It is where dense tropical rainforest occurs in particularly remote areas and islands that human influence is minimal (Figure 2.1.1). Similarly high rainfall only acts as a major constraint on population in middle latitudes in really remote areas such as some parts of south east Alaska, such as the Tongass National Forest (see Figure 2.1.2), or some parts of southern Chile.

High rugged mountains seldom attract permanent settlement of people. In tropical regions, mountain systems such as the Andes and the Himalayas carry quite dense populations at fairly high levels, but the true wildernesses are found in the very highest parts of mountain areas such as the Karakoram or the Cordillera Real in Peru and Bolivia. Desert mountains are wildernesses not only by virtue of their ruggedness, but also by their aridity and remoteness (Figure 2.1.3). In higher latitudes it is often a combination of these same environmental factors that creates wilderness in mountain areas.

FIGURE 2.1.3 Saharan Mountains

Student Activity 2.1

1 Some major environmental factors responsible for wilderness have been identified above. Discuss the inter-relationships between these factors. Why is it difficult to isolate the most important?
2 Other environmental factors may also contribute to the existence of wildernesses. Make a list of such factors and draw a diagram to show how they are related to those discussed above.

FIGURE 2.1.2 (*far left*) Tongass National Forest, South East Alaska

For example in the Brooks Range in northern Alaska, relief is not only particularly rugged in the Arrigetch Mountains (Figure 2.1.4), but they are also extremely remote and suffer far harsher climatic conditions than mountain areas in lower latitudes. The most extreme conditions are found in the mountain areas of Antarctica, such as the Transantarctic Mountains and the Vinson Massif (see Figure 3.8.4, page 49).

It has been noted in Chapter 1 that a visual comparison of a global map of wilderness areas, and a map of world biomes shows some clear relationships. Again, it is difficult to say that certain types of vegetation are, of themselves, the only environmental factor responsible for wilderness. In some countries of West Africa, little rainforest now survives, and it is necessary to protect remaining areas. It is only in remote parts of Amazonia, and perhaps Zaire and Brunei that the wilderness dimension is apparent. Much more extensive areas of the boreal forest and the tundra coincide with wilderness areas when the maps of wilderness and biome are compared (see Chapter 1, pages 9 and 11). Harsh climate and remoteness combine with vegetation to create wilderness in these regions.

FIGURE 2.1.4 Arrigetch Mountains, Brooks Range in Alaska

2.2 Case studies of aspects of the wilderness environment

In Section 2.1 various factors responsible for the wilderness environment were discussed, together with the manner in which they interacted to intensify wilderness. In this section some examples are studied in more detail.

1 The Antarctic Climate.
2 The Climate of the Sahara.
3 The Andean Mountains.
4 The Canadian North.

The Antarctic climate

'We hoped that we were rising on the long snow cape that marks the beginning of Mount Terror. That night the temperature was down to −75 F (sic); at breakfast −70 F (sic); at noon nearly −77 F (sic). The day lives in my memory as that on which I found that records were not worth making ... this was our tenth day out and we hoped to be away for 6 weeks.'

Apsley Cherry-Garrard, *The Worst Journey in the World*, 5 July 1911

Antarctica's unique climate results from a combination of factors – its latitude, its perpetual snow cover, its altitude and its continental size. Almost all of Antarctica lies within the Antarctic Circle, which means that, on balance, the continent loses more solar energy than it gains over the year. Snow and sea ice reflect away nearly 80 per cent of the solar energy reaching Antarctica. Its continental dimensions (14 million km², twice as large as Australia) and its height mean that the polar plateau of the interior has extreme weather conditions for much of the year. With an average elevation of some 2300 m, Antarctica is the highest of the continents. This is not so much due to the height of its mountains, but to the thickness of the polar ice sheet which has an average thickness of 2.3 km, and a maximum known thickness of nearly 5 km.

The two maps in Figure 2.2.1 show the distribution of temperature in January and July in Antarctica. As expected there are obvious differences between the coastal zones and the

FIGURE 2.2.1 Mean surface temperatures in Antarctica, January and July

FIGURE 2.2.2 (*below*) Annual mean temperature variations selected weather stations in Antarctica

FIGURE 2.2.3 (*below right*) Captain Scott and his team at the South Pole

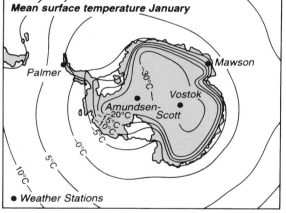

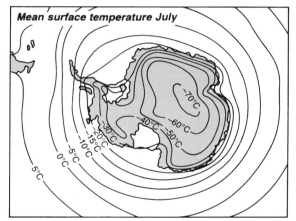

interior, and the variations are shown in graphical form in Figure 2.2.2. Antarctica has only two seasons, the so-called 'pointed summer' and the 'coreless winter', conditions which are much accentuated on the polar plateau. The sharp decline in temperatures after the brief summer maximum no doubt contributed to the tragic end to Scott's polar journey. Only Shackleton had previously been on the polar plateau when Scott planned his journey and he had recorded temperatures in January between −23°C and −40°C, with an average of −29°C. Amundsen, who reached the South Pole before Scott, was only on the plateau at the height of summer, whilst Scott was still there in late January, when temperatures were falling rapidly and imposed appalling physical strain on Scott and his team (Figure 2.2.3).

The polar plateau of Antarctica is a cold desert, with less than 50 mm water equivalent of snow falling throughout the year. On the coast, amounts are somewhat higher, with figures reaching some ten times the level of the interior. Strong winds are another feature of the Antarctic (Figure 2.2.4) and these are particularly violent where very cold, dense air flows off the polar plateau and is channelled along glaciers, such as the Beardsmore Glacier, followed by Scott and more recent expeditions. Such 'katabatic' winds can gust up to 300 km per hour. In some areas these winds can blow uninterruptedly for days and even weeks. The Australian explorer, Mawson wrote the following in his diary.

'Looking through my diary I notice that "on March 24 we experienced a rise in spirits because of the improved weather". Referring to the records, I find the average velocity of the wind for the day to have been 45 miles per hour, corresponding to a strong gale on the Beaufort scale. This tells its own story.'

It is not surprising that Antarctica is often referred to in the popular press and travel books as 'The Last True Wilderness'. It is the only continent with no permanent population, with an over-wintering population of less than 1000 scientists, which rises to 4000 in the brief summer.

Student Activity 2.2

'Antarctica is colder than the Arctic.' Using a good atlas and a suitable climate textbook, explore some of the reasons why this might be so, and discuss some of the wilderness implications.

The climate of the Sahara

'Suddenly, after hardly any twilight, the sun rises in the clear sky. In this dry atmosphere its rays are already scorching in the early morning, and under the influence of the reflection from stone and sand the layer of air next the ground is warmed rapidly. There is no active evaporation to moderate the rising temperature. After nine o'clock the heat is great and goes on increasing till 3 or 4 o'clock in the afternoon, when the quivering mirage is sometimes seen, produced by the vibration of the air, heated as in an oven. It gets slowly cooler towards the evening, and the sun, just before it sets, suffuses the cloudless sky with a glow of colour. In the transparent night the rocks and sand lose their heat almost as quickly as they acquired it, and the calmness of the atmosphere, which is so still that a flame burns without a tremor, also favours the cooling of the air. We shiver with cold and it is no uncommon thing in winter to find water on the surface of the ground frozen in the morning.'

Schirmer, *Le Sahara*

Schirmer's description of the daily regime in the Sahara will be familiar to all who work or travel in the Sahara. Its climate is sometimes referred to as 'A cold climate where the sun burns'. This summarises the extremes of temperature that can be experienced during the course of the day and night. In July in the central Sahara, average daily mean temperatures can reach 35–45°C, with daily maxima rising to 55–60°C. At night temperatures may fall as much as 30°C or even 50°C on occasions. In the winter temperatures of 25–30°C are common in the day, but at night temperatures at Tamanrasset have fallen to −5−−7°C. On the summit of Assakrem, the highest point in the Hoggar mountains (2585 m) temperatures will fall as low as −25°C.

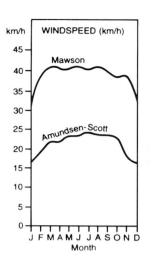

FIGURE 2.2.4 Wind speed variations at two weather stations in Antarctica

FIGURE 2.2.5 The Saharan anticyclone

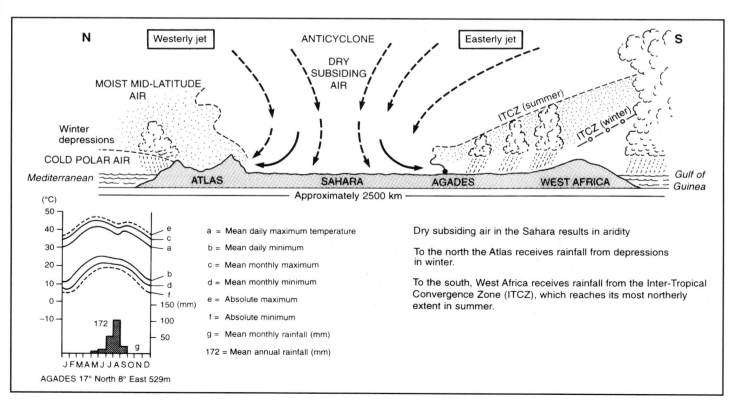

a = Mean daily maximum temperature
b = Mean daily minimum
c = Mean monthly maximum
d = Mean monthly minimum
e = Absolute maximum
f = Absolute minimum
g = Mean monthly rainfall (mm)
172 = Mean annual rainfall (mm)

Dry subsiding air in the Sahara results in aridity

To the north the Atlas receives rainfall from depressions in winter.

To the south, West Africa receives rainfall from the Inter-Tropical Convergence Zone (ITCZ), which reaches its most northerly extent in summer.

AGADES 17° North 8° East 529m

Rainfall over the Sahara is extremely low, with many locations recording hardly any over periods as long as ten years. The air over the Sahara is extremely dry, partly as a result of subsidence within the persistent anticyclone and partly because of the distance from the sea (see Figure 2.2.5). Rainfall usually comes in the form of violent downpours. In Tamanrasset, in the central Sahara, 44 mm fell in three hours (the mean annual rainfall is 40 mm!). Such sudden falls of rain can cause flooding in **wadis**, and travellers have often been drowned while camping in valley bottoms.

Strong winds are often experienced in the Sahara, particularly during the summer. Because of the vast open spaces, they blow with great force, and are usually charged with dust or sand.

The Andean mountains

'No single chain dominates the landscape of a continent as does the Andes of South America ... these mountains run in a practically unbroken chain from near the Panama Canal to Cape Horn, a distance of some 4,500 miles. Along this vast distance there are many sub-ranges of great beauty and breathtaking peaks, as well as convoluted ridges, nondescript hilly terrain, isolated volcanoes, and miscellaneous transverse ridges of minor importance.'

Leo Le Bon, *Majestic Mountains*

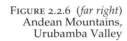

FIGURE 2.2.6 (*far right*) Andean Mountains, Urubamba Valley

From the above comments on the Andes by Leo Le Bon, it is clear that they are unlikely to be a mountain range of unbroken wilderness. This is confirmed when the map of global wildernesses is consulted in Chapter 1, page 9. The largest areas of wilderness occur on the eastern slopes of the Andes in Peru (often drained by the headwaters of the Amazon and its tributaries (see Figure 2.2.6), in parts of central and southern Bolivia, and in a much more continuous zone in southern Chile, where the Andes, although lower, carry ice caps and glaciers.

Mountain wildernesses in the Andes result from

a combination of the physical factors noted in Section 2.1. Ruggedness, remoteness and harsh climatic conditions are responsible for the wilderness of southern Chile, but it is high altitude that also plays an important role in the wilderness areas of Peru and Bolivia. These two environmental aspects of mountain wildernesses are now examined.

The Paine National Park, southern Chile

The Torres del Paine is a relatively compact mountain wilderness (see Figure 2.2.7). It is described in the extract in Figure 2.2.8 from Paine Grande in Leo le Bon's *Majestic Mountains*.

FIGURE 2.2.7 Torres del Paine

Student Activity 2.3

1 How far do you think that the use of the term wilderness is justified in describing the Torres del Paine?
2 What other information about the area would be needed in order to confirm its wilderness status?

The effect of high altitude in the Andes on human activity

High altitude in the Andes stresses the human system in a number of ways, but the most serious is the reduced levels of atmospheric oxygen associated with lower atmospheric pressure. Such reduced terrestrial oxygen pressure is known as **hypoxia**. Other adverse conditions that may interact with hypoxia include, cold, low humidity, high wind flow, and high levels of solar and cosmic radiation.

FIGURE 2.2.8 Extract from Paine Grande, Leo Le Bon

Torres del Paine, Chile

Near the southern tip of South America, where the Andes' 5,000-mile-long chain of mountains comes to an abrupt end and plunges into the stormy South Pacific, surges the Paine Range – a spectacular array of huge spires and sharp peaks with gleaming, smooth walls rising for 6,000 vertical feet out of the undulating Patagonian grasslands.

This is a wild land of wind-whipped lakes, billowing skies, and rolling hills, with the bleak aspect of Yorkshire moors on a stormy day in midwinter.

The Paine mountains, which enchant trekker, climber, and tourist alike with their incomparable, stark beauty, are a distinct range of peaks connected to the main Andean chain by a mountain pass, the Paso Paine. The range runs in a west–east direction, as opposed to the Andes' north–south axis. The length, slightly less than 30 miles, makes it a compact and easily accessible range.

The Torres del Paine, as the area is known in Chile, is an upthrusted batholith that rose from the center of the earth long ago and later was covered with large glaciers that came streaming off the continental icecap during the Ice Age. In time, the glaciers retreated, carving huge towers and deep gashes. What remains today are the alpine peaks and wondrous Towers of Paine.

One would be hard-pressed to find anywhere in the world a more compelling, savagely beautiful array of peaks than the Towers of Paine. The steepness and size of the smooth granite walls defy the imagination. The mountains are surrounded by strings of many large and small lakes of different color and shape, varying from bright blue to turquoise green to pale gray. The hills and valleys that surround the peaks are heavily forested and support a wealth of indigenous flora, including wind-twisted beech trees (both Magellan and Haya, or Southern beech).

The wildlife at Paine is abundant, with over 4,000 guanacos (cousins of the llama) roaming the park. Armadillo, puma, fox, Patagonia hare, and rhea (the Patagonian version of the ostrich) can also be seen. But most bountiful are the avian species, of which upland geese, parrots, flamingos, and Andean condors are the most visible. Here one can see the regal condor, the world's largest flying bird, effortlessly riding the wind currents around the peaks and towers on its 12-foot wingspan.

The only way in which to relieve this reduced oxygen pressure stress is by the use of bottled oxygen, as is the case on most major mountaineering expeditions in the Himalayas and other high mountain wildernesses, although ascents of Everest and other peaks are now regularly accomplished without the benefits of oxygen.

For people that live at low altitudes exposure to high altitudes above 2500 m or 3000 m produces a variety of symptoms that may include the following.

Shortness of breath; headache; fatigue; sleeplessness; rapid pulse rate; nausea; mental disorientation; general malaise.

Such symptoms will be felt at relatively low levels, e.g. 2500–3000 m after vigorous exercise, and at much higher levels they are experienced while at rest. After a period at higher elevations those accustomed to living at lower levels will not experience these symptoms while resting, but they are likely to recur after exercise. For this reason those participating in high level mountaineering expeditions in the Himalayas and other mountains must acclimatise at low levels before proceeding to the higher mountain environments. After a considerable period at high levels the low-level residents will have acquired a fair degree of adaptation to hypoxia. However they still will not have the capacity for work possessed by indigenous peoples. Thus nearly all Himalayan expeditions use Sherpas for carrying heavy loads into the remote mountain wildernesses (Figure 2.2.9).

It is apparent that indigenous peoples have developed special physical characteristics that enable them to function more efficiently at high levels in mountain environments. In the high Andes chest size and lung capacity is great relative to body size and to the size of the lowland residents.

Cold is another factor that affects people in high mountain environments. Night frosts become increasingly frequent with altitude, and low temperatures are first encountered in late afternoon shortly after the sun goes down, and continue into early morning. The indigenous people of the Andes have little to combat these low temperatures but shelter, home-spun wool clothing and the heat generating and conserving capacities of the human

FIGURE 2.2.9 Sherpas in the Gokyo Valley, Khumbu Himalayas

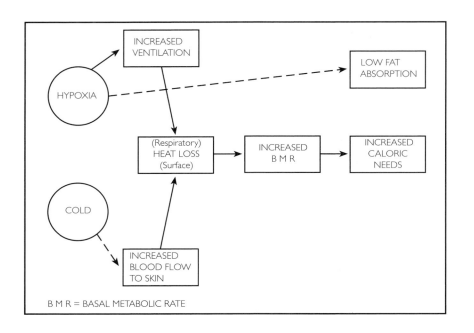

B M R = BASAL METABOLIC RATE

NATION	TOTAL POPULATION ('000s)	% RURAL POPULATION	POPULATION ABOVE 2500 M('000s)	% POPULATION ABOVE 2500 M
Venezuela	10 755	28	105	0.9
Colombia	22 160	42	5 666	25.6
Ecuador	6 028	54	2 047	34.0
Peru	13 586	51	5 774	42.5
Bolivia	4 658	65	3 676	78.9
Chile	9 780	30	55	0.6
Argentina	24 352	21	149	0.6
Total	91 319	37	17 472	19.1

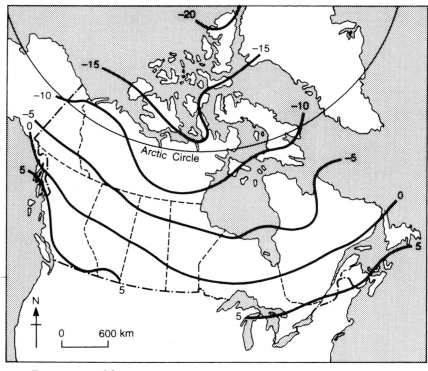

FIGURE 2.2.13 Mean annual air temperature in Canada

body. There are no apparent relationships between hypoxia, cold and the need for calorie intake summarised in the diagram Figure 2.2.10.

Figure 2.2.11 shows details of populations in the Andean republics. It can be seen that substantial numbers of Andean peoples live above 2500 m. The highest level of permanent settlement in the Andes appears to be in scientific research stations on Chalcataya in Bolivia, at some 5300 m. Permanent settlement based on agriculture stops well short of this level probably between 4000–4250 m. The true mountain wildernesses of Peru and Bolivia where hypoxia, cold and rugged relief prevent all human settlement probably begin at about 4500 m.

The Canadian North

Much of the Canadian North appears as wilderness on Figure 1.3.1 (page 9). Once again a combination of circumstances has contributed to wilderness in this vast region (see Figure 2.2.12). Figure 2.2.13 shows mean annual air temperature, and Bone suggests that the north may best be delimited by the 0°C mean annual isotherm. A quick comparison with Figure 1.3.1 shows that there is a marked coincidence between the line of the 0°C isotherm and the southern limit of the huge wilderness area covering much of northern Canada and Greenland.

Variable	Polar units
1 Latitude	
90°	100
80°	77
50°	33
45°	0
2 Summer heat	
0 days above 5.6°C	100
60 days above 5.6°C	70
100 days above 5.6°C	45
>150 days above 5.6°C	0
3 Annual cold	
6650 **degree days** below 0°C	100
4700 degree days below 0°C	75
1950 degree days below 0°C	30
550 degree days below 0°C	0
4 Types of ice	
Frozen ground	
Continuous **permafrost** 475 m thick	100
Continuous permafrost <475 m thick	80
Discontinuous permafrost	60
Ground frozen for less than 1 month	0
Floating ice	
Permanent pack ice	100
Pack ice for 6 months	36
Pack ice <1 month	0
Glaciers	
Ice sheet >1523 m thick	100
Ice cap 304 m thick	60
Snow cover <2.5 m	0
5 Annual precipitation	
100 mm	100
300 mm	60
500 mm	0
6 Natural vegetation cover	
Rocky desert	100
50% tundra	90
Open woodland	40
Dense forest	0
7 Accessibility by land or sea	
No service	100
For 2 months	60
By 2 means	15
>2 means	0
8 Accessibility by air	
Charter, 1600 km	100
Regular service, weekly	25
Regular service, daily	0
9 Population	
Settlement size	
None	100
About 100 people	85
About 1000 people	60
>5000 people	0
Population density	
Uninhabited	100
1 person per km²	50
4 persons per km²	0
10 Degree of economic activity	
No production	100
Exploration	80
20 hunters/trappers	75
Inter-regional centre	0

Clearly there are other factors that contribute to wilderness in northern Canada, and here it is useful to look at the work of the Canadian geographer Hamelin. He devised an index to show 'nordicity', which although not precisely the same as wilderness, has a broad approximation to it. Hamelin selected ten physical and human variables which represent various facets of the Canadian North. Each variable was assigned a range of 'polar values', and the sum of polar values is taken as the 'nordicity' of a place. The maximum number of polar units can only be obtained at the North Pole, and the 200 polar value line acts as the southern limit of the Canadian North.

The ten variables are shown in Figure 2.2.14. For variables **4** (Types of ice) and **9** (Population) options are given and the selection of the best option is determined by the particular location of the site.

Hamelin used the calculated polar units to divide Canada into five regions (Figure 2.2.15). The southern limit of the middle north corresponds more or less with the limit of wilderness in northern Canada. The idea of nordicity was put to good use. Hamelin used the nordicity index to calculate the isolation allowances for state workers from the south working in the north. Hamelin's nordicity index successfully shows how wilderness arises from a whole combination of factors.

FIGURE 2.2.14 (*far left*) Measures of Nordicity

FIGURE 2.2.15 Nordicity in Canada

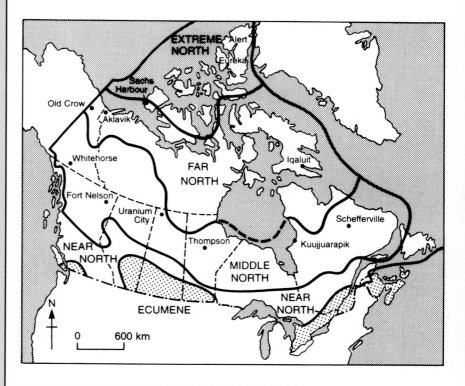

Student Activity 2.4

1 How effective is the nordicity index in delimiting wilderness?
2 What variables of the nordicity index would be unsuitable for calculating a 'wilderness index' on a global basis? Suggest some suitable replacements.

2.3 People in wilderness regions

It has been suggested that, in defining wilderness, there are very few regions that remain untouched by people. Some wilderness areas, such as parts of Antarctica and the Siberian and Canadian Arctic, still remain unexplored but elsewhere the trace of humans is apparent. Indigenous peoples have long inhabited parts of the Arctic, the tropical rainforests, the world's deserts, and high mountain regions. Exploration has revealed the existence of these peoples to the outside world, and for many of them the links with modern civilisation are still tenuous. However, as other people have sought to develop wilderness areas, the indigenous groups have inevitably become involved. Management of the areas within which these indigenous groups live must consider how their mode of existence may best be integrated into an overall plan for the region. Such management clearly has the potential for conflict between groups with different attitudes and values.

People from established centres of population have long expressed interest in wilderness regions. Initial exploration was always followed by political interest in securing new territories as witnessed by the so-called scramble for Africa in the nineteenth century, and the division of South America between Spanish and Portuguese interests in the fifteenth century. Commercial exploitation of resources in wilderness areas began in the late nineteenth century with the rubber booms in Amazonia, the gold rushes in Yukon and Alaska (Figure 2.3.1) and the appearance of the first rash of mining camps in the Australian outback at places such as Coolgardie in Western Australia, and Cloncurry in Queensland. With the increasing demand for forest products and water and mineral resources in the twentieth century, the whole pace of survey (increasingly from the air in remote locations), exploitation and production has quickened. This has brought the need for proper management sharply into focus, an issue that is addressed fully in Chapter 6.

FIGURE 2.3.1 Skagway, Alaska

2.4 Case studies of indigenous people in wilderness environments

Indigenous groups in Amazonia

The voice of the indigenous peoples

'There are many Yanomami who live in Brazil and Venezuela. We think that there are more than 20 000. We are all one people because we understand the language of them all.'

'The Yanomami do not go out from their villages and so most of them only speak Yanomami. I Davi, first studied my own language, I have started to read and write in Yanomami. I have never been in a school for white people and so I can't speak Portuguese well. The other Yanomami also don't speak Portuguese. We were invited to this meeting to tell you of our situation. Our lands have not been demarcated. That is why we are being invaded by whites who are taking gold from our lands and bringing diseases and contaminating the Yanomami. We call the white man's disease xawara. These diseases kill our people.'

'At first we didn't know that the miners were invading our land. Now we know: those that live near the miners and ranchers, the Yanomami of the Aranji, the Catrimani, the Demini, the Couto do Magalhaes and the Erico. There are Yanomami who know that it is bad for them and are sorry because they are stricken with illnesses. There are others who think that it is good because they receive machetes, axes, pans and matches that they use in the forest.'

'But we, who know that the miners deceive us, are telling the others. So that they know what is happening. The miners want to take our Yanomami women to keep them and they are deceiving us and stealing our gold.'

'I am telling you this because I am worried and angry. I want you to know of our situation, to understand our worries and to join our struggle.'

FIGURE 2.4.1 Indigenous peoples and territories in Amazonia

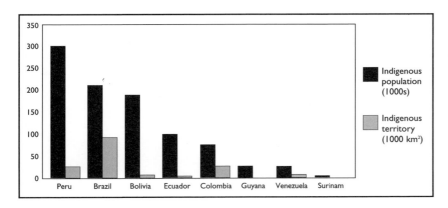

'We Yanomami want the demarcation of our Yanomami Park. A continuous area, that is very important for us Yanomami.'

Statement issued by Davi, Yanomami from Toototobi in Carreira, Yanomami headman of Wakathaotheri, and Rubi, Yanomami from the lower Catrimani, at a meeting at Surumu, 7–9 January 1985.

The above comments indicate Indian feelings concerning the exploitation of their lands by various developers. Major development programmes in the 1970s saw distribution of land for rubber production, for agriculture, for livestock and timber production without any reference to the indigenous groups.

The Yanomami (see Figure 2.4.2) have suffered particularly badly as a result of incursions into their territory. The Yanomami live in an area on the Brazil-Venezuela border on the drainage divide between the Orinoco and the Amazon (see Figure 2.4.3). Much of this land could be described as true wilderness:

'of streams and swiftly falling rivers interrupted by innumerable small waterfalls, making navigation impracticable; of steep valleys and mountains whose summits sometimes shake clear of the enclosing vegetation to reveal their worn and stony crowns, and above all of dense cool rainforest.'

from Johnson, Knowles and Colchester in *Rainforest, Land Use Options for Amazonia*

Yanomami existence depends on hunting, fishing, collecting and 'slash and burn' agriculture. Some 21 000 Yanomami live in over 360 settlements in an area about the size of Wales. Small communities of 50 Indians are dispersed throughout the rainforest and the only communication between them is along remote forest tracks. Canoes are only used for transport on the edges of the Yanomami lands where rivers are wider. Most of the food for the Yanomami's diet is grown in their own gardens (see Figure 2.4.4), but the main protein supply comes from the birds and animals killed in the forest by hunters. They appear to live in sustainable equilibrium in their wilderness environment.

In the 1950s their territories were invaded by missionaries and miners, who reached areas that

were inaccessible to non-Indians before the use of outboard motors, and monoplanes. In the 1970s a road was built across Yanomami territory, which resulted in considerable loss of life in communities in the contact zone. Very high death rates in Yanomami villages resulted from diseases brought into the area as a consequence of the road building programme – up to 90 per cent in some cases. The

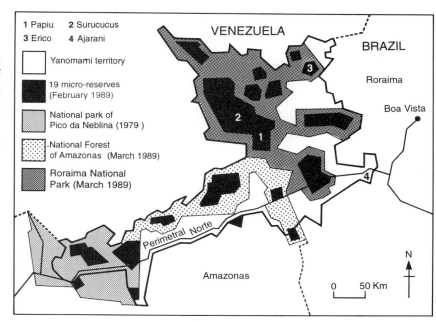

FIGURE 2.4.3 Yanomami territory

FIGURE 2.4.2 (*far left*) Yanomami Indians, Amazonia

FIGURE 2.4.4 A Yanomami garden

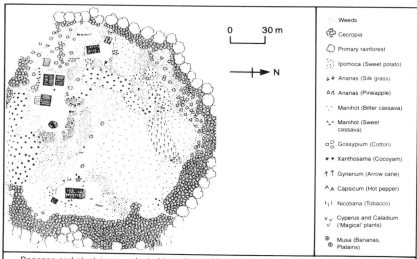

Bananas and plantains are planted in wetter and lower parts of the garden. This mature garden has been heavily invaded by weeds. Quick growing softwoods, of the genus *Cecropia*, have already completely taken over the outer margins of the garden. Other parts of the garden have also already been given over to weeds. The garden was in fact completely abandoned about 18 months after this drawing was made.

FIGURE 2.4.5 Ethnic groups, indigenous populations and lands set aside for their use in the member countries of the Amazon Co-operation Treaty (signed 3 July 1978)

COUNTRY	NUMBER OF ETHNIC GROUPS	ESTIMATED AMAZONIAN INDIGENOUS POPULATION	EXTENT OF LANDS SET ASIDE FOR ETHNIC GROUPS (ha)
Bolivia	31	171 827	2 053 000
Brazil	200	213 352	74 466 149
Colombia	52	70 000	18 507 793
Ecuador	6	94 700	1 918 706
Peru	60	300 000	3 822 302
Guyana	9	40 000	NA
Surinam	5	7 400	NA
Venezuela	16	386 700	8 870 000
TOTAL	379	935 949	109 637 950

NA: Not available

FIGURE 2.4.6 Yanomami lands in Venezuela and Brazil (1991)

The Yanomami lands in Venezuela and Brazil

After several years of unsuccessful attempts to create a binational agreement on protection of the Yanomami, Brazil and Venezuela issued separate decrees which constitute an advance in the protection of Yanomami rights.

On November 15, 1991, President Fernando Collor de Mello of Brazil ended a long-standing dispute by creating the Yanomami Indigenous Park. The park is the largest of its kind in Brazil and, with Kayapó Park, doubles the territory assigned to indigenous peoples during this century.

In August 1991, meanwhile, Venezuela's presidential decree No 1635 created the Alto Orinoco-Casiquiare Biosphere Reserve. This reserve covers 8 million ha and includes the territory of the Yanomami and other zones, among them a segment of the territory of the Ye'Kuanas and, to the west, the Cerro de la Neblina National Park.

The creation of the park represented a victory for the Indians living in the territory and for the agencies which have supported them. In the case of Venezuela, the reserve offers certain legal protection to the Yanomami in that they cannot be relocated, the area cannot be divided, colonisation is explicitly prohibited, and approval of the national executive is required to carry out any activity involving the use of resources. Still, the management plan outlined in the decree, which has not yet been edited, will determine the priority that will be assigned to protection of the Yanomami on the Venezuelan side. On the Brazilian side, the establishment of a large and contiguous area signifies, above all, the prevalence of Indian rights in the dispute. Earlier proposals would have established indigenous reserves around the settlements while opening the rest of the area to the exploitation of natural resources. Other interests, among them those of mining and lumber companies and certain political or military sectors in Brazil, must now be resolved in common accord with the indigenous authorities who have gained legitimacy in the process.

Other battles must be waged to achieve total protection for the Yanomami. Regulations must be enacted governing use of the areas and governments must lend their support to demarcation of the Yanomami territory. Also, the safety of the peoples in the future must be assured.

The governments could add a final grace note to the project were they to adopt the indigenous philosophy that, as the rivers of the Amazon flow freely without regard to borders, all elements of nature (including people) are interdependent. In the meantime, the governments should institute Article 32 of the Agreement on Indigenous Peoples and Tribes of the International Labour Organization (ILO) 1989 which reads: "*Crossborder Contacts and Cooperation.* The Governments will take appropriate measures, if necessary by international treaty, to facilitate crossborder contacts and co-operation between indigenous and tribal peoples, including activities in the economic, social, cultural, spiritual and environmental spheres."

Respective decrees of Venezuela and Brazil, Arvelo-Jimenez and Cousins (1991)

1980s saw more miners moving into Yanomami territory, searching for and exploiting gold and tin. Government initiatives in Yanomami territory in the late 1970s and 1980s, motivated mainly by conservation pressures, served to fragment the territory (see Figure 2.4.3) without recognising the need for the delimitation of a Yanomami Park.

Figure 2.4.5 shows the increasing recognition of the need for the indigenous peoples of Amazonia to have lands of their own where they can practice their traditional way of life.

Student Activity 2.5

1 Study Figure 2.4.6.
(a) Summarise the major advantages for indigenous groups of these parks.
(b) What difficulties still have to be resolved?

2.5 Case studies of the use of wilderness regions by non-indigenous groups

In Section 2.3, the past and current demands on wilderness regions by non-indigenous groups were briefly reviewed. This section examines the use of wilderness land for mining and strategic defence policies. Use of wilderness areas for tourism and forestry are discussed fully in Chapters 5 and 6.

Weipa: the development of a bauxite mine in the Cape York Peninsula, Northern Queensland

Much of the Cape York Peninsula is remote wilderness country, and the Weipa **bauxite** mine is located on the west coast (Figure 2.5.4). Much of the land to the north and south of Weipa is Aboriginal Reserve (see Figure 2.5.1) and thus Weipa presents an interesting case of mining development that is likely to have a significant impact on indigenous people. Several issues arise:

- under what conditions should mining development occur within Aboriginal lands;
- what opportunities would exist for the employment of Aborigines in the mining complex;
- what social and welfare benefits would be made available to Aborigines;
- what attempts would be made to integrate Aborigines with the non-indigenous groups in Weipa;
- what provisions would be made for social stability in the area after mining had ceased?

Early difficulties arose when initial negotiations began over the development of the mine. Vast areas of the Cape York peninsula were reserved for the use of Aboriginal peoples in the nineteenth century. However, the rights and interests of the Aboriginal owners of the land were not protected in the mid-

1950s when mining companies were seeking permission to develop the mineral resources of the region. At that time Aborigines neither possessed citizenship of Australia nor enjoyed basic human rights. Special legislation (the Comalco Act of 1957) revoked the land's reserve status in favour of mining leases.

Employment of Aborigines in the mine was seen in the 1950s to be a major benefit of the Weipa project. Figure 2.5.2 shows details of Aboriginal employment at Weipa from 1973–88. Current levels of employment in the mid-1990s would appear to conform to the 7–10% of the Comalco workforce achieved since the early 1970s. This level of Aboriginal employment is substantially better than many other Australian examples (in the eastern gold-fields of Western Australia Aboriginal employment was only 4 per cent, and in Western Australia as a whole the level was only 0.775 per cent across the mining industry). Comalco has

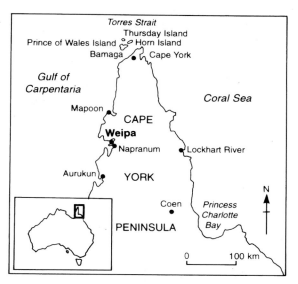

FIGURE 2.5.1 Location of Weipa, Queensland

FIGURE 2.5.2 Aboriginal employment in Weipa, 1973–1988

YEAR	TOTAL WORKFORCE (ACTUAL)	ABORIGINAL EMPLOYEES (ESTIMATED ANNUAL AVERAGE)	ESTIMATED % TOTAL WORKFORCE ABORIGINAL
1973	860	65	7.56
1974	917	68	7.42
1975	1074	81	7.54
1976	1144	80	6.99
1977	1150	96	8.35
1978	1152	97	8.42
1979	1143	108	9.45
1980	1119	106	9.47
1981	1112	89	8.00
1982	1025	78	7.61
1983	972	73	7.51
1984	1050	73	6.95
1985	1061	76	7.16
1986	980	81	8.27
1987	1049	80	7.63
1988	1047	74	7.07

consistently been the major employer of men from the township of Napranum on the Weipa peninsula. Inevitable difficulties arose in the employment of Aborigines in a modern industrial society, including problems over attendance, health, training, work practices and community relations, management and supervisor attitudes. In the late 1960s there was some evidence that Comalco was attempting to discriminate against the Aborigines in terms of pay and benefit packages.

The Weipa Aboriginal Society was established in 1973, with the aim of improving relations through the provision of a range of social and welfare initiatives. Funding was shared between Comalco (50 per cent) and the State and Federal Governments (25 per cent). The projects funded in the period 1973–88 are shown in Figure 2.5.3. The Weipa Aboriginal Society has increasingly focused its programme on Aboriginal priorities and aspirations. The fish farm is an attempt to provide alternative employment for Aborigines utilising the abundant marine resources of the western Cape York peninsula coast.

FIGURE 2.5.3 Projects funded: Weipa Aboriginal Society

1973	Town Plan	77 000
1974	Pre-School	349 000
1976	Sewerage	751 000
1977	Roads and drainage	310 000
1978	Community Hall	125 000
1979	Accommodation for pre-school teachers	52 000
1981	Convenience store and laundromat	180 000
1982	Alcohol rehabilitation and workshop training	260 000
1984	Useful skills training (annual operating costs)	100 000
1986	Pre-school expenses (annual costs)	65 000
1986	Training centre	108 000
1986	Fish farm feasibility study	1 000
1986	Snack bar renovation	55 000

Note: All figures in Australian dollars.

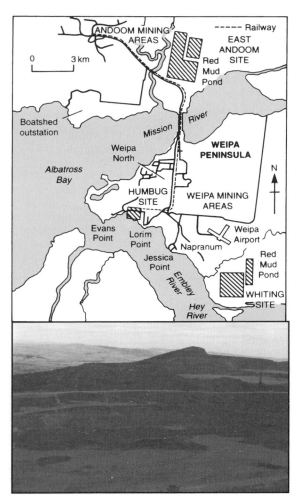

FIGURE 2.5.4 The Weipa area: photo of Comalco bauxite mines at Cape York, North Queensland

FIGURE 2.5.5 (*below*) *The Guardian*: Outback Aussies

There has, to date, been little evidence of any successful integration of the Aborigines with the non-indigenous groups in the area. Weipa North is the company mining town. In the mid-1980s Comalco had identified 'normalisation' as its policy for running the town, whereby there would be greater local participation through the establishment of a town council. As an example Napranum Council were offered a chance to purchase the lease for the town's shopping complex, with Commonwealth Government funding available. The proposal was rejected because the political costs were perceived as being too high: '*why should the community pay to lease facilities which were built on their land without their approval?'*

New proposals for an alumina refinery in the Weipa area are now being considered. Initial Aboriginal opposition to the Whiting site has been successful, and two other sites have been investigated, but any final selection will have to meet stringent environmental and social criteria. Existing law in Queensland means that approval of the new plant could occur against the wishes of the Aboriginal community, but opposition would be far better organised now than in the past. There would be some benefits for the Aboriginal community, but it seems that the fish farm and similar ventures, based on the marine and coastal resources, are the best future option for the Aboriginal community.

Although there has been some important movement on the part of Comalco to recognise the interests and aspirations of Aborigines in the Weipa community, much still remains to be achieved. Marginalisation of the Aboriginal communities is still a fact of life in Queensland, and the co-operation of Comalco and the Aboriginal community at Weipa may mark the beginning of a greater level of Aboriginal integration into the social and economic structure of Queensland.

Student Activity 2.6

1 Study Figure 2.5.5.
(a) Why does the situation in Tennant Creek make integration of communities more difficult?
(b) Is such a ban likely to be effective? What alternatives could achieve better results?

Wilderness frontiers in Amazonia: geopolitical issues

Figure 2.5.6 shows the unstable nature of Brazil's frontier regions, and the degree of Brazilian expansion into the wilderness areas that exist along the boundaries with other South American states. It can be seen that most of this territorial expansion occurred in the nineteenth century, and much was development-led, as the Amazon was opened up to traffic, and the rubber boom reached its height between 1890 and 1912.

Brazil's military leaders have played a leading role in its territorial policy for much of the present

Outback Aussies lament ruling that bans 'grog' one day a week

One of the thirstiest towns in the Australian outback has introduced a "grog-free" day each week.

But the ban on alcohol sales at Tennant Creek on Thursdays – at the request of Julalikari Aborigines – has angered some white residents who allege racial discrimination.

The Northern Territory's Liquor Commission approved the restrictions for the small mining town, about 500 miles south of Darwin, to stem alcohol-related street crime. It is the first time all residents in a mainly white town will face such curbs.

Five liquor outlets on the main street are banned from all bar and off-licence sales on Thursdays, the social security pay day, for a six-month trial period. In addition, there is a total ban on four-litre wine casks and flagons of fortified wines.

The owner of the Tennant Creek Hotel, Frank Martin, said the ban discriminated against the two-thirds of the 3,000 residents who are non-Aboriginal and could cause racial tension.

The commission says the town's rate of per capital alcohol consumption is almost twice that of the Northern Territory, which is the highest of any Australian region.

Police say almost all crime in the town is alcohol-related and about 95 per cent of crimes are committed by male Aborigines. The Julalikari said an alcohol-free day was needed to break the cycle of abuse.

The move comes after a report by the Human Rights and Equal Opportunities Commission said publicans could discriminate against Aborigines, whose elders did not want them to drink, by refusing to sell them alcohol.

The Guardian, June 1995

century. The remote territory of Acre was annexed in 1903 and in the first part of the twentieth century Marshal Rondon supervised the building of roads and of telegraph links to the interior. He was also responsible for organising the Government's supervision of Indian affairs, and founded the Indian Protection service in 1940.

In the 1950s General Golbery do Couto e Silva became the successor to Rondon, and influenced geopolitical thinking in the country for almost two decades. 'Security and development' was the motto that encouraged much of the activity in Amazonia in the 1960s and 1970s (see Figure 2.5.7). Road building that linked the frontier wildernesses with the centre of Brazil was fundamental to the geopolitical strategy and includes the following.

■ The Belem–Brasilia Highway built in 1956 and tarmacked in 1974.
■ The Cuiaba–Porto Velho Highway built in 1964, and tarmacked in 1980.
■ The Transamazonia Highway built to Iquitos and giving access to Lima in Peru.
■ The Cuiaba–Santarem Highway, built in 1975, with a later extension to Paramaribo in Surinam.
■ The Porto Velho–Manaus–Boa Vista Highway, eventually linking to Caracas in Venezuela and Georgetown in Guyana.
■ The Perimetral Norte linking Amapa with Bogota in Colombia, although still incomplete.

The completion of these highways encouraged a wider concept – that of Panamazonia. Its further development was inherent in the signing of the Treaty of Amazonian Co-operation in 1978.

Current interest focuses on the Calha Norte project, presented to President Sarney in 1985, by General Rubens Denys, Head of the National Security Council. Sarney actively supported the Calha Norte Project, which aims at securing and developing the wilderness regions between the channels of the Solimoes and the Amazon and the northern frontier (see Figure 2.5.8) during his term of office.

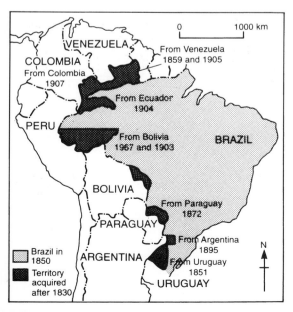

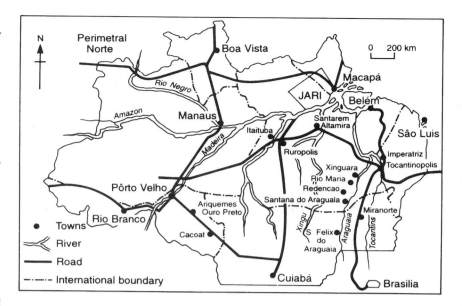

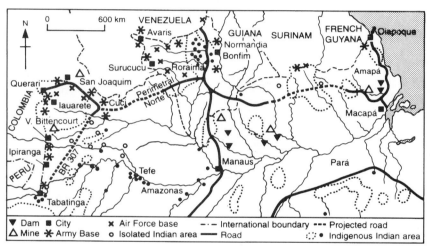

The successor to President Sarney, Fernando Collor do Mello insisted on a much lower military profile in this frontier region, and was instrumental in the establishment of the Yanomami Park (see Figure 2.4.5, page 26). However, the armed forces still have a fundamental role to play in the frontier areas. Under the Brazilian constitution, drawn up in 1988, the military have responsibility for proposing the terms, conditions and use of all areas of national security, including the frontier wildernesses.

Territorial disputes continue to simmer in other Amazon territories. Ecuador and Peru are in dispute over an area in the Cordillera del Condor, and fighting broke out over rival territorial claims in both 1981 and more recently in 1995.

FIGURE 2.5.7 (*top*) The road network in Amazonia

FIGURE 2.5.8 (*above*) The Calha Norte Project

Student Activity 2.7

Border disputes in the Sahara are equally common. Nearly all boundaries within the Saharan wilderness are heavily guarded military zones. Attempt to find out which of the zones are most unstable, and examine the reasons for territorial disputes in the Sahara.

FIGURE 2.5.6 (*far left*) Brazil's troubled frontier

The strategic significance of a wilderness island: South Georgia

'Just rejoice at the news and congratulate our forces and the marines ... Rejoice, rejoice.'
Mrs Thatcher, Prime Minister, meeting reporters in Downing Street, after receiving news of the Argentinian surrender on South Georgia on 26 April 1982.

FIGURE 2.5.9 South Georgia

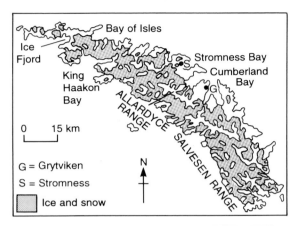

FIGURE 2.5.10 The entrance to Cumberland Bay, South Georgia

South Georgia is one of the largest of the wilderness islands of the South Atlantic, which lie between the Antarctic Peninsula and Cape Horn (see Figure 2.5.9). Captain Cook landed on the Island of South Georgia on 17 January 1775. The island is about 170 km long and between 2–30 km wide, half of which is covered in ice and snow. South Georgia has been described as 'the Alps in mid ocean' (Figure 2.5.10). Two mountain ranges form the spine of the island, with Mount Paget rising to approximately 3000 m. Its coastline is spectacular, but forbidding, consisting of high sea cliffs, broken by glaciers and fjords. The only level ground exists at the heads of some of the bays and fjords, and it was here that whaling stations were established in the early twentieth century.

The strategic importance of the wilderness islands of the south Atlantic was first apparent in the 1914–18 war in two major fleet actions fought for control of the shipping lanes around Cape Horn. In the 1939–45 war, Operation Tabarin was set up for two main reasons, to deter the use of South Atlantic and Antarctic anchorages by German raiders and to strengthen the claims of Britain to sovereignty over the Falkland Islands Dependencies (now South Georgia and the South Sandwich Islands, shown in Figure 2.5.11). Bases were set up, meteorological work was carried out, and much preliminary survey work was done.

Argentina's interest in South Georgia was first apparent in the early twentieth century when a whaling station was established at Grytviken for an Argentine company. The station operated until 1960, when it was sold to a company registered in the Falkland Islands. The British claim to sovereignty was established principally through discovery, occupation and effective government. Argentina had made vague claims to sovereignty in the twentieth century, but these were more to do with South Georgia as part of the Falkland Islands Dependencies rather than South Georgia itself. After dubious incursions into South Georgian waters and illegal landings by Argentinian forces, a serious invasion of South Georgia followed on 3 April 1982.

After some fierce resistance from British marines, the forces surrendered to the Argentines. On 25 April British forces subdued the Argentinians on the island who surrendered on the following day. A permanent garrison is now maintained on South Georgia, and its continued existence is likely while strategic matters in the South Atlantic remain unresolved.

FIGURE 2.5.11 Falkland Islands Dependencies and British Antarctic Territories

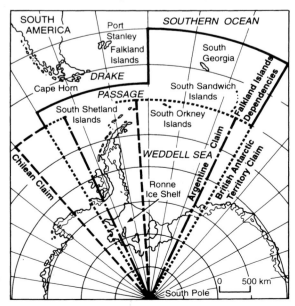

Student Activity 2.8

1 Discuss the use of wilderness areas for military purposes. On what grounds can it be justified?
2 Why is it difficult to manage the use of wildernesses for these purposes?

ESSAYS

1 Discuss why environmental factors make it so difficult for people to establish permanent settlements in wilderness regions.
2 Explain why strategic interests will continue to demand a military presence in wilderness zones.

3
WILDERNESS
LANDSCAPES

*'And nature, left undisturbed and unhindered, has a
way of ruling with a hand that is graceful and restrained,
even while giving us a land that is wild, colourful, and
beautiful beyond description.'*

John Bezy

KEY IDEAS

■ Wilderness landscapes occur on a range of
scales, and possess great variety in physical form.
■ Variety in wilderness landscapes results from
the distinct physical processes operating in
different climatic regimes.
■ Wilderness landscapes possess great scenic
appeal, which has encouraged the growth of
tourism.

■ Wilderness landscapes are increasingly in need
of protection, because of the expansion of people's
activities.
■ Increased awareness of the value of wilderness
landscapes has seen the growth of local
national and international policies for their
conservation.

3.1 *Scale and variety in wilderness landscapes*

The scale and variety of wilderness landscapes
constitute their major appeal to people. If we
consider the great expanses of wilderness shown on
a global map little remains over much of Europe
and the USA. Yet few would deny that within these
regions, areas exist whose landscapes have
wilderness qualities but are limited in scale. Viewed
from the peak of Skala to the north, the Jotunheim
in Norway is a true Scandinavian wilderness.
Equally a survey of the Assynt landscape of ice-
scoured rock, bog and lochan from the summit of
Canisp in north west Scotland reveals another land
virtually untouched by people (Figures 3.1.1 and
3.1.2). Compared with the views from the air of the
Wrangell-St Elias Mountains of south eastern
Alaska (Figure 3.1.3) or the prospect of the George
Gill Ranges in central Australia from an outback
track (Figure 3.1.4), the European examples lack
something in scale, but still possess certain
wilderness qualities.

Wilderness landscapes owe their variety to their
widespread distribution across the globe. In
different latitudes different physical processes are at
work. Polar landscapes in the Arctic and Antarctic
reveal the work of ice, and in the sub-arctic lands of
Eurasia and North America, together with some of
the remote islands of the South Atlantic, periglacial

processes are partly responsible for their distinctive
scenery. Desert landscapes in the Sahara and in the
Australian interior reflect the work of physical
weathering (Figure 3.1.5), wind erosion and
deposition and the occasional contemporary work
of water.

FIGURE 3.1.1 The
Jotunheim ice cap,
Norway

FIGURE 3.1.2 Assynt from the summit of Canisp

FIGURE 3.1.3 (*far right*) Wrangell-St Elias Mountains

FIGURE 3.1.4 George Gill Ranges in the Northern Territory, Australia

FIGURE 3.1.5 (*far right*) The Devil's Marbles, south of Tennant Creek in Northern Territory, Australia

These areas often show evidence of erosion which has occurred under wetter conditions existing in the past. Savanna landscapes show their characteristic combination of wide, gently sloping plains broken by sharply defined **inselberg** over considerable parts of the sub-Saharan wildernesses in Africa (Figure 3.1.6). Mountain landscapes display much variety in themselves, depending on whether they are high enough and cold enough for glacial processes to operate. Many desert mountains, such as those of the Hoggar and the Tibesti in the Sahara, and the Macdonnell ranges in Australia show their own distinctive landscapes,

FIGURE 3.1.6 Inselberg, Tsavo West National Park, Africa

quite different from the glacially sharpened peaks of the southern Andes or eastern Greenland. Finally, in the great wildernesses of Amazonia, physical form is partly obscured by the dense mantle of tropical rainforest, only to reappear in the Roraima massif to the north or the rising slopes of the eastern Andes to the west.

Wilderness landscapes are important for a number of reasons.

■ They possess enormous scenic appeal, by virtue of their untouched nature;

■ they provide an opportunity for earth scientists to study geology where outcrop and structure are easily revealed;

■ they allow a study of physical processes in a wide variety of environments;

■ they form the physical environment for some of the world's most distinctive, rich and fragile ecosystems;

■ they provide an opportunity for 'spiritual refreshment' for those that live in populated areas;

■ they are often the homelands of truly indigenous peoples. Because wilderness landscapes are of such high aesthetic and scenic quality, it is important to realise that they are likely to come under increasing threat from a number of sources:

■ their scenic appeal will inevitably attract the attention of the tourist industry. The lack of a sensitive approach could cause lasting damage to the very landscapes that people have come to visit;

■ scarce resources exist within these wilderness landscapes, and development of these resources needs careful and sensitive planning (it may be necessary to ban development completely as in the case of the 50-year mining ban in Antarctica);

■ the visual impact of new transport routes could damage wilderness landscapes;

■ geopolitical considerations may necessitate a high profile military presence in such areas, which could spoil their intrinsic qualities;

■ threats from global warming (wilderness wetlands), acid rain (boreal forest) could damage the ecosystems of wilderness landscapes.

These threats to wilderness landscapes are fully covered in Chapters 5, 6 and 7.

3.2 Case studies of wilderness landscapes

In Section 3.1 scale and variety were shown to be important features of wilderness landscapes. These case studies are arranged in ascending order of scale, and illustrate the variety of wilderness landscapes that can be found across the globe.

1 Fisherfield Forest: the 'Whitbread Wilderness' (north west Scotland);
2 Yellowstone National Park (Wyoming, USA);
3 Svalbard (Spitzbergen);
4 Glacier Bay Alaska and Brooks Ranges (Alaska, USA);
5 The Central Australian Deserts;
6 Antarctica.

FIGURE 3.3.1 (*left*) Western fringe of Fisherfield Forest from Slioch

3.3 Fisherfield Forest, north west Scotland

FIGURE 3.3.2 Fisherfield Forest

'The atmosphere in this corrie is one of utter seclusion, and the scenery has a strange beauty.'
                    Tom Strang in the Northern Highlands,
                    Scottish Mountaineering Club,
                    District Guide.

Fisherfield Forest is one of the deer forests of north west Scotland. Today it has no forest cover at all, although hunting and shooting deer is still practised. It was known as the 'Whitbread Wilderness' after one of the former owners of the Fisherfield estate. The name seems to have been retained among the climbing and walking fraternity, who, apart from the sports people who still hunt and shoot in the area, are the only people to penetrate one of the most remote wilderness areas in Britain. Figure 3.3.2 shows its location between two glacially deepened lochs, Loch Maree and Loch na Sealga. The centre of the 'Wilderness' is some 10 km from the nearest road as the crow flies and about the same distance from permanent settlements on Loch Broom. Within this radius there

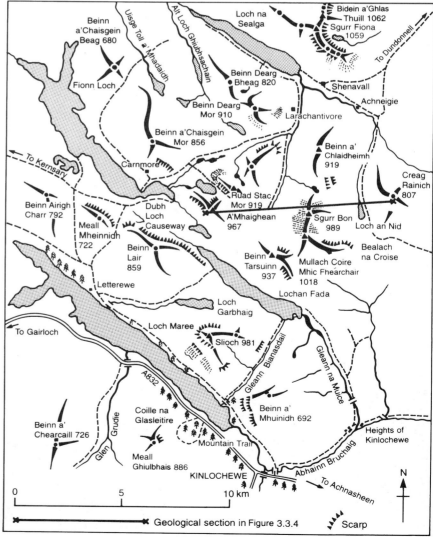

FIGURE 3.3.5 (*far right*)
Fionn Loch from the
summit of
A'Mhaighdean

is the occasional mountain bothy and a few ill-
defined tracks, but the area is dominated by its
soaring mountains (A'Mhaighdean is said to be the
most remote of the Scottish Munros – the peaks
above 915 m), deep glacial lakes and fast-flowing
and treacherous rivers. Figure 3.3.1, taken from
Slioch on its western fringe, shows the desolate
nature of Fisherfield Forest and the water colour
sketch in Figure 3.3.3 from David Bellamy's *Wild
Places of Britain* well portrays its bleak winter aspect.

FIGURE 3.3.3 Water
colour study: Beinn
a'Chaidheimh

was probably buried by the ice which moved over
the area from south east to north west. The legacy of
glacial erosion includes some of the finest
landforms in north west Scotland (see Figure 3.3.5).
Much of the outcrop of the Lewisian gneiss displays
a glacially roughened surface, sometimes referred to
as knock-and-lochan topography. This landscape
forms a striking contrast with the stark and massive
Torridonian mountains to the south east. In the later
glacial stages many of the peaks of the area would
have nourished their own small **corrie glaciers**,
such as those on An Teallach, and Beinn Dearg
Bheag (see Figure 3.3.6).

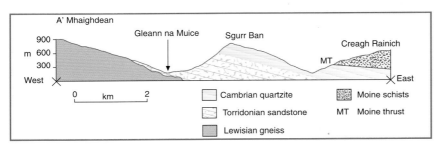

FIGURE 3.3.4 Geological
cross-section of
Fisherfield Forest from
A'Mhaighdean to Creagh
Rainich

Fisherfield owes its striking wilderness
landscape to its geology and the glacial and
periglacial processes that have shaped its scenery.
Figure 3.3.4 is a sketch geological cross-section
across the area. Most of the rocks are **Pre-Cambrian**,
but there is a small strip of Cambrian rocks running
through the centre. The oldest rocks, the Lewisian
gneiss, dominate the north west of the area, and
they reach their highest point in A'Mhaighdean. To
the south east they are overlain by the Torridonian
sandstone, which forms many of the peaks in the
area, including its highest, An Teallach. Some of the
Torridonian peaks carry a small capping of
Cambrian quartzite, such as Beinn a'Chaidheimh.
Beyond the narrow zone of the Cambrian rocks lies
the Moine thrust zone where more Pre-Cambrian
rocks, principally the Moine series of **schists**, have
been bodily thrust over the other rocks.

In the **Pleistocene** Period much of Fisherfield

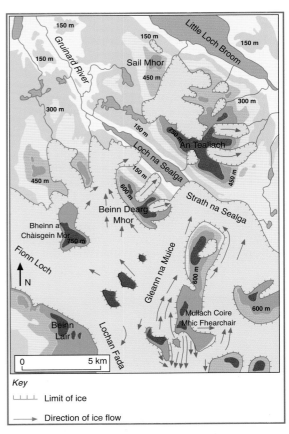

FIGURE 3.3.6 Late stage
glaciation of Fisherfield
Forest

After the last corrie glaciers disappeared from the area, periglacial processes began to operate and have continued to the present day. Although **periglacial** processes are normally associated with Arctic and sub-arctic regions, the higher parts of Fisherfield Forest do experience conditions that promote a range of periglacial activity. Rather than enduring the extreme cold, frequent freezing and thawing and the deeply frozen ground (**permafrost**) common in the Arctic, the Fisherfield mountains experience extreme wetness, heavy precipitation, prolonged snow-cover and frequent strong winds. Thus periglacial activity will be different in scale and character in these mountains. Figure 3.3.7 shows some of the periglacial features to be found in the Fisherfield Forest area.

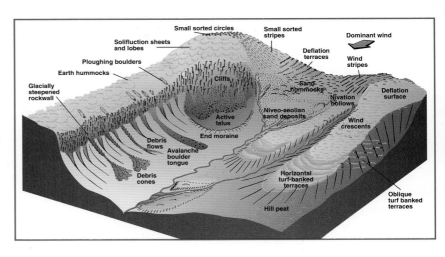

FIGURE 3.3.7 Range of periglacial features found in Fisherfield Forest

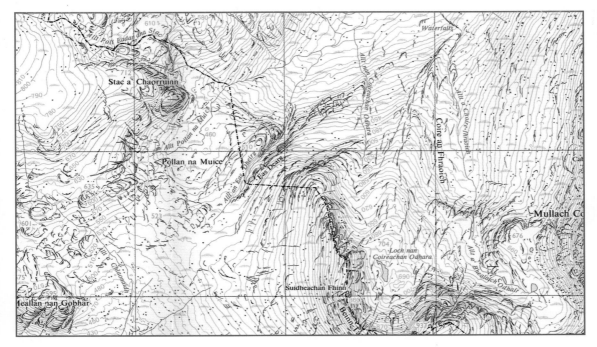

FIGURE 3.3.8 Ordnance Survey extract 1:25 000 NH 07/17 Loch a'Bhraoin © Copyright

---

Student Activity 3.1

Using the extract from Loch a'Bhraoin (NH07/17) in Figure 3.3.8 and the diagrams and photographs in the Fisherfield Forest section, explain how you would convince a sceptical friend that the Fisherfield Forest is a true wilderness area. You will need to consider such things as distance from access routes and settlements, the total dominance of the physical landscape and the absence of human activity.

3.4 Yellowstone National Park

'We were compelled to content ourselves with listening to marvellous tales of burning plains, immense lakes, and boiling springs, without being able to verify these wonders.'
Captain W F Raynolds, US Corps of Topographical Engineers on being unable to reach Yellowstone in the 1850s because of deep snow

Raynolds was one of an increasing number of surveyors, speculators and adventurers who explored the wilderness of Yellowstone in the mid-nineteenth century. Such was the interest stimulated by their reports that people's attention turned increasingly towards the idea of keeping Yellowstone as an area that people could 'travel through as freely and enjoy the region as we did', (Charles Cook, on returning from a visit to the

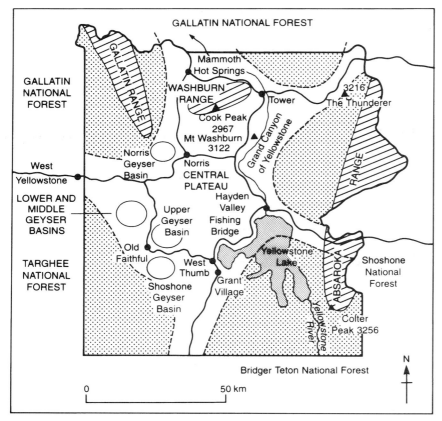

FIGURE 3.4.1 (*top*) Yellowstone National Park

FIGURE 3.4.2 (a)

FIGURE 3.4.2
Yellowstone Park
(a) Mammoth Springs,
(b) Grand Canyon of the
Yellowstone River
(c) Old Faithful

Figure 3.4.3 shows the geology of the Yellowstone National Park. The oldest rocks (Pre-Cambrian and **Palaeozoic**) occur mainly in the north west of Yellowstone where they form the Gallatin Mountains, some of the most remote uplands within the Park. Although **Mesozoic** rocks do occur within the Park, it is the Tertiary volcanic rocks that are responsible for much of the spectacular scenery. In the south east of the Park the eruption of huge piles of lava some 55–50 million years ago have contributed to the landforms of the Absaroka Range and the Washburn Range in the interior. Later volcanic activity was responsible for the formation of a huge **caldera** in what is now the central part of the Park. Part of the caldera is occupied by Yellowstone Lake itself.

FIGURE 3.4.2 (b)

geysers of Yellowstone). Thus in 1871 the United States Congress introduced a bill to 'set aside a certain tract of land lying near the headwaters of the Yellowstone River as a public park'. The following year the bill became law, and Yellowstone became the first designated National Park in the USA.

Yellowstone National Park (see Figure 3.4.1) occupies an area of some 8992 km², and although, today it is not the remote location that it was in the mid-nineteenth century, it still retains some of the finest wilderness landscapes in the USA. Yellowstone National Park receives over 2 million visitors a year now, but relatively few venture beyond the familiar sites of Mammoth Springs, the Grand Canyon of the Yellowstone and Old Faithful (Figure 3.4.2).

In the collapsed centre of the caldera eruption of lava flows continued until 60 000 years ago.

Although glaciation has not resulted in landforms such as the sharp peaks of the Grand Tetons to the south of Yellowstone or the deeply-cut glacial troughs of Yosemite in California, it has played an important role in the shaping of the scenery of Yellowstone. Glaciers invaded the park in three different periods from the higher areas of the Absaroka Mountains to the south east and the Gallatin Mountains to the north west.

Important contributions to the wilderness landscapes of Yellowstone are made by the deeply-incised canyons, such as that of the Yellowstone River and the thermal features of the hot springs and geysers. Marked contrasts exist between various sections of the Yellowstone Valley (see Figure 3.4.4). The river meanders over a broad plain in the Hayden Valley before plunging into the deep canyon at Lower Falls. Figure 3.4.5 shows the evolution of the canyon over the last 600 000 years.

The thermal systems captivated the early explorers of the Yellowstone area and Charles Cook wrote, as they watched a geyser erupt, 'we could not contain our enthusiasm; with one accord we all took off our hats and yelled with all our might.'

FIGURE 3.4.2 (c)

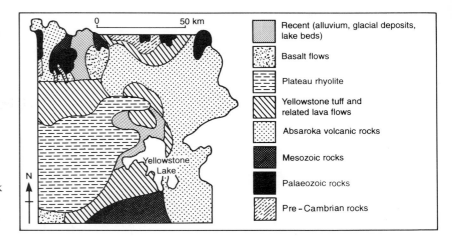

FIGURE 3.4.3 (above) Geology of Yellowstone

FIGURE 3.4.4
Yellowstone Park
(a) (left) Fishing Bridge,
(b) (below)Lower Falls

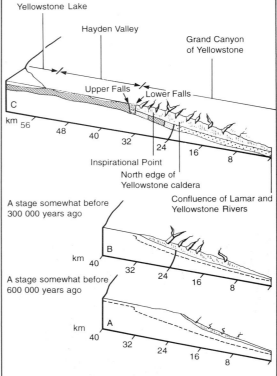

Today they can hardly be said to be part of the true wilderness of Yellowstone, simply because they are easily accessible from the main roads that run through the Park. However, they were part of the essential wilderness that the nineteenth century explorers found. The thermal features are related to the past volcanicity of the region. Most hot springs discharge water in a steady, regular fashion, although various factors are responsible for differing levels of activity – some hot springs boil violently and emit vast clouds of vapour, whilst in others hot water wells up gently. Where the **conduits** are too narrow, or the hot water and steam are under great pressure, a geyser will erupt (see Figure 3.4.6).

Development of Grand Canyon of Yellowstone river. Profiles along the floor of the Grand Canyon of the Yellowstone as it appears today (C) and as it appeared at two older stages in its development (A and B). Note particularly the various kinds of rocks through which the canyon has been cut, and how rock differences have influenced the location of the two falls ▒ unaltered rhyolite; ▓ rhyolite with much volcanic glass; ░ hydrothermally altered rhyolite ⋰ Absaroka volcanic rocks

FIGURE 3.4.5 Evolution of the Grand Canyon of the Yellowstone River

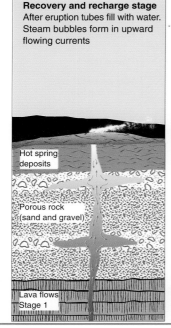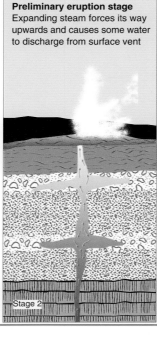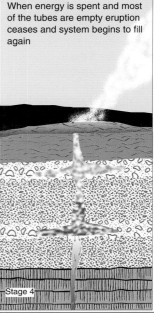

Recovery and recharge stage
After eruption tubes fill with water. Steam bubbles form in upward flowing currents

Preliminary eruption stage
Expanding steam forces its way upwards and causes some water to discharge from surface vent

Full eruption stage
Large amounts of water inside chambers flash into steam and full eruption occurs

Steam stage
When energy is spent and most of the tubes are empty eruption ceases and system begins to fill again

Hot spring deposits

Porous rock (sand and gravel)

Lava flows
Stage 1

Stage 2

Stage 3

Stage 4

FIGURE 3.4.6 Geysers in Yellowstone

Student Activity 3.2

1 Why was the Yellowstone wilderness chosen as the first National Park of the USA in 1872?

2 In the late twentieth century Yellowstone might be described as a wilderness that has been lost. Explain why. Can you suggest and justify any management policies by which it might become a wilderness regained?

FIGURE 3.5.1 (*below*) Magdalene Fjord, the crest of Svalbard (Spitzbergen)

FIGURE 3.5.2 (*below right*) Green Harbour, Svalbard: mean monthly temperature and precipitation

3.5 Svalbard: A wilderness landscape of the Arctic

Svalbard (Spitzbergen) lies well within the Arctic Circle extending from just south of 77N to beyond over 80N. Figure 3.5.2 shows the temperature and precipitation regimes for Svalbard, with much of the precipitation falling as snow.

Most of the Svalbard archipelago (62 400 km²) is covered by ice cap, with only bare, periglacially affected ground exposed in the major valleys and around the coast (see Figure 3.5.1).

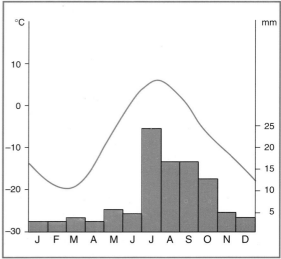

Few people have the opportunity to visit the Arctic wilderness landscapes of Svalbard. It has never had any indigenous population, and, although there has been intermittent activity by hunters and trappers, it is the coal resources of Spitzbergen that have been exploited by both Norway, which exercises sovereignty over the islands, and Russia. These coal resources have led to the growth of a few small settlements along the coasts of Isfjorden and Van Mijentfjorden (see Figure 3.5.3), but the remainder of Svalbard is still a pristine wilderness of glacier and fjord (Figure 3.5.4).

FIGURE 3.5.3 (*far left*) Svalbard (Spitzbergen)

FIGURE 3.5.3 (*far left*) Svalbard (Spitzbergen)

FIGURE 3.5.4 (*above*) Glacier and fjord on Svalbard

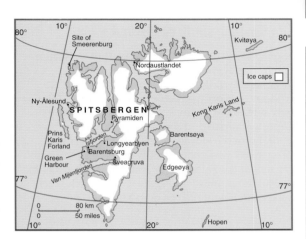

Glaciation increases from south west to north east across the Svalbard archipelago. On the main island the **firn line** decreases from 700 m in the south west to 350 m in the north east, where high ice cliffs meet the sea along considerable stretches of the coast. Nordaustlandet is almost completely covered in ice cap, and the east and south coasts are almost Antarctic in nature, with continuous ice cliffs for over 100 km.

Figure 3.5.5 shows the distribution of permafrost in the circumpolar north. Svalbard lies well within the line of continuous permafrost, and the depth varies between 75 and 450 m. In the Fisherfield Forest wilderness it was seen that past and present periglacial activity plays an important part in the wilderness landscape. In Svalbard the tundra surfaces around the coast are dominated by periglacial features, which can sometimes display bewildering complexity in a relatively small area. **Patterned ground**, with **polygons** and **stripes**, occupies much of the surface, together with a whole range of **hummocks** and **frost blisters**.

Periglacial landscapes dominate much of the wilderness region of both the Canadian and the Siberian Arctic. They are rarely spectacular, and are often bleak and lonely plains or plateaux. However they are of great importance to those scientists studying the physical processes that operate in these Arctic conditions of permafrost, and seasonal thawing and freezing in the surface layers. Understanding these processes, as will be shown in Chapter 6, is of vital importance to controlling the development of resources in these regions.

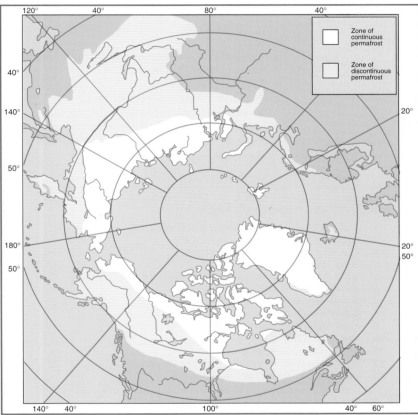

Additionally the sensitive and fragile tundra ecosystem in these wilderness regions needs particular care and understanding if it is not to be damaged in future developments.

FIGURE 3.5.5 Permafrost in the circumpolar north

Student Activity 3.3

1 Explain why the wilderness landscape of Svalbard is under much less threat than the Yellowstone landscape.
2 In what ways is the landscape of Svalbard likely to come under increasing threat in the future?
3 Consider what steps the Norwegian Government might take to counteract these threats. You will need to reconsider some of the issues raised in the study of South Georgia in Chapter 2, Section 2.5.

3.6 The wilderness landscapes of Alaska

'Now hidden, now partly revealed, the whole making a picture of icy wilderness, unspeakably pure and sublime.'
John Muir, on seeing Glacier Bay in 1879.

The landscapes

It has already been noted that there are very few sizeable areas of wilderness in the contiguous part of the USA or, as it is called in Alaska, the 'Lower 48'. Wilderness regions probably occupy about one-third of Alaska's 1 536 610 km². Figure 3.6.1 shows the distribution of the so-called National Interest Lands, the (D)2 lands, which broadly coincide with the wilderness regions of Alaska as shown in Figure 1.3.1. There are four categories of National Interest Lands:

1 National Parks, Preserves and Monuments;
2 National Wildlife Refuges;
3 National Forests;
4 Bureau of Land Management areas.

Most of the National Parks are in the south, either in the Alaska Range or on the coast. National Wildlife Refuges are in the more remote areas such as the North Slope, the Aleutian Islands or in the huge delta of the Yukon River. The National Forests are mainly in the south east in the Alaskan Panhandle, with its very high levels of precipitation, and in the lands around Prince William Sound.

Three Alaskan wilderness landscapes are selected for study in this section:
1 The Glacier Bay wilderness in south east Alaska;
2 the Mount McKinley Massif in the Denali National Park;
3 the Brooks Range in the Alaskan north.

Glacier Bay, south east Alaska

Nearly 80 per cent (over 11 000 km²) of the Glacier Bay National Park and Preserve is officially designated wilderness land. Access to the wilderness is only possible by sea or air, and the only settlement of any size is Gustavus, with its important airstrip, at the entrance to Glacier Bay itself. From the entrance at Sikataday Narrows, Glacier Bay penetrates deeply into the icefields and glaciers of the Fairweather and Alsek Ranges of the coastal mountains (see Figure 3.6.2), which reach a maximum height of 4663 m in Mount Fairweather

FIGURE 3.6.1 Alaska: National Interest Lands

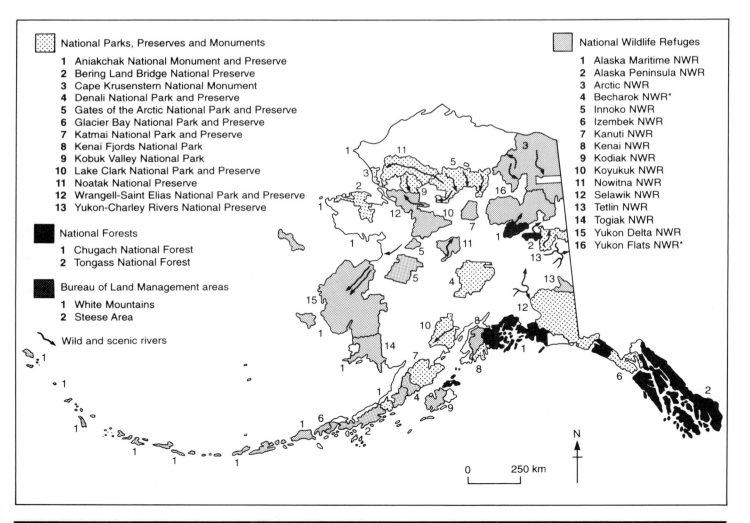

National Parks, Preserves and Monuments
1 Aniakchak National Monument and Preserve
2 Bering Land Bridge National Preserve
3 Cape Krusenstern National Monument
4 Denali National Park and Preserve
5 Gates of the Arctic National Park and Preserve
6 Glacier Bay National Park and Preserve
7 Katmai National Park and Preserve
8 Kenai Fjords National Park
9 Kobuk Valley National Park
10 Lake Clark National Park and Preserve
11 Noatak National Preserve
12 Wrangell-Saint Elias National Park and Preserve
13 Yukon-Charley Rivers National Preserve

National Forests
1 Chugach National Forest
2 Tongass National Forest

Bureau of Land Management areas
1 White Mountains
2 Steese Area

Wild and scenic rivers

National Wildlife Refuges
1 Alaska Maritime NWR
2 Alaska Peninsula NWR
3 Arctic NWR
4 Becharok NWR*
5 Innoko NWR
6 Izembek NWR
7 Kanuti NWR
8 Kenai NWR
9 Kodiak NWR
10 Koyukuk NWR
11 Nowitna NWR
12 Selawik NWR
13 Tetlin NWR
14 Togiak NWR
15 Yukon Delta NWR
16 Yukon Flats NWR*

0   250 km

N

itself. The quality of this wilderness landscape is shown in Figure 3.6.3. Sharply glaciated peaks rise from the huge icefields, from which glaciers stream down to Glacier Bay, its inlets such as Tarr Inlet, John Hopkins Inlet (Figure 3.6.5) and Muir Inlet or the Pacific coast. Within the Park 16 glaciers empty into tidewater, with a pattern of characteristic advance and retreat. At the moment six of the glaciers appear to be advancing (in particular the John Hopkins and the Grand Pacific), three

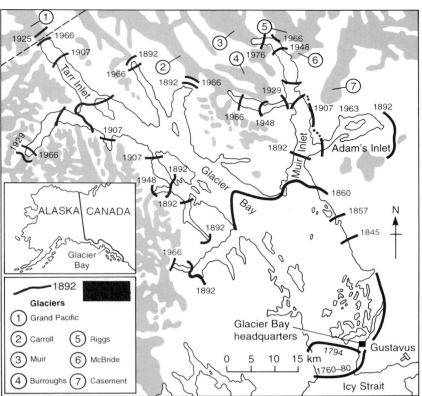

FIGURE 3.6.2 (*above*) Glacier Bay

retreating and seven are more or less stationary. Only one glacier, La Perouse, discharges directly into the Gulf of Alaska. Others such as the Fairweather and the Grand Plateau pour ice into the fault zone of Desolation Valley, or spread their ice out in huge lobate patterns on the narrow coastal plain (Figure 3.6.4).

Apart from the thousands of visitors who view the glaciers and peaks from the safety and security of their cruise ships (Figure 3.6.6), few enter the wilderness of Glacier Bay. Since Muir's first exploration in 1879 only backpackers and climbers venture beyond the shores of Glacier Bay.

FIGURE 3.6.3 (*top left*) Wilderness landscape: Glacier Bay, from the air

FIGURE 3.6.4 (*middle left*) Coastal glaciers from Gulf of Alaska

FIGURE 3.6.5 (*above*) John Hopkins Inlet

FIGURE 3.6.6 (*bottom left*) Cruise vessel in John Hopkins Inlet

The Mount McKinley Massif

FIGURE 3.6.7 (*right*)
Mount McKinley, Denali

Mount McKinley (Figure 3.6.7) occupies a central position in the Denali National Park (22 784 km², of which 7600 are a designated wilderness area). Figure 3.6.8 shows that the wilderness area extends from the entrance to the Park on the Nenana River south westwards to include all of the highest parts of the McKinley massif. Although the wilderness quality is highest in the McKinley area, many other landscapes in this wilderness area, such as those around Polychrome Mountain and Primrose Ridge are much valued (see Figure 3.6.9). Tourist access is via a track that runs from the Visitor Access Centre in Denali village to Eielson Visitor Centre, some 100 km into the wilderness area, but some 40 km short of Mount McKinley.

FIGURE 3.6.8 Denali National Park

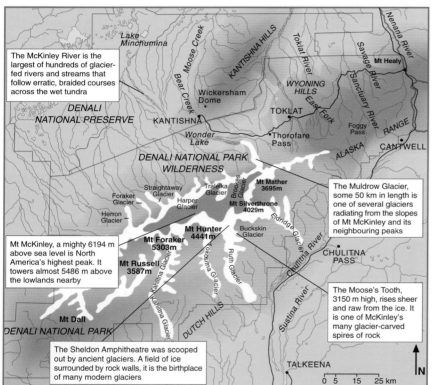

- The McKinley River is the largest of hundreds of glacier-fed rivers and streams that follow erratic, braided courses across the wet tundra

- Mt McKinley, a mighty 6194 m above sea level is North America's highest peak. It towers almost 5486 m above the lowlands nearby

- The Sheldon Amphitheatre was scooped out by ancient glaciers. A field of ice surrounded by rock walls, it is the birthplace of many modern glaciers

- The Muldrow Glacier, some 50 km in length is one of several glaciers radiating from the slopes of Mt McKinley and its neighbouring peaks

- The Moose's Tooth, 3150 m high, rises sheer and raw from the ice. It is one of McKinley's many glacier-carved spires of rock

Mount McKinley (6194 m) is the highest point in North America, and dominates the landscape in the central part of the massif. Figure 3.6.10 shows the principal features. McKinley and the surrounding peaks are cut in granite, and form a vast complex of classic glacial landforms with corries, and high precipitous ridges through which ice spills from one valley into another. Fed by a heavy snowfall, the Massif gives rise to a series of glaciers that flow away to the north and south. On the south east side of the Massif (Figure 3.6.11) there is heavier snowfall, and thus the snowfields are much larger (the Don Sheldon Amphitheatre), and the glaciers longer (the Kahiltna Glacier is nearly 50 km long). Surprisingly the longest glacier is the Muldrow glacier (Figure 3.6.12) which flows north east from Mount McKinley for some 52 km before it becomes almost unrecognisable under the cover of thick masses of surface moraine. It is a glacier prone to sudden surges, which may be due to the build up of water between the base of the ice and the bedrock channel.

Away from the McKinley Massif, the surrounding wilderness region displays many of the important features of a periglacial regime, with rivers such as the Toklats and the Savage following braided courses across the tundra landscape.

The Brooks Range

If wilderness is measured by means of access, then the Brooks Range is the most remote of the three Alaskan wildernesses studied in this section. Access to Glacier Bay is mainly by water, or by air to the landing strip at Gustavus. Visitors to Denali arrive on the Anchorage–Fairbanks railroad or on the George Parks Highway, which is closed in winter over long stretches. Apart from the point where the Brooks Range is crossed by the Dalton Highway (see Section 1.4) there is virtually no access at all to this wilderness except on foot from the floatplane base at Bettles, 65 km to the south, or from the airstrip at Anaktuvuk Pass. Charter floatplanes will fly out from Bettles to designated lakes and rivers.

FIGURE 3.6.9 Landscape around Polychrome Mountain

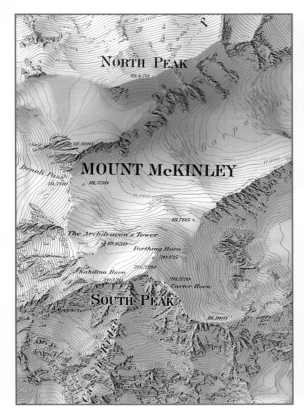

FIGURE 3.6.10 (*far left*) Map extract from the US Geological Survey

FIGURE 3.6.11 Ruth Glacier

FIGURE 3.6.12 Muldrow Glacier

The Brooks Range is covered by three National Park Service Units (Figure 3.6.13):

■ The Gates of the Arctic National Park and Preserve;
■ the Noatak National Preserve;
■ Kobuk Valley National Park.

There are some 51 400 km² of total wilderness land within this area, six and a half times as large as the whole of Yellowstone National Park, and over four-fifths the size of Svalbard. The Brooks Range runs from the Canadian border to the Chukchi Sea, rising to a height of 2612 m at Mount Igikpak in the Schwatka Mountains to the west and to a height of 2749 m at Mount Chamberlin in the Romanzof Mountains to the east. Much of the Brooks Range receives little precipitation, with as low as 200 mm in places. This accounts for the lack of ice fields and glaciers except in a few parts of the Romanzof Mountains, although there is sufficient evidence of an earlier glaciation in the landforms of the higher areas. However, much of the area suffers from permafrost, which keeps parts of the low-lying areas in the valleys ill-drained and boggy throughout the summer.

FIGURE 3.6.13 Brooks Range

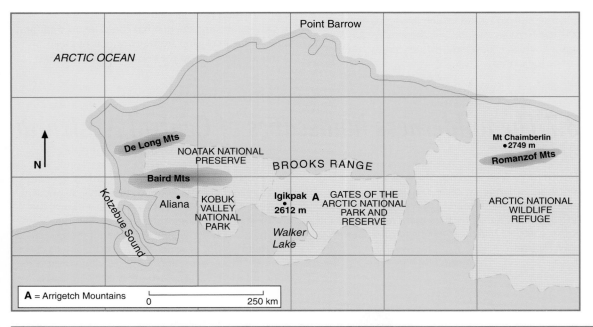

Landforms vary enormously in such a vast wilderness (Figure 3.6.14), with each of the individual groups of mountains having distinctive forms. In the east the high peaks of the Romanzofs are cut in limestone, granite and volcanics, whilst the sharp and rugged Arrigetch Mountains in the west are again granitic.

FIGURE 3.6.14 Brooks Range

Although both Eskimos and Athabascan Indians practised a nomadic way of life in the Brooks Range in the past, most have moved out into more permanent settlements in the valleys to the north and the south. Exploration of the Brooks Range by white people did not begin seriously until the turn of the century. For some years the central Brooks Range was worked for gold, but Wiseman in the Koyukuk valley, close to the Dalton Highway is the only settlement that survives. A young forester, Robert Marshall, explored much of the central Brooks Range in the early 1930s and probably did more than anyone to promote the concept of wilderness in northern Alaska. He advocated the designation of the entire northern half of Alaska, from the Yukon River to the Arctic Ocean as one huge wilderness preserve. Although this proposal was never put into practice, much of the wilderness landscape of the Brooks Range is now protected. The Noatak Preserve is a designated biosphere reserve under the United Nation's Man and the Biosphere programme, which aims to recognise pristine ecosystems, and use them as controls against which ecosystems influenced by humans can be measured.

Outside the preserves, in the west of the Brooks Range, both the De Long and the Baird Mountains contain mineral deposits of major international importance. One of the world's richest copper belts runs between Walker Lake and Kiana in the Baird Mountains. The most promising zone between the Gates of the Arctic and Kobuk valley National Parks was purposely excluded from these areas so that development problems would be simplified. This obviously raises some important conflict issues over designation of National Parks in wilderness areas.

Alaska wilderness landscapes are administered by the National Park Service, the US Fish and Wildlife Service and the US Forest Service. Wilderness, as defined by the Wilderness Act of 1964, is '*land sufficient in size to enable the operation of natural systems without undue influence from activities in surrounding areas, and should be places in which man himself is a visitor who does not remain.*' In the continental USA wilderness management restricts the use of mechanised transportation – wilderness is assumed to be '*land maintained in a natural state, roadless, without maintained trails and without man-made structures . . .*'

In Alaska the Wilderness Act was amended by the Alaska Lands Act in 1980, which was specifically designed for Alaska conditions.

The rules in Alaska are considerably modified to make allowances for Alaska conditions, particularly with reference to transportation access, artificial structures and the use of mechanised vehicles.

Student Activity 3.4

1 Using all of the resources in Section 3.6, compare the quality of the three wilderness landscapes selected. You could do this by using a matrix to score wilderness landscape qualities and then by ranking the three areas.
2 Explain why all three of the landscapes need the protection afforded by their inclusion within the provisions of the Alaska National Interest Lands Conservation Act.
3 Outline the arguments that could be used for and against the exclusion from protection of those mineral-rich areas to the west of the Brooks Range.

3.7 The wilderness landscapes of Central Australia

'*From an aeroplane, the South Australian outback looks varied but menacing: an endless red desert, the nothingness broken here and there by tufts of grass and curious craters. Rarely the presence of intruders becomes visible: a narrow track as straight as a ruler, destination indeterminate.*'

From *Discover Australia*, Berlitz

In their survey, McCloskey and Spalding estimate that approximately 2 500 000 km², some 30 per cent of Australia is wilderness. Figure 3.7.1 shows the location of the major wilderness areas in the continent, although some of the smaller ones are omitted because of scale. The Australian Conservation Federation suggest that a wilderness zone should consist of two areas of a core and a buffer zone. The core should be at least 25 000 ha,

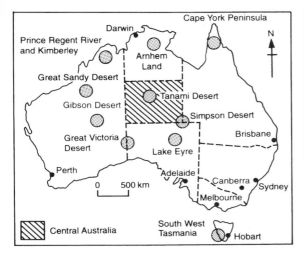

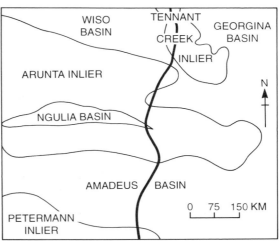

FIGURE 3.7.1 (*far left*)
Wilderness of
Australia

FIGURE 3.7.1 (*far left*)
Wildernesses of
Australia

FIGURE 3.7.3 Geology of
Central Australia

and the buffer zone approximately the same size. Clearly the wilderness areas shown on the map are much bigger than that – the Prince Rupert River and the Kimberley wilderness area is one and a half times as big as the state of Victoria and six times as big as Tasmania! Considerable variety exists within the wilderness areas of Central Australia, as defined by the Geological Survey of Northern Territory (see Figure 3.7.2). The map shows that within the area defined as Central Australia (nearly 1 million km²), two of the major wilderness areas shown on Figure 3.7.1 are located. Besides the Tanami and the Simpson Desert, several other smaller wilderness areas can be recognised, such as parts of the Macdonnell Ranges, and the areas around Lake Amadeus and Lake Neale, as shown on Figure 3.7.2.

The simplified geology of Central Australia is shown in Figure 3.7.3. Three **inliers** of igneous and metamorphic rocks, the Petermann, Arunta and Tennant Creek structures, are surrounded by sedimentary basins. Generally the mainly igneous and metamorphic rocks of the inliers form the mountain ranges and uplands of Central Australia, whilst the sedimentary basins are the sites of major sand dune formations, such as those in the Tanami and Simpson Deserts. Three contrasted landscapes from Central Australia are selected to illustrate the variety of scenery:
■ the Western Macdonnell Ranges;
■ the Uluru National Park (Ayers Rock and Kata Tjuta);
■ the Simpson Desert.

Of these the Simpson Desert is the only true wilderness landscape. As was seen in the case of the Yellowstone National Park, the building of access roads and, in the case of Uluru, an airstrip, has inevitably meant the loss of some wilderness quality in the Macdonnells and Uluru. Nevertheless Uluru is a World Heritage site, and is one of 12 Australian Biosphere Reserves.

The Western Macdonnell Ranges

FIGURE 3.7.2 (*far left*)
Wilderness areas of
Central Australia

FIGURE 3.7.4 Western
Macdonnells

The Western Macdonnells are a series of narrow steep-sided ridges that extend east–west across the relatively flat surrounding plains. Folding and uplifting of the rocks in these ranges, steeply tilted the sedimentary layers. Where these rocks are tough and resistant, such as the Heavitree quartzite, they form the sharp, rugged ridges that characterise the Western Macdonnells (Figure 3.7.4). Rivers have cut striking gaps through the ridges, as at Standley Chasm, where softer **dolerite** has been eroded away between walls of the more resistant **quartzite**.

FIGURE 3.7.5 (*below right*) Original sketches of Ayers Rock and the Olgas

Uluru and Kata Tjuta

'After a long and anxious scrutiny through the smoke and haze, far, very far away, a little to the south of west, I descried the outline of a range of hills, and right in the smoke of one fire an exceedingly high and abruptly ending mountain loomed.'

Ernest Giles, on sighting Mount Olga (Kata Tjuta) on 13 October 1872. He was the first European to see the mountain.

Ernest Giles, and his contemporary, W G Gosse were two early explorers of the wilderness of Uluru and Kata Tjuta; their original sketches convey some of the physical dominance of these features (Figure 3.7.5). Today the two inselbergs or bornhardts are known as Ayers Rock and The Olgas.

FIGURE 3.7.6 (*top*) Ayers Rock (Uluru)

FIGURE 3.7.7 (*above*) The Olgas (Kata Tjuta)

Giles summed up his feelings about them: *'Mount Olga is the more wonderful and grotesque, Mount Ayers the more ancient and sublime.'* Ayers Rock (348 m) (see Figure 3.7.6) dominates the surrounding plains. The Olgas (Figure 3.7.7), a group of steep-sided rounded hills, lie 36 km to the west and rise to a height of 546 m. Both are made of the tough Mount Currie Conglomerate, which is much coarser at the Olgas and at Ayers Rock it is an **arkose**. Figure 3.7.8 indicates the likely mode of formation of both Ayers Rock and the Olgas and details of the weathering of Ayers Rock are shown in the inset.

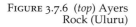

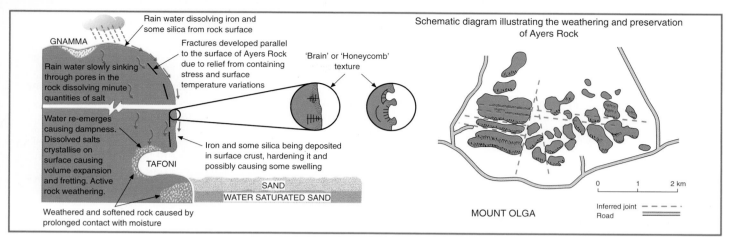

Schematic diagram illustrating the weathering and preservation of Ayers Rock

Rain water dissolving iron and some silica from rock surface

GNAMMA

Rain water slowly sinking through pores in the rock dissolving minute quantities of salt

Fractures developed parallel to the surface of Ayers Rock due to relief from containing stress and surface temperature variations

'Brain' or 'Honeycomb' texture

Water re-emerges causing dampness. Dissolved salts crystallise on surface causing volume expansion and fretting. Active rock weathering.

TAFONI

Iron and some silica being deposited in surface crust, hardening it and possibly causing some swelling

SAND
WATER SATURATED SAND

Weathered and softened rock caused by prolonged contact with moisture

MOUNT OLGA

0   1   2 km

Inferred joint – – –
Road

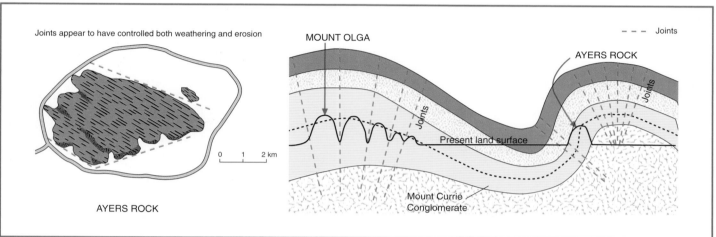

Joints appear to have controlled both weathering and erosion

MOUNT OLGA

– – – Joints

AYERS ROCK

Joints

Joints

Present land surface

Mount Currie Conglomerate

AYERS ROCK

0   1   2 km

Wilderness landscapes of the Simpson Desert

'No river, but the trace as of dried tears on a worn face.'
Frederick T Macartney, Desert Claypan

The Landsat image in Figure 3.7.9 shows part of the Simpson Desert.

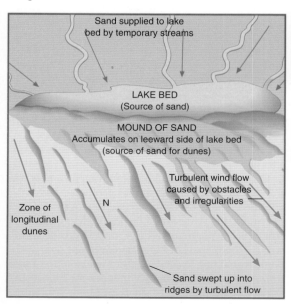

Sand supplied to lake bed by temporary streams

LAKE BED
(Source of sand)

MOUND OF SAND
Accumulates on leeward side of lake bed
(source of sand for dunes)

Zone of longitudinal dunes

N

Turbulent wind flow caused by obstacles and irregularities

Sand swept up into ridges by turbulent flow

FIGURE 3.7.8 Ayers Rock and the Olgas: weathering and development

FIGURE 3.7.9 Landsat image of Simpson Desert, Australia

The Simpson Desert occupies the driest part of Australia, with an average rainfall of 100–150 mm and temperatures that rise to 50°C in the summer. The dunefields cover an area of some 159 000 km²: individual dunes are up to 10–35 km high, and some 200 km long, running parallel in a north north west–south south east direction. The dune slopes appear to be stable, since they are covered with vegetation, but the crests are mobile and are shaped daily by the wind. The Desert lies within a great depression into which water-borne sediment has been transported for millions of years, but particularly between 50 000 and 30 000 years ago. Figure 3.7.10 explains their formation.

FIGURE 3.7.10 (*far left*) Formation of dune ridges: Simpson Desert

To the south east lies the wilderness of the Stony Desert, first discovered by Charles Sturt, the intrepid Australian explorer in 1845, when he complained about the *'heated and parching blasts'*. The surface is covered everywhere with bare, red, iron-oxide coated gravel (gibber). This material appears to have been derived from the breakdown of underlying material (often tough sandstone). Finer material is winnowed away by the wind, which then polishes the remaining fragments, stained red with a coating of iron oxide.

Student Activity 3.5

1 Suggest some criteria that might have been used for the designation of Uluru as a World Heritage site.
2 The Simpson Desert has been described as 'the driest region of the driest habitable continent'. Explain why part of it has been designated a National Park.
3 Compare the wilderness qualities of the Alaskan Mountains with those of the Central Australian Desert. Which do you find the more appealing?

3.8 The landscapes of Antarctica

'It was a wonderful night ... Sounds carried an immense distance. The stillness was almost uncanny. One could imagine oneself in another dead planet. I could easily imagine we were standing not on the Earth, but on the Moon's surface. Everything was so still and cold and unearthly.'

Edward Wilson, Antarctic explorer in his diary,
22 May 1902

than any other. The nearest continent, South America, is nearly 1000 km away, and Australia some 4000 km distant. It is possible that some parts of Antarctica remain unexplored (see Figure 3.8.1) but, with the number of scientific bases around the coast and in the interior, it is only some parts of the polar plateau that remain inviolate. Satellite technology (see Figure 3.8.2) now enables scientists to have a complete view of the continent.

FIGURE 3.8.1 Unexplored Antarctica

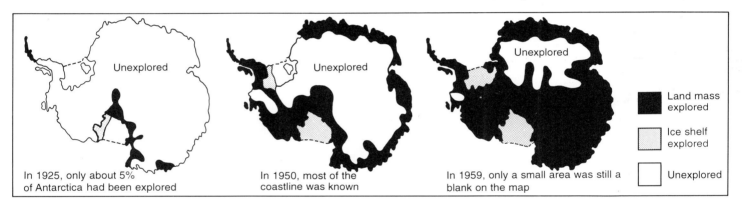

In 1925, only about 5% of Antarctica had been explored

In 1950, most of the coastline was known

In 1959, only a small area was still a blank on the map

Land mass explored

Ice shelf explored

Unexplored

FIGURE 3.8.2 Landsat image of Antarctica

Compared with the 30 per cent of Australia's area that is regarded as wilderness, nearly all of Antarctica's 14 million km² presents wilderness landscapes on a scale unparalleled elsewhere on the globe. The Antarctic wilderness is far more remote

In order to understand the variety of Antarctica's landscapes it is first necessary to examine the structure of the continent. Broadly it consists of two landmasses: East Antarctica and West Antarctica. East Antarctica makes up two-thirds of the area of the continent, bounded on the west by the Transantarctic Mountains that stretch some 5000 km from the Ross Sea to the Weddell Sea. West Antarctica is much smaller, and if the ice sheet were to be removed, it would be revealed as a series of small land areas that formed an archipelago (Figure 3.8.3).

Only about 2 per cent of the continent is now ice-free, and it is in these areas that geologists have gathered details that have enabled them to determine the structure of the land. Most of East Antarctica is made up of Pre-Cambrian rocks and was originally part of the supercontinent **Gondwanaland**. West Antarctica is made up of five different blocks: the Haag Nunataks; the Ellsworth-Whitmore Mountains; Marie Byrd Land; Thurston

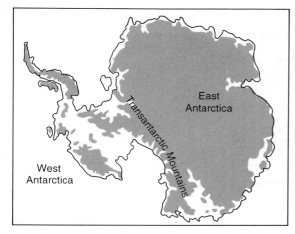

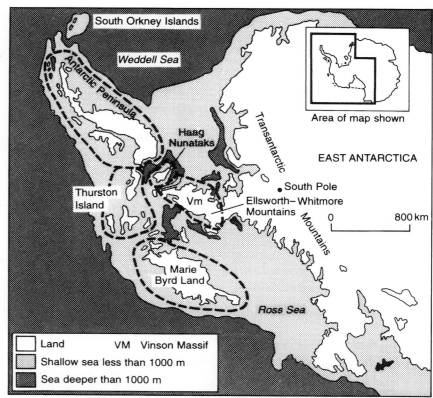

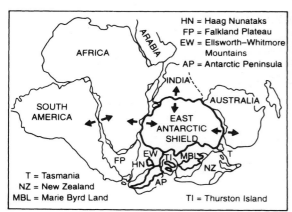

Island; and the Antarctic Peninsula (see Figure 3.8.4). These may well be **micro-continental plates** that were also part of Gondwanaland, but they appear to have moved into place quite independently (see Figure 3.8.5).

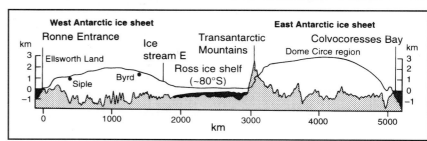

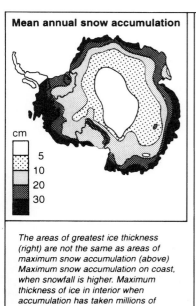

The areas of greatest ice thickness (right) are not the same as areas of maximum snow accumulation (above). Maximum snow accumulation on coast, when snowfall is higher. Maximum thickness of ice in interior when accumulation has taken millions of years.

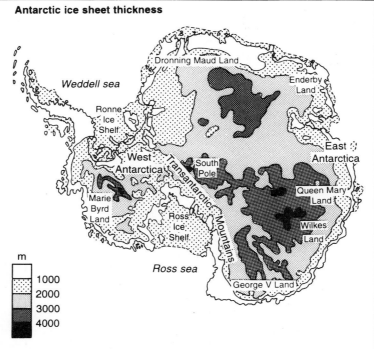

FIGURE 3.8.3 (*top left*) Antarctica after removal of ice

FIGURE 3.8.4 (*top*) Structure of West Antarctica

FIGURE 3.8.5 (*middle left*) Micro-continental plates of Antarctica and Gondwanaland

FIGURE 3.8.6 (*above*) Cross-section of Antarctica

FIGURE 3.8.7 Variations in thickness of ice and snow accumulation

FIGURE 3.8.8 Minimum and maximum extent of ice: Antarctica

Most of Antarctica is covered by a huge ice sheet (see Figure 3.8.6). 30 million km³ of ice covers the continent, with 26 million km³ in East Antarctica, 3.3 km³ in West Antarctica, and the remainder in the permanent ice shelves around the continent. Figure 3.8.7 shows the variations in thickness of the ice sheet in Antarctica. Little snow falls over the polar plateau because the air is so cold, and it therefore cannot hold much moisture, and only about 2–5 cm accumulates there annually. As snowfall is much higher round the coast, rates of accumulation are much higher, up to 2 m a year. With such slow rates of accumulation, the ice sheet has obviously taken millions of years to form.

Sea ice covers much of the sea around Antarctica for most of the year. Figure 3.8.8 shows the minimum and maximum extent of the ice. It reaches its maximum extent in September (20 million km² of the Southern Ocean) and recedes to a minimum of 4 million km² at the end of February. Icebergs are also a major feature of the Southern Ocean, and break off from the ice sheets and glaciers where they reach the seas around Antarctica.

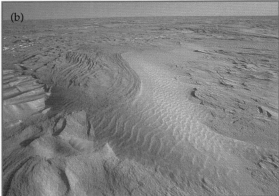

Maximum and minimum sea ice extent between 1973 and 1981. The maximum limit represents the furthest north ice has been found in this period, while the minimum limit shows areas where there is always a probability of between 80 and 100% of finding ice

Even in a continent like Antarctica, wilderness landscapes do possess some variety. There appear to be four main elements in the Antarctic landscape.
- The South Polar plateau.
- The Transantarctic Mountains.
- The Antarctic Peninsula.
- The coastal ice shelves.

Figure 3.8.9 illustrates the various landscapes.

Much of the polar plateau is relatively featureless, although the surface is broken up by **sastrugi**, ridges carved by the wind, and a variety of crevasses indicate that the ice is moving rather than static. It is sometimes not realised that the polar plateau rises to a height of over 4000 m, and explorers have often been affected by the height.

The landscape of the Transantarctic Mountains is physically much more powerful. Ice buries the lower parts of the Transantarctic Mountains, and its major peaks protrude to form **nunataks**, or more continuous ranges. Glaciers, such as the Beardsmore and the Byrd cut through the Transantarctic Mountains, carrying the ice from the polar plateau to the coast or to the ice shelves. Unusual features of the Transantarctic Mountains are the so-called dry valleys, areas in the Queen Maud land that are free of ice. These seem to have been caused by the uplift of the area exceeding the rate at which glaciers could cut down. Eventually the glaciers seem to have been trapped behind a rock lip at the valley heads. Dry winds from the polar plateau keep these valleys free of snow, and, for a short period in summer the River Onyx flows through the Wright valley to Lake Vanda.

The Antarctic Peninsula has much more in common with the Andes, some 750 km distant across Drake Passage, than it does with the rest of Antarctica. It is the eroded remnant of a volcanic arc, that only ceased to be active some 10 million years ago. There is a remarkable difference between its west and east coasts. On the west coast, spectacular mountains rise above a network of channels that run between the coast and off-shore islands. By way of contrast the east coast is fringed by the Larsen Ice Shelf.

The ice shelves make up the fourth of Antarctica's landscapes. Ice shelves form an intermittent fringe around the coast of Antarctica, although the two most prominent are the Ronne Ice Shelf and the Ross Ice Shelf. These masses of ice float on the sea, and are thinner towards the ice front. They are the fastest flowing parts of the ice, with speeds of several kilometres a year in places. Their surface is a rather flat featureless plain, which terminates in hugh ice cliffs. Great icebergs break off from the ice shelves, and large segments sometimes become detached such as the one covering 31 000 km² in 1956.

How vulnerable are these wilderness landscapes of the Antarctic? It is unlikely that the scientists in the bases scattered around the continent will damage the landscapes in any way, since all of their activities are now subject to a very strict environmental protocol (see Chapter 7). Although tourism is growing in importance, numbers were still only of the order of 8000 in 1994, and no tourists venture beyond some of the off-shore islands on brief visits to the Antarctic Peninsula. Although it is thought likely that Antarctica does have valuable mineral resources, all mining is banned for 50 years (see Chapter 7, page 22). It remains speculative as to how global changes in the climate might affect the Antarctic landscapes. There is some evidence that global warming may be encouraging plant growth on some of the subAntarctic islands. However, the effects of global warming on the ice masses of Antarctica are uncertain: it is possible that warmer ocean temperatures could weaken the attachment of the floating ice shelves around the coasts. Large segments of the shelves could break off resulting in mega-icebergs. Generally the wilderness landscapes of Antarctica seem unlikely to lose any of their remote and forbidding character in the foreseeable future.

DECISION-MAKING EXERCISE

You have been asked, as a geographer studying wildernesses, to give a short talk to a local environmental group on the importance of wilderness landscapes. You have been invited to speak for about 20 minutes, and will not, therefore, be able to speak in detail on more than three wilderness landscapes.

Decide which three of the landscapes discussed in this chapter you would use to illustrate your talk. You will need to use a ranking technique, similar to the one suggested in the exercise on the Alaskan wildernesses.

When you have selected the three wilderness landscapes for your talk justify your choice, and give the reasons why you did not select the other landscapes.

ESSAYS

1 Explain why some wilderness landscapes are much more vulnerable than others.

2 Explain why wilderness quality can vary so much from one landscape to another.

4

THE ECOSYSTEMS OF WILDERNESS REGIONS

*'Wilderness or primitive bushland . . . one of the really
indispensable necessities of modern existence in its
soundest sense . . . for where else can man go to escape his
civilisation . . . more and more people want back the
forested and mountainous wilderness which has been
lost . . . to preserve for the human race that connection
with things natural and wholesome which is now more
than ever necessary.'*

Myles Dunphy, 1934

KEY IDEAS

■ Important links exist between wilderness
ecosystems and wilderness landscapes.
■ Wilderness ecosystems still cover considerable
areas and display a wide range of habitats.
■ Wilderness ecosystems are important for their
biodiversity, and the richness of their gene pool.
■ Wilderness ecosystems provide the opportunity
for animal communities to remain in their natural
environments.

■ Wilderness ecosystems are under threat
because of their indigenous resource value, and
the importance of the physical resources that exist
within the area of the ecosystem.
■ Wilderness ecosystems need protection from
the various human activities that threaten their
future existence.

4.1 Landscapes and ecosystems

The link between wilderness landscapes and
ecosystems is perhaps an obvious one. To the
physical geographer, landscape presents an overall
view of relief and landforms, and its study requires
an explanation of the processes responsible for the
formation and shaping of these features. This

concept was largely used for the discussion in the
previous chapter of wilderness landscapes. It was
pointed out, however, that wilderness landscapes,
in the strictly physical sense, provide the essential
relief and landform background for wilderness
ecosystems. From this standpoint we could move

FIGURE 4.1.1 Landscape
and ecosystems

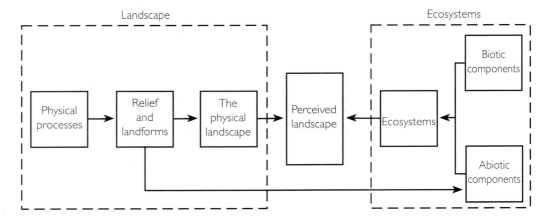

FIGURE 4.1.2 The landscape-ecosystem continuum

Physical landscape dominant				Ecosystem dominant
Landscape continuum				
South Polar Plateau	Simpson Desert (Australia)	Tundra North Slope Alaska	Coniferous forest Coastal British Columbia	Tropical rainforest Amazon Basin

on to a more overall view of landscape, the 'perceived' landscape, in which relief and landforms combine with ecosystems. The relationship between the two is illustrated in Figure 4.1.1.

The role of ecosystem in the overall concept of landscape can be briefly pursued by again considering the idea of a continuum, from landscapes where ecosystem plays a minimum role, such as that of the Antarctic polar plateau, to that where the ecosystem plays a dominant role in the landscape as in the tropical rainforests in parts of the Amazon Basin. Such a continuum is illustrated in Figure 4.1.2.

4.2 Wilderness ecosystems

In Chapter 1 it was suggested that one way of classifying wildernesses was to relate wilderness regions to major world biomes. It was thus possible to identify the ecosystems that were important in wilderness regions.

- Tropical rainforest.
- Tropical grassland and savanna.
- Deserts.
- Temperate grasslands.
- Northern coniferous forest.
- Tundra.
- Mountain.

The scale and importance of the present wilderness ecosystems depends on their global distribution and the extent to which the original ecosystem has been cleared or developed by people. In some regions, such as the temperate grasslands of North America, very little remains of the wilderness that was settled in the nineteenth century. By way of contrast, considerable areas of the northern coniferous forest, and the tundra are relatively untouched and remain important wildernesses today.

Wilderness ecosystems are important because of the following:

- their extent, and the range of habitats and **niches** that they provide;
- their **biodiversity** and the richness of their gene pool, particularly in the tropical rainforest;
- the opportunity to use them as controls against which other managed or mismanaged ecosystems elsewhere may be compared;
- the opportunities that they provide for animal communities to remain in their natural environment;
- the opportunities that they provide for scientific study of their organisms and their structure and functioning.

As with wilderness landscapes, their ecosystems are also under increasing threat because:

- resources within the ecosystem (such as timber) are of commercial value, and their uncontrolled exploitation could cause irreversible damage;
- physical resources that occur within the area occupied by the ecosystem are of commercial value, and similar damage could be done to the ecosystem if these resources were exploited in a manner detrimental to the ecosystem;
- the uncontrolled and insensitive development of tourism in the area could result in damage to the ecosystem;
- global climatic change could have a damaging effect on ecosystems.

Management of wilderness ecosystems is clearly important, not only where they are under present threat, as in the tropical rainforest of Amazonia (Figure 4.2.1), but also in areas that, as yet, remain relatively untouched as in parts of the tundra ecosystems of the Arctic.

FIGURE 4.2.1 Clearance of tropical rainforest, Amazon Basin

4.3 Case studies of wilderness ecosystems

Four case studies of wilderness ecosystems are presented here to illustrate their outstanding global importance. Because of their rich biodiversity, tropical rainforests are examined in a number of different locations, and options for management are studied in the Amazonian rainforest. Since most of the tundra ecosystem of the Arctic is wilderness, but could come under increasing threat from mineral developments in both North America and Russia, it is appropriate to study its particular features. The ecosystem of the mulga woodlands and spinifex grasslands of the Australian outback complement these studies. Finally the marine ecosystem of the Antarctic, one of the globe's richest resources, is examined.

4.4 The tropical rainforest

'The glossy green of the foliage but above all the general luxuriance of the vegetation filled me with admiration . . .'
Charles Darwin, on experiencing tropical rainforest near Salvador on the north-east coast of Brazil, 29 February 1832

FIGURE 4.4.1 Projected loss of species in tropical rainforest

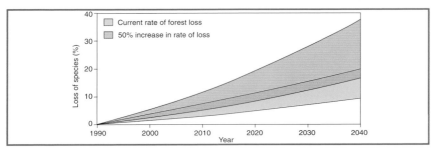

Tropical rainforests are one of the world's most valuable wilderness ecosystems. Their outstanding biodiversity probably concentrates more than half of the world's gene pool. This results from the particular concentration of ultraviolet-B radiation at the equator, which encourages more frequent **mutations**, and thus more species are likely to evolve. Other factors which encourage this wealth of species include the opportunities for species' immigration within the low latitude forests, and the opportunities for co-existence within the forest. Apart from the genetic richness of biodiversity, many species are extremely useful for their medicinal and nutritional value and for a range of other economic uses. In the Amazon rainforest, 2000 species have been identified as useful. Loss of the rainforest from various human activities could seriously reduce the gene pool. Figure 4.4.1 shows how current forest loss rates and a 50 per cent increase in the rate of loss will affect species in the tropical rainforests.

The loss of rainforest is also linked to global climatic change. Burning of the tropical rainforest, and the consequent release of CO_2 contribute to the greenhouse effect, and thus to global warming. Deforestation may also result in increased **albedo**, which can trigger other climatic changes.

It is for these reasons that proper management of tropical rainforests is a vital concern for all those who live and work in this ecosystem. The case studies of Belalong and Queensland stress the importance of biodiversity, and sustainable development is considered in the Amazon rainforest study.

The Belalong Forest, Brunei

The Belalong Forest (Figure 4.4.2) lies within the Batu Apoi Forest Reserve, which occupies much of the district of Temburong in the east of Brunei (Figure 4.4.4). The climate details for Kuala Belalong are shown in Figure 4.4.3. It will be seen that there are two maxima of rainfall associated with the overhead passage of the **Inter-Tropical Convergence Zone (ITCZ)**, and two relatively dry spells in February and March, and in July and

FIGURE 4.4.2 Belalong rainforest

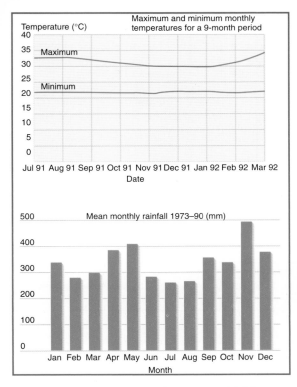

Temperature (°C)

Maximum and minimum monthly
temperatures for a 9-month period

Maximum

Minimum

Jul 91 Aug 91 Sep 91 Oct 91 Nov 91 Dec 91 Jan 92 Feb 92 Mar 92
Date

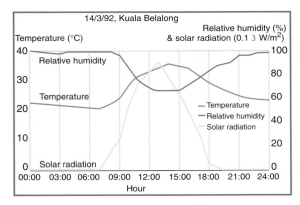

Mean monthly rainfall 1973–90 (mm)

Jan Feb Mar Apr May Jun Jul Aug Sep Oct Nov Dec
Month

FIGURE 4.4.3 Mean
monthly temperature
and precipitation: Kuala
Belalong

FIGURE 4.4.4 (*right*)
Location of Batu Apoi
Forest Reserve in
Temburong, Brunei

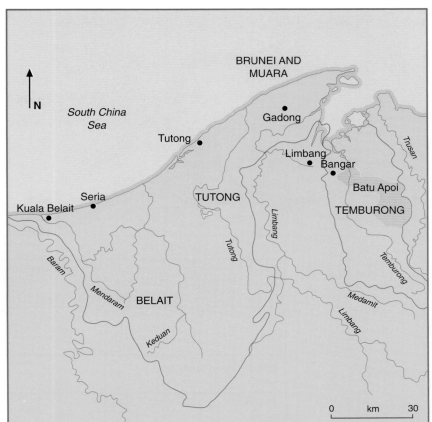

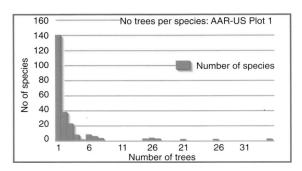

FIGURE 4.4.5 Diurnal
variation of temperature:
Kuala Belalong

August. Although monthly means of temperature
do not vary a great deal from one time of the year to
another, the daily variation of temperature is quite
high as shown in Figure 4.4.5.

Biodiversity in the Belalong Forest

Belalong well illustrates the richness in species to be
found in the tropical rainforest. The profile in
Figure 4.4.6 shows a small section of the Belalong
Forest (a strip 70 m long and 8 m wide). This is a
mixed **Dipterocarp** forest. In the Belalong Forest
several trial plots of 1 ha were enumerated to
examine the biodiversity of the forest. Figure 4.4.7
shows the results for one of the plots.

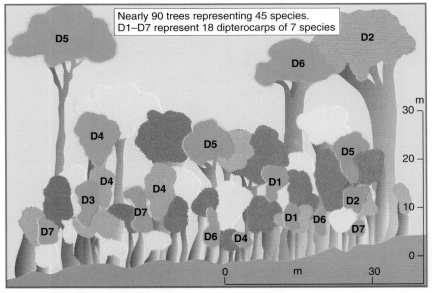

FIGURE 4.4.6 (*above*)
Profile: Belalong
rainforest

FIGURE 4.4.7 Tree species
frequency histogram for
1 ha plot

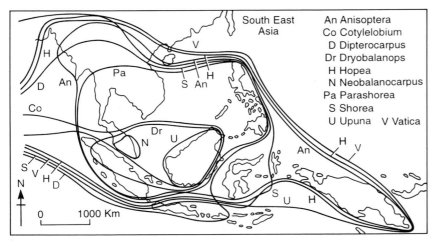

An Anisoptera
Co Cotylelobium
D Dipterocarpus
Dr Dryobalanops
H Hopea
N Neobalanocarpus
Pa Parashorea
S Shorea
U Upuna   V Vatica

South East Asia

Student Activity 4.1

1 Comment on the biodiversity shown in Figures 4.4.6 and 4.4.7.
2 Consider the distribution of Dipterocarps in South East Asia (Figure 4.4.8). Compare the number of genera in Brunei, with numbers in Hainan (Ha) and Java (J). What does this tell us about the Brunei rainforest and diversity?

Research into species richness in the Belalong Forest suggests that it may be determined by certain physical factors.
1 On soils with a high nutrient content biodiversity seems to be related to frequency and size of gap formation in trees.

FIGURE 4.4.8 (*above*) Distribution of Dipterocarps in South East Asia

FIGURE 4.4.9 Species diversity: plants and animals

FIGURE 4.4.10 (*below*) Species diversity: variations in latitude, termites and swallow-tail butterflies

Estimates of biodiversity			
Known and estimated world totals of living species of selected groups of plants, fungi and animals, showing numbers already described and best estimates of the total numbers likely to exist.			
GROUP	DESCRIBED SPECIES	ESTIMATED TOTAL SPECIES	PERCENTAGE OF TOTAL ALREADY DESCRIBED
Micro-organisms Bacteria	3000	2 500 000	0.1
Plants Algae	40 000	350 000	11
Bryophytes (mosses, liverworts)	17 000	25 000	68
Vascular plants	220 000	270 000	81
Fungi (including lichens)	69 000	1 500 000	5
Animals Nematodes (roundworms)	15 000	500 000	3
Arthropods, e.g. insects, spiders and crustaceans	80 000	6 000 000	13
Fish	22 500	35 000	64
Birds	9040	9100	99
Mammals	4000	4020	>99

2 On soils with relatively low nutrient levels maximum diversity seems to coincide with low concentrations of aluminium and very low concentrations of phosphorus.
3 Loss of seeds from specific host trees may lead to low densities of that particular tree which enables other competitive species to flourish.

In the number of species world-wide, animals greatly exceed plants (see Figure 4.4.9). Species diversity of animals is generally higher at equatorial latitudes than elsewhere (Figure 4.4.10). Figures 4.4.11 and 4.4.12 display the species diversity of moths at Belalong and birds netted at Pondok Bujat in the Belalong forest.

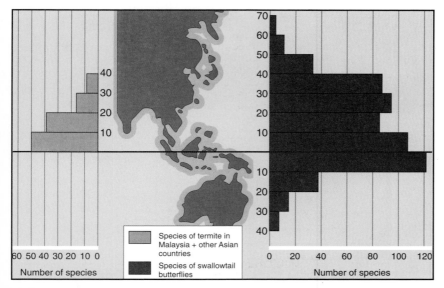

Species of termite in Malaysia + other Asian countries

Species of swallowtail butterflies

Number of species

Number of species

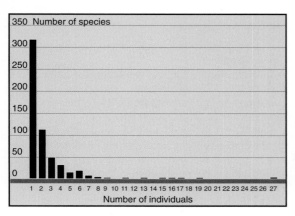

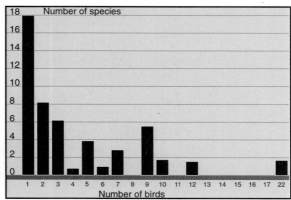

Student Activity 4.2

1 Comment on the species diversity shown in Figures 4.4.11 and 4.4.12.
2 How does it compare with the species diversity of trees in Figure 4.4.7?

World Heritage rainforest wilderness: the wet tropics of Queensland

Figures 4.4.13 and 4.4.14 show the setting of the Queensland wet tropics in Australia, and the decline in forest cover in Australia over a period of 200 years.

Student Activity 4.3

1 Calculate the percentage decline of forest cover between the period prior to European settlement and the present for each state.
2 Use a simple correlation test to see if there is any relationship between percentage decline, and the original area of forest.
3 Offer an explanation of your findings.

Figure 4.4.15 shows the distribution of rainforest in the so-called wet tropics of Queensland (Figure 4.4.16).

FIGURE 4.4.11 (*above left*) Species diversity: moths at Belalong

FIGURE 4.4.12 (*above*) Species diversity: birds netted at Pandok Bujat

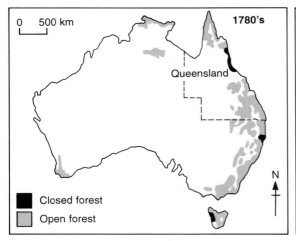

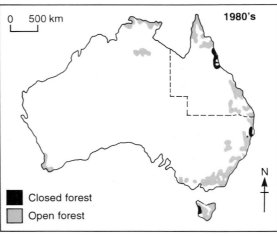

FIGURE 4.4.13 Queensland rainforest in Australian setting

FIGURE 4.4.14 Australia: decline in forest cover

STATE	1	2	3	4	5
New South Wales	801.2	157.4	20	62.4	8
Victoria	227.6	85.9	38	35.5	16
Queensland	1727.9	355.4	21	201.8	12
Western Australia	2527.6	20.3	1	11.8	0.5
South Australia	983.5	2.1	0.2	.1.4	0.1
Tasmania	68.3	32.2	47	20.9	31
Northern Territory	1353.6	47/41	4	47.3	3
Australian Capital Territory	2.5	1.5	59	1.0	39
Australia	7692.3	702.2	9	381.0	5

1 State total area 100 000 ha; 2 Area forested prior to European settlement 100 000 ha; 3 % of state; 4 Current forest cover 100 000 ha; 5 % of state.

FIGURE 4.4.15
Distribution of rainforest
in Queensland's wet
tropics

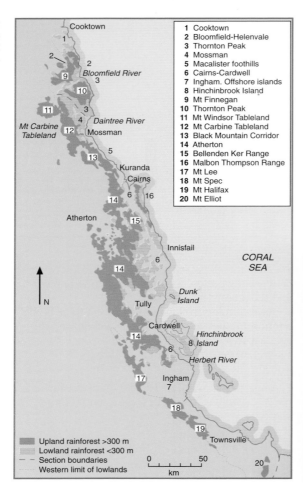

1	Cooktown
2	Bloomfield-Helenvale
3	Thornton Peak
4	Mossman
5	Macalister foothills
6	Cairns-Cardwell
7	Ingham. Offshore islands
8	Hinchinbrook Island
9	Mt Finnegan
10	Thornton Peak
11	Mt Windsor Tableland
12	Mt Carbine Tableland
13	Black Mountain Corridor
14	Atherton
15	Bellenden Ker Range
16	Malbon Thompson Range
17	Mt Lee
18	Mt Spec
19	Mt Halifax
20	Mt Elliot

FIGURE 4.4.16 (*far right*)
Tropical rainforest,
Eungella in Queensland

Upland rainforest >300 m
Lowland rainforest <300 m
Section boundaries
Western limit of lowlands

0   50
km

'*This area contains the oldest continually surviving rainforest on earth ... It is estimated that some 50 to 100 million years ago, the entire continent was covered with vegetation similar to that found in these forests today. Some of the more beautiful plants found in these forests include the beautiful and unusual fan palm; 13 different types of one group of plants out of a world total of 36; over 90 species of orchids, many found in very limited areas; one of the largest cycads in the world, as well as one of the smallest, and the richest concentration of ferns in Australia.*'

Masterworks of Man and Nature, Preserving our
World Heritage

Student Activity 4.4

1 Figure 4.4.17 shows conservation areas in Queensland.

How well does the wet tropical coast (which includes the World Heritage area) fare in conservation status compared to the other biogeographical regions in the table?

2 The extract in Figure 4.4.18 gives details of a hydro-electric scheme that was planned for the area of the tropical wet forests of Queensland. Who do you think has the stronger case: the Minister for Resource Industries; or the Minister for Environment and Heritage?

FIGURE 4.4.17
Conservation areas in
Queensland

BIOGEOGRAPHIC REGION	AREA	% OF QUEENSLAND	NUMBER OF PARKS	PARK AREA
North-west highlands	6 967 510	4	1	12 200
Gulf plains	21 304 680	12.3	2	507 100
Cape York Peninsula	11 531 360	6.7	9	1 472 660
Mitchell grass downs	23 788 550	13.8	1	13 800
Channel country complex	23 705 800	13.7	3	613 500
Mulga lands	21 764 650	12.6	4	344 952
Wet tropical coast	1 901 840	1.1	20	232 261
Central Mackay coast	1 151 720	0.7	11	117 879
Einsleigh uplands	12 923 100	7.5	6	63 333
Desert uplands	6 881 790	4.0	1	86 600
Brigalow belt	32 352 480	18.7	25	552 648
South East Queensland	8 104 020	4.7	25	251 530
New England tablelands	342 490	0.2	2	25 189

Proposal for Hydro-Electric Scheme

FIGURE 4.4.18 *The Conservation News*

The Queensland Electricity Commission (QEC) is planning to build a hydro-electric scheme in north Queensland, by damming the Tully River and flooding 1400 hectares of the Wet Tropics World Heritage area.

Plans for the $600 million Tully–Millstream Hydro-Electric Scheme have been floating around Queensland Government Departments for some time, but were never seriously considered until the region was listed as World Heritage, in late 1988. Bob Katter, the Minister for Mines and Energy at the time, then deemed the Scheme essential to meet Queensland's rising energy requirements. The Scheme would increase the State's energy supply by 550 megawatts.

... For many years it has been argued and demonstrated that energy conservation is cheaper than building new power production schemes. Recent Victorian studies show that by spending 10 per cent of the dam's cost on energy conservation four times the electricity the dam could produce would be saved ...

The QEC were forced to decrease their estimates of demand for power in the late 1980s. The forecasted increases in demand for 1983–87 were over twice the actual increases, while the 1989 maximum demand was actually 1370 mw less than installed capacity of 5093 mw ...

Located in the wild and remote mountains between Ravenshoe and Tully, the scheme would reduce many creeks and rivers to a fifth of their normal flow, thus seriously impairing recreational and scenic values of the area. White-water rafting would be out! But so would many of the northern Yellow-bellied Gliders, the vertebrate most at risk from the flooding; and nobody really knows the effect it would have on the tiny Atherton Antechinus. When doing their research the QEC did not realise this creature lived in trees, so based its data on a trapping programme for terrestrial animals. The Brush-tailed Bettong is also at risk ... Conservationists believe that failure to find several rare or endangered species likely to occur in the affected area, may simply represent a failure to conduct appropriate surveys.

The Goss Government was elected to office promising to defer a final decision on the scheme until energy conservation options were fully considered. However, some members of the Government disagree with this delay. Ken Vaughan, State Minister for Resource Industries announced in December that the scheme would proceed. He faces opposition from his colleague, Pat Comben, Minister for Environment and Heritage, who feels further study should be done on the environmental viability of the project ...

The Conservation News, April 1990

In many parts of the wet tropics of Queensland eco-tourism (Figure 4.4.20) has now become very important. Both Mossman, and the Daintree River have become important foci of this activity (see Figure 4.4.19).

Student Activity 4.5

1 What should be the principal environmental aims of ecotourism in an area like the Daintree River?
2 What would you consider to be the main difficulties in the achievement of these aims?
3 Complete the compatibility/conflict matrix shown in Figure 4.4.21 for the rainforests of the wet tropics of Queensland.

FIGURE 4.4.19 (*far left*) The Daintree River

FIGURE 4.4.20 Tourist brochures for ecotourism

FIGURE 4.4.21
Compatibility matrix for
rainforests of wet tropics,
Queensland

CONDITION OR USE	OTHER POTENTIALLY LIMITING USES	SITE OF SPECIAL SCIENTIFIC INTEREST	GENETIC POOL	WATER CATCHMENT	TIMBER EXTRACTION	WOODCHIP	CLEAR-FELLING	PICNICS	HIKING	FISHING	TRAIL BIKE RIDING	MOTOR RALLIES
Site of special scientific interest												
Genetic pool												
Water catchment												
Timber extraction												
Woodchip												
Clear-felling												
Picnics												
Hiking												
Fishing												
Trail bike riding												
Motor rallies												

• Major limitations to full development or enjoyment of use
× Incompatible conditions or uses

Options for the future of the Amazonian rainforest

The tropical rainforest of the Amazon has probably received greater media publicity than any other rainforest area. Attention has been particularly focused on deforestation within the region.

Student Activity 4.6

Figure 4.4.22 shows the amount of forest cleared in the Brazilian Amazon between 1975 and 1988.
1 Use bar charts to plot the percentage cleared in the various states on a blank map of the Amazon Basin for 1975 and 1988.

2 Use bar charts to plot the absolute amount of cleared forest in 1975 and 1988.
3 From the first map that you have constructed, identify the states that appear to have been the worst affected.
4 From your second map, identify the states that appear to have been the worst affected.
5 What are the important differences between the two maps, and how would you attempt to explain them?
6 Of what importance are these figures to the Brazilian Government?

The main effects of deforestation on the environment of the Amazonian rainforest are shown in Figure 4.4.23.

FIGURE 4.4.22
Deforestation of the
Amazon rainforest

STATE OR TERRITORY	AREA IN LEGAL AMAZONIA (km²)	AREA CLEARED (KM²)				% OF STATE OR TERRITORY CLASSIFIED AS CLEARED			
		1975	1978	1980	1988	1975	1978	1980	1988
Amapá	140 276	152.5	170.5	183.7	571.5	0.1	0.1	0.1	0.4
Pará	1 248 042	8 654.0	22 445.3	33 913.8	120 000.0	0.7	0.8	2.7	9.6
Roraima	230 104	55.0	143.8	273.1	3 270.0	0.0	0.1	0.1	1.4
Maranhão	257 451	2 940.8	7 334.0	10 671.1	50 670.0	1.1	2.8	4.1	19.7
Tocantins (Goiás)	285 793	3 507.3	10 288.5	11 458.5	33 120.0	1.2	3.6	4.0	11.6
Acre	152 589	1 165.5	2 464.5	4 626.8	19 500.0	0.8	1.6	3.0	12.8
Rondônia	243 044	1 216.5	4 184.5	7 579.3	58 000.0	0.3	1.7	3.1	23.7
Mato Grosso	881 001	10 124.3	28 355.0	53 299.3	208 000.0	1.1	3.2	6.1	23.6
Amazonas	1 567 125	779.5	1 785.8	3 102.2	105 790.0	0.1	0.1	0.2	6.8
Legal Amazonia (total)	5 005 425	28 595.3	77 171.8	125 107.8	598 921.5	0.6	1.5	2.5	12.0

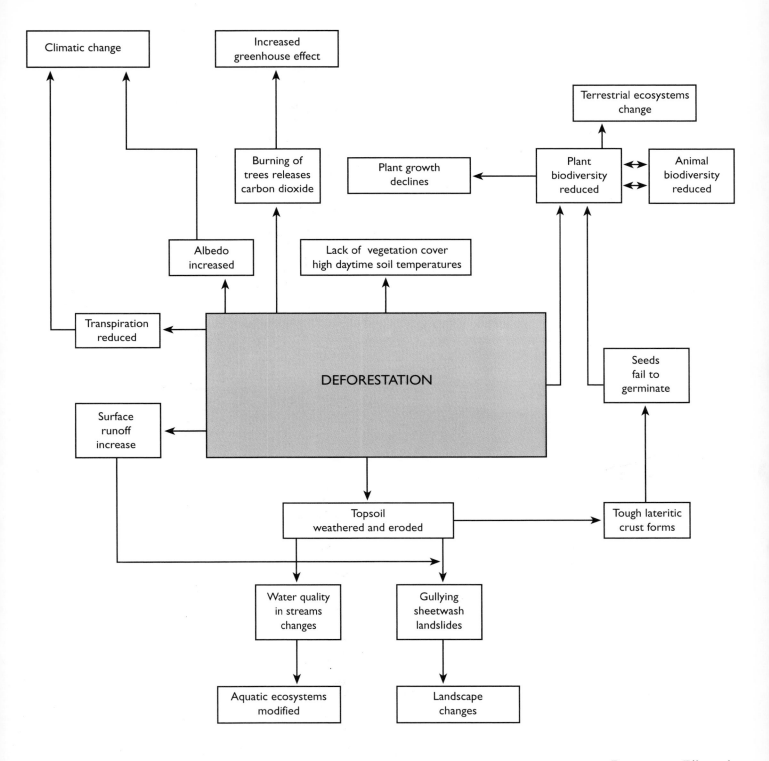

Climatic change		Increased greenhouse effect	

Climatic change

Increased greenhouse effect

Terrestrial ecosystems change

Burning of trees releases carbon dioxide

Plant growth declines

Plant biodiversity reduced

Animal biodiversity reduced

Albedo increased

Lack of vegetation cover high daytime soil temperatures

Transpiration reduced

DEFORESTATION

Seeds fail to germinate

Surface runoff increase

Topsoil weathered and eroded

Tough lateritic crust forms

Water quality in streams changes

Gullying sheetwash landslides

Aquatic ecosystems modified

Landscape changes

FIGURE 4.4.23 Effects of deforestation

Objectives for an Amazonian development strategy

Dr Philip Fearnside, an American working in the Department of Ecology at the Manaus Institute has proposed a series of options for future land use in Amazonia. These options are a response to a set of development criteria that they must fulfil.

Development criteria

■ Agricultural sustainability: a reasonable balance of nutrients in the system; prevention of soil compaction; renewable energy resources.

■ Social sustainability: a particular land use system must be maintained by society; it must be profitable.

■ Unsubsidised economic competitiveness: the agricultural system should be self-supporting.

■ Maximum self-sufficiency: although there will be a need for some goods to be brought in from outside, there must be self-sufficiency in products that can be grown locally.

■ Fulfilment of social goals: minimum standards of hygiene and welfare must be sustained.

■ Consistency with maintenance of areas for other uses: the strategy must be compatible with other uses of the area.

■ Retention of development options: consideration must be given to future development options for the area.

■ Minimal effect on other resources: development must be compatible with surrounding areas.

■ Minimal macro-ecological effects: no loss of species diversity.

Fearnside then listed nine possible land uses as follows.

1 Untouched forest.
2 Forest products extraction.
3 Agroforestry.
4 Shifting cultivation.
5 Annual crops in continuous planting.
6 Pasture with fertiliser.
7 Pasture without fertiliser.
8 'Highgrading' with replanting.*
9 Clear-cutting without replanting.

FIGURE 4.4.24 Location of Amerindian forest management settlements

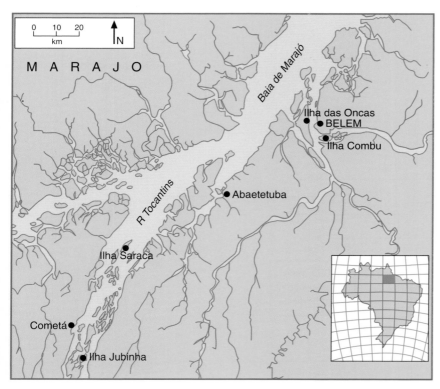

* 'Highgrading' refers to an exploitation system where only the most valuable of forest trees are removed and the remainder are left untouched.

Student Activity 4.7

1 How realistic are the development objectives?
2 Discuss each of the development options in terms of the objectives. You should construct a matrix showing the objectives along the left hand side, and the options along the top. Place a tick in the appropriate box if you think it meets the objective. In this way you may be able to rank the different options.

Case study 1: extraction and forest management by forest Indians in the Amazon Estuary

Figure 4.4.24 shows the location of this case study. The plots on the Amazonian floodplain or *varzea* are managed by the local *caboclos*, Amerindians, generally regarded as lazy, and having a 'collecting' mentality. Conditions for agriculture in the floodplain are not particularly favourable, and agricultural production is chronically low. The environment is well-suited to extractive economy; regular flooding produces water-logged soils for much of the year, and biodiversity is low, yet there is a number of species of considerable economic importance. There is a high frequency of tree falls, and forest regeneration appears to be swift.

There are four land use zones associated with the isolated dwellings found on the islands in the rivers (Figure 4.4.25).

1 The house garden or *terreiro* where domesticated animals are reared, and a range of both exotic and native plants is grown.
2 Swidden plots or *rocas* are used for the cultivation of subsistence crops, such as rice, corn and beans, or for cash crops such as sugar cane and rice.
3 Managed forest, in which certain species are encouraged at the expense of others. The less desirable trees are thinned, or, in the case of larger trees, ringed. Another form of management is to promote certain trees by planting seeds or transplanting seedlings.
4 Unmanaged forest, the dense floodplain forest, where there is no form of discernible management.

Important differences exist between the managed and unmanaged forests. The unmanaged forest has greater biodiversity, and greater biomass. Figure 4.4.26 shows the relative importance of species and resources in areas of managed and unmanaged forest on the Ilha das Oncas.

DECISION MAKING EXERCISE

Three land use options actually in practice in Amazonia are described in detail below. As a student, seconded temporarily to work in the Ecology Institute in Manaus, you have been asked to make a report on the three systems, and rank them in order of sustainability.

1 Classify each of them into one of the nine options defined by Fearnside.
2 Use the Fearnside objectives to test their sustainability, and put them in rank order.
3 Write a report on the merits of each one in rank order.

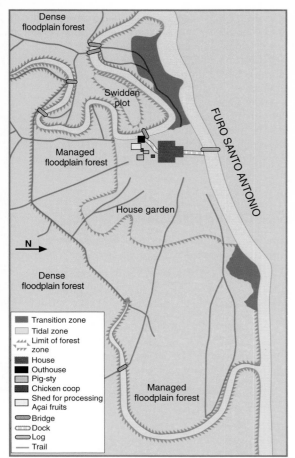

ITEM	IMPORTANCE	
	MANAGED FOREST	UNMANAGED FOREST
Species (20)	96.4	84.9
Food	64.0	40.1
Drink	48.4	33.8
Medicine	59.2	55.1
Wood	36.8	52.5
Game attractant	46.0	36.2
Energy	29.3	47.0
Fertiliser	29.3	27.1
Utensils	30.1	38.1
Fibres	29.2	27.1
Other uses	21.4	10.3

FIGURE 4.4.25 (*far left*) Land use around settlements on the Ilhas das Ongas

FIGURE 4.4.26 Relative importance of species and resources in managed and unmanaged floodplain forests

Case study 2: the Celos management system for sustained timber production

This system of land use requires large stretches of wilderness forest (Figure 4.4.27), with only a sparse indigenous population. The system was developed in Surinam, where it was tested over a few hundred hectares, but never put into operation for political reasons.

Six main principles guide the Celos operation.
1 Harvesting operations and silvicultural treatments are integrated.
2 Forest inventory is the basis for all forest operations.
3 Timber extraction is restricted in order to maintain ecological balance within the forest.
4 The system is polycyclic, with rotations of 15–25 years, depending on growth rates and timber dimensions expected.
5 Management units function as forest districts with an infrastructure of tracks and settlements for labourers.
6 Strict forest laws maintain the legal position of management units.

The Celos system differs from conventional systems, in that it cares for the remaining ecosystem after the required timber has been removed. Felling and skidding damage can be reduced by careful organisation of operations. After controlled logging the remaining forest is subject to refinement, whereby unwanted trees are killed off with arboricide to encourage growth of commercially valuable trees. Second and third refinements may be necessary.

FIGURE 4.4.27 Virgin Amazonian rainforest

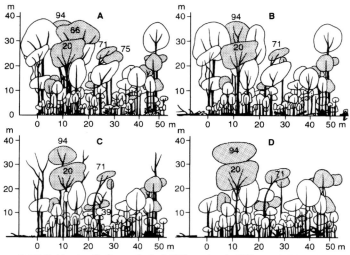

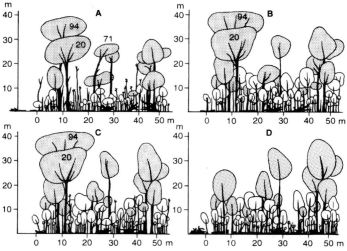

Hypothetical forest profile diagrams for the first felling cycle under CMS, years 0–7. A = prior to harvesting (year 0); B = after felling of two trees (year 0); C = after initial refinement (year 2); D = prior to second refinement (year 7). Crowns of economic species are shaded.

Hypothetical forest profile diagrams for the first felling cycle under CMS, years 9–20. A = after second refinement (year 9); B = prior to third (light) refinement (year 15); C = after third refinement (year 17); D = after second felling (year 20). Crowns of economic species are shaded.

Figure 4.4.28 shows hypothetical forest profiles after years 0–7 and 9–20 years in the felling cycle. Ecological sustainability is a major issue with the Celos system, and the maintenance of a high level of biomass is important because of its high nutrient content.

Celos needs several hundred hectares of potentially productive forest, and even larger areas may be necessary simply because not all forest areas are suitable for such timber production. It is likely that neighbouring areas may well be suitable for alternative uses, and will be unaffected by the operation of Celos.

Case study 3: Japanese agroforestry

Japanese immigrants have been farming parts of Amazonia since the 1920s and rely on the intensive cultivation of relatively small plots of land. One

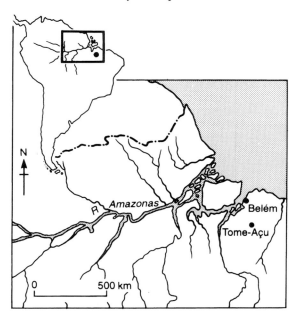

FIGURE 4.4.28 (*above*) Hypothetical forest profiles in Celos system of land management

FIGURE 4.4.29 (*above right*) Location of Tomé Açu

FIGURE 4.4.30 Range of crops sold in Japanese agroforestry unit

	RECEIVED BY CAMTA		SOLD BY CAMTA		
PRODUCT	AMOUNT (KG)	PRODUCERS	VALUE ($CZ)*	VALUE ($US)	% OF TOTAL
Black pepper	885 093	163	174 802 168.37	3 884 492.63	78.42
Cacao	288 652	138	23 457 000.00	521 266.67	10.52
Passion fruit	1 870 900	108	16 167 931.04	359 287.36	7.25
Cupuaçu	50 383	30	2 143 191.55	47 626.48	0.96
Rubber (raw)	12 410	13	1 310 611.95	29 124.71	0.59
Papaya	232 067	18	1 216 091.00	27 024.24	0.55
Eggs	–	1	1 011 781.13	22 484.03	0.45
Pumpkin	135 931	37	809 951.18	17 998.92	0.37
Graviola	30 140	10	736 169.96	16 359.33	0.33
Lime	98 740	29	685 978.20	15 243.96	0.31
Cucumber	29 256	4	183 581.63	4 079.59	0.08
Bell pepper	7413	7	118 914.48	2 642.54	0.05
Guaraná	1262	7	56 480.00	1 255.11	0.03
Melon	1483	3	23 437.32	520.83	0.01
Other	–	–	173 340.76	3 852.02	0.08
TOTAL		196	222 896 628.57	4 953 258.42	100.00

CAMTA Tomé Açu Agricultural Co-operative. * $ Cruzeiros (Brazilian)

Japanese colony is the settlement of Tomé Açu (see Figure 4.4.29), some 115 km south of the city of Belém. Soils are of low nutrient status, and it has an annual rainfall of 2600 mm. (Moisture deficits are likely during a five-month period of reduced rainfall.) Most of the rainforest has been removed from the area, except for a few small patches.

Commercial production of black pepper began in the late 1940s and has proved to be economically successful. Falling pepper prices on the world market, and fungal infections of the pepper plant have led to diversification of the cropping programme since the 1960s.

Most holdings are 100–150 ha, but only an average of 20 ha per plot is cultivated, the remainder existing as secondary or virgin forest. The range of crops sold through the co-operative is shown in Figure 4.4.30. Intercropping is widely practised, with annuals being planted between the rows of the perennial crops. Fertiliser is essential in such an operation: the amount varies according to the crop. Management of crops that are price-sensitive tends to be complex, and has evolved on many of these farms over a number of years. Figure 4.4.31 shows a typical unit of agroforestry in the Tomé Açu area.

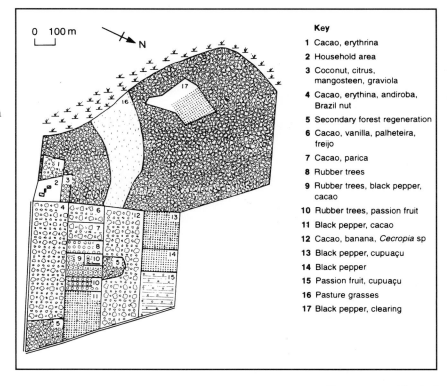

Key
1 Cacao, erythrina
2 Household area
3 Coconut, citrus, mangosteen, graviola
4 Cacao, erythrina, andiroba, Brazil nut
5 Secondary forest regeneration
6 Cacao, vanilla, palheteira, freijo
7 Cacao, parica
8 Rubber trees
9 Rubber trees, black pepper, cacao
10 Rubber trees, passion fruit
11 Black pepper, cacao
12 Cacao, banana, *Cecropia* sp
13 Black pepper, cupuaçu
14 Black pepper
15 Passion fruit, cupuaçu
16 Pasture grasses
17 Black pepper, clearing

FIGURE 4.4.31 Typical unit of agroforestry in Tomé Açu

4.5 The Arctic Tundra

'The low profile of the landscape gives a sense of unobstructed vastness and exposure to the elements.'
Description of the Bering Land Bridge National Preserve in Alaska National Interest lands

No wilderness ecosystem could show a greater contrast with the tropical rainforest. The description of the bleak Alaskan landscape above conveys a totally different impression to the very limited fields of view within the tropical rainforest. It is only when one rises above the canopy layer in the tropical rainforest that the vastness of the wilderness becomes comparable with that of the tundra (Figure 4.5.1).

'Tundra' appears to have different meanings in different languages. To the Finns it means 'barren land', and to the Russians is means 'marshy plain'. A glance at the climatic statistics for Sachs Harbour on Banks Island in the Canadian Arctic (Figure 4.5.3) will help to clarify the alternative meanings. The average temperatures from September through to May are below 0°C. In addition to the permanently frozen ground of permafrost, surface layers will also be frozen and covered in snow, indeed a 'barren land' (Figure 4.5.2). Summer is brief, but the surface layers will thaw, and water is abundant enough at the surface for low-lying areas to be waterlogged, the 'marshy plain'.

FIGURE 4.5.1 View of Arctic Tundra at ground level

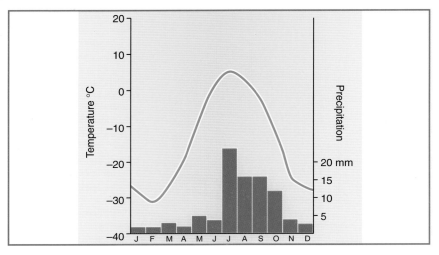

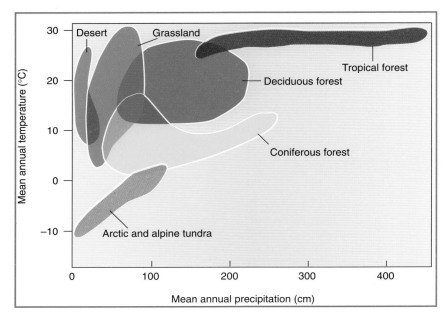

Figure 4.5.4 compares the tundra biome with that of other major world biomes. It indicates that there are very limited opportunities for primary production, compared to other world biomes. Figure 4.5.5 compares net primary productivity for the major world biomes, and it can be seen that only the wildernesses of the world's deserts, and the rock and ice of polar regions have a lower net primary productivity than the tundra. Figure 4.5.6 illustrates the differences in incoming solar radiation between tundra locations and those in lower latitudes. Temperature can be seen to be a major limiting factor in plant productivity in the tundra biome.

Student Activity 4.8

1 Compare net primary productivity in the main wilderness biomes, as shown in Figure 4.5.5.
2 Discuss some of the factors that might be responsible for these variations.

FIGURE 4.5.2 (*above right*) Aerial view of Arctic Tundra

FIGURE 4.5.3 (*top*) Mean monthly temperatures and precipitation: Sachs Harbour on Banks Island in the Canadian Arctic

FIGURE 4.5.4 (*above*) Mean annual temperature and total precipitation of six major biomes

FIGURE 4.5.5 (*right*) Net primary productivity: major biomes

	AREA (10^6 KM^2)	NET PRIMARY PRODUCTIVITY PER UNIT AREA (DRY G M^{-1} YR^{-1}) NORMAL RANGE	MEAN	WORLD NET PRIMARY PRODUCTIVITY (10^9 DRY TONNES PER YEAR)
Lake and stream	2	100–1500	500	1.0
Swamp and marsh	2	800–4500	2000	4.0
Tropical forest	20	1000–5000	2000	40.0
Temperate forest	18	600–2500	1300	24.4
Boreal forest	12	400–2000	800	9.6
Woodland and shrubland	7	200–1200	600	4.2
Savanna	15	200–2000	700	10.5
Temperate grassland	9	150–1500	500	4.5
Tundra and alpine	8	10–400	140	1.1
Desert scrub	18	10–250	70	1.3
Extreme desert, rock and ice	24	0–10	3	0.07
Agricultural land	14	100–4000	650	9.1
Total land	149		730	109.0
Open ocean	332	2–400	125	41.5
Continental shelf	27	200–600	350	9.5
Attached algae and estuaries	2	500–4000	2000	4.0
Total ocean	361		155	55.0
Total for earth	510		320	164.0

Plants must adapt to the low temperatures, drought and high winds of the tundra biome if they are to survive. Some of these adaptations are listed below (adapted from Billings).

1 Life forms: mainly perennial herbs, prostrate shrubs, lichens and mosses.

2 Seed dormancy: seeds will remain dormant for long periods of time since temperatures well above freezing are needed for germination.

3 **Photosynthesis** and respiration: these are at high rates for only a few weeks when temperature and light conditions are favourable. Optimum photosynthesis rates are at lower temperatures than for ordinary plants. In some plants respiration and photosynthesis can occur below 0°C.

4 Growth: very rapid even at low positive temperatures.

5 Food storage: important in all tundra plants with carbohydrates mostly stored underground in perennials. Much of the biomass is underground (in the New Siberian Islands the above:below biomass ratio is 1:7.19).

6 Winter survival: frost resistance and survival good after hardening.

The main groups of plants that are found in the tundra are shrubs, herbs, grasses and sedges, mosses and lichens (see Figure 4.5.7). The habitats of these different plants vary according to slope, drainage and exposure, as shown in Figure 4.5.8.

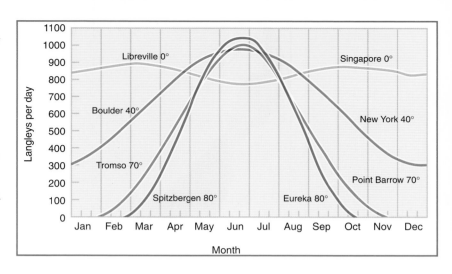

FIGURE 4.5.6 Variations in insolation between tundra and other locations

FIGURE 4.5.7 Tundra vegetation (arctic poppy)

Animal life in the tundra inevitably shows both anatomical and behavioural adaptations to the severe environment.

1 Warm-blooded animals which live above the snow have a cover of fur which retains warmth. Moulting allows modification of this insulation in warmer weather.

2 Special pads on the feet enable animals to cross snow-covered ground, e.g. the snow-shoe hare.

Student Activity 4.9

1 One of the main reasons put forward for conserving the wilderness of the tropical rainforest is its rich biodiversity. What arguments could be put forward for protecting the tundra biome wilderness which shows lower levels of biodiversity in its plants?

2 'The flora of the tundra are far less threatened than those of the tropical rainforest.' To what extent do you think this is true?

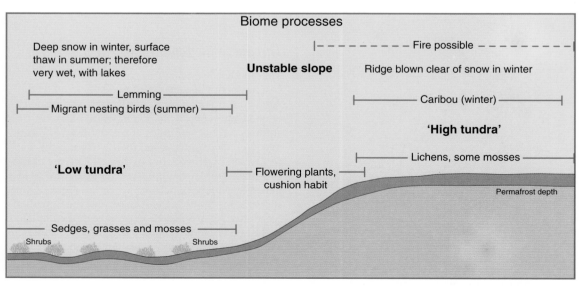

FIGURE 4.5.8 Habitats of tundra plants

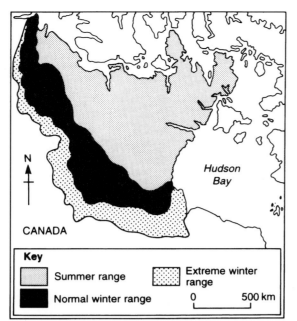

Figure 4.5.9 Caribou migration limits

Figure 4.5.10 Food webs in the Arctic tundra

3 Hibernation, although the difficulty of finding a location is hampered by permafrost (the arctic ground-squirrel is the only true hibernator of the tundra).

4 Many large herbivores are very sensitive to the depth and density of the snow cover. Caribou therefore either migrate to areas of relatively soft snow or areas where the snow has been blown away, or leave the tundra altogether and move to the taiga. Figure 4.5.9 shows the various limits of caribou migrations. Ptarmigan will find pockets of soft snow in which to burrow, but the majority of birds that nest in the tundra migrate southwards during the winter.

Food webs of the tundra are shown in Figure 4.5.10. The first part of the diagram illustrates one of the simplest webs, where the lemmings are the only herbivores. The other food web is much more complex and includes marine as well as terrestrial fauna.

Student Activity 4.10

1 Explain the differences between the two webs.
2 Discuss the ways in which the complex food web could be modified by removal of various elements from it.

Antarctic tundra

Tundra-type vegetation in the Antarctic is very restricted. It is confined to the narrow coastal regions, which are devoid of ice and snow in summer. Lichens dominate the plant communities in the drier and more exposed locations, whilst mosses and algae occur in moister and more sheltered localities. Only two flowering plants are found south of 60°S, the pearlwort and Antarctic hair grass. Interestingly, both of these plants have shown a significant increase in numbers over the last 30 years. This is thought to be the result of an increase in summer temperatures in the region since the late 1940s.

Threats to the tundra ecosystem

Mention has been made of some of the environmental hazards that are likely to affect the Arctic tundra ecosystem, particularly in Sections 1.4 on the Dalton Highway. Exploitation of Arctic animals for meat supplies in the last two centuries may well have unbalanced food webs and the ecosystem in general, but in the last 50 years of the twentieth century a whole new range of threats to the ecosystem have become apparent. Figure 4.5.11 shows some of the 'mega-projects' in the Canadian North that have either been proposed or completed in the late twentieth century. Figure 4.5.12 shows some of the proven and likely environmental pollution in the Canadian North.

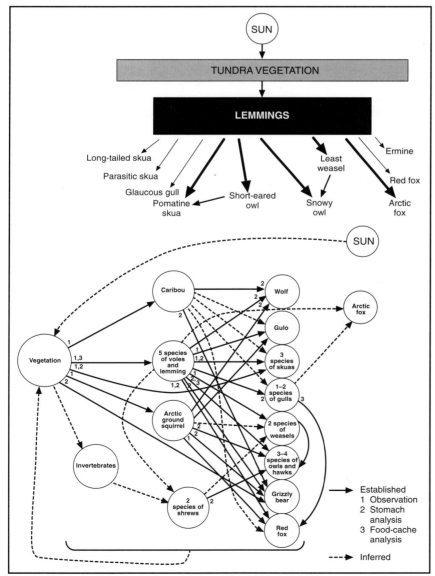

The use of the snowmobile

The one-person snowmobile was developed in Canada in the late 1950s. It was first imported into Finland in 1962, and within two years was widely in use for reindeer herding. Herds are no longer regularly tended as they used to be, and the snowmobile is most useful in the roundup. Figure 4.5.13 shows the pattern of reindeer sales and herd growth in Utsjoki (northern Finland) before and after the introduction of the snowmobile.

Student Activity 4.11

Comment on the changes in the reindeer sales and herd growth after the introduction of the snowmobile.

The Mackenzie Valley pipeline enquiry

The proposal for a Mackenzie Valley pipeline involved the building of a pipeline to bring gas from the Prudhoe Bay oilfields in Alaska through the Mackenzie Valley to markets in Southern Canada and the USA (see Figure 4.5.11). The cost of the Arctic Gas Proposal was some $8 billion. Three main issues surfaced during the course of the enquiry.

1 The problem of burying a pipeline in the area of permafrost.
2 The threat to the Arctic environment along the Yukon Coast.
3 The potential disruption of the life of the indigenous peoples, and the impact on traditional Eskimo culture.

The enquiry found that the environmental soundness of burying the pipeline beneath the permafrost was fraught with technical problems of thawing of the permafrost. The report was also concerned that the pipeline route along the Arctic coast of Yukon would pass through the calving area of the Porcupine caribou herd, and would affect the animals during their calving period. Chief Justice Thomas Berger found that *'the preservation of the herd is incompatible with the building of a gas pipeline and the establishment of an energy corridor through its calving ground.'*

The proposal was rejected, although a later one for an alternative route was approved. The Mackenzie enquiry was the first one to place firm emphasis on public participation in the hearings, and it gave a particularly high profile to environmental issues affecting indigenous peoples. Although the Norman Wells pipeline project was allowed to go ahead, it is significant that in the same area in the early 1980s, after the first year of operation, subsidence around the pipeline was much more than expected.

FIGURE 4.5.13 Reindeer Sales and herd growth at Utsjoki, Finland

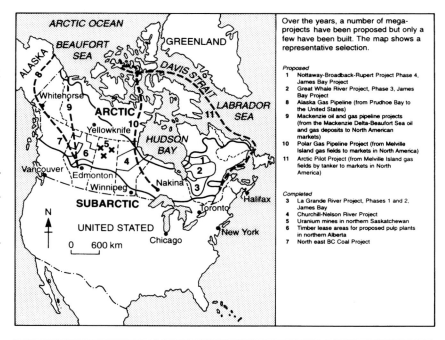

FIGURE 4.5.11 (*top*) Mega-projects in the Canadian North

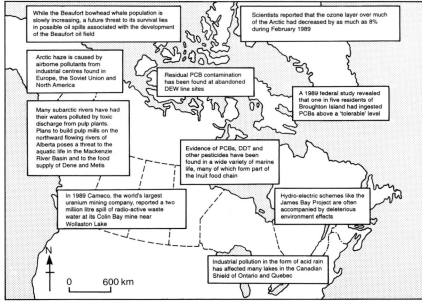

FIGURE 4.5.12 (*above*) Environmental pollution in the Canadian North

PERIOD	REINDEER SLAUGHTERED AND SOLD	NET INCREASE IN HERDS
	(%)	(%)
1956–61		
Owner A	25.5	1.7
B	15.5	34.3
C	22.7	13.5
Total association (104 members)	23.7	7.8
1963–9		
Owner A	43.7	−16.8
B	32.6	−17.4
C	43.0	−20.2
Total association (111 members)	32.7	−10.0

4.6 *Mulga woodlands and Spinifex scrub in the Australian outback*

Mulga scrub

'We had great difficulty in getting through, from the quantity of dead timber, which had torn our saddlebags and clothing to pieces.'

John McDouall Stuart, Australian explorer

Mulga scrub occupies some 1.6 million km², or some 20 per cent of Australia, and much of this area is true wilderness (Figure 4.6.1) with only a small Aboriginal population. It sits uneasily across the boundaries of major biomes, part desert, part savanna and part temperate grassland. In some ways its very distinctiveness demands a category all its own. Mulga (*Acacia aneura*) grows across the extensive plains that grade away imperceptibly from the high ranges of the Australian interior. Mulga reaches particularly high densities over much of the interior, up to 300 per hectare, and in south west Queensland up to 5000 per hectare. Mulga woodland grows in areas where the rainfall is totally unreliable, and there the shrub must adapt to the lack of moisture.

FIGURE 4.6.1 (*far right*) Mulga scrub, Australia

FIGURE 4.6.2 (*below*) Mulga and spinifex distribution

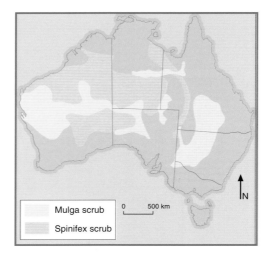

Mulga scrub

Spinifex scrub

0   500 km

N

Spinifex grasslands

'A land, as far as the eye can see,
where the waving grasses grow
Or the plains are blackened and burnt and bare, where the false mirages grow.'

A B (Banjo) Paterson, The Plains

The distribution patterns of mulga and spinifex, when seen together, make up a mosaic on the map of Australian outback. Spinifex covers 22 per cent of Australia (Figure 4.6.2), and it is the essential desert ecosystem in the outback. About 30 different species of spinifex exist. They can be broadly divided into 'hard' and 'soft' varieties. Soft spinifex grows on the sand plains to the north and west of Alice Springs: hard spinifex is the most drought resistant and grows south west of Alice Springs and in the vast emptiness of the Simpson Desert and the Victoria and Great Sandy Deserts of Western Australia. Spinifex grows in clumps (Figure 4.6.3). Root

■ Its leaves are vertically aligned to reduce heatload.
■ Sunken **stomata**, reduced leaf size, and abundant leaf hairs reduce transpiration.
■ Foliage colour, silvery blue-green increases reflectance from the leaves.
■ The overall shape of the tree encourages channelling of water so that it is concentrated at the base of the trunk.
■ It possesses a deep root system to reach water at depth within the soil.

FIGURE 4.6.3 (*right*) Spinifex, Australia

Grasses, and other flowering plants form an understorey to mulga.

systems extend down for 3 m, and the roots develop from the same nodes as the shoots and therefore each stem has its own direct supply of water and nutrients.

Fires are a frequent feature of spinifex grasslands, and since the biomass of spinifex does not break down, spinifex retains much of its biomass, highly flammable, throughout its lifetime. Fires are thus of unparalleled ferocity and speed, and ecosystem recovery depends on special characteristics of the plants. Some spinifex resprout quickly, and others complete their life cycles quickly from seed. Ernest Giles, the explorer who first discovered Kata Tjuta (The Olgas) wrote *'the natives were about burning, burning, ever burning; one would think that they were of the fabled salamander race, and lived on fire instead of water.'*

Fire was perhaps the earliest form of management of spinifex, and mulga. Aborigines used fire for hunting regeneration of food plants, signalling and for clearing paths through the spinifex. The firing produced a range of habitats for flora and fauna that required different stages of regeneration. It also eliminated large-scale wildfires by providing firebreaks.

Mulga and spinifex occupy vast areas of wilderness in Australia, and some parts receive little management at present. Figure 4.6.4 shows Australian landscapes in the 1990s. It should be compared with the distribution of mulga and spinifex (Figure 4.6.2). It will be seen that four main landscapes are found in the mulga and spinifex lands.

1 Extensive farming: mainly large cattle and sheep stations.
2 Aboriginal lands and reserves.
3 National Parks and Reserves.
4 Vacant lands.

Areas 2, 3 and 4 are the wilderness lands of the mulga and spinifex ecosystems. Aboriginal lands make up 14.5 per cent of Australia in the 1990s, and over considerable areas, as Heathcote says *'the scene has changed little since 1770 in terms of flora and fauna'*. National Parks and Reserves make up 4.5 per cent of the continent, and in the more remote areas

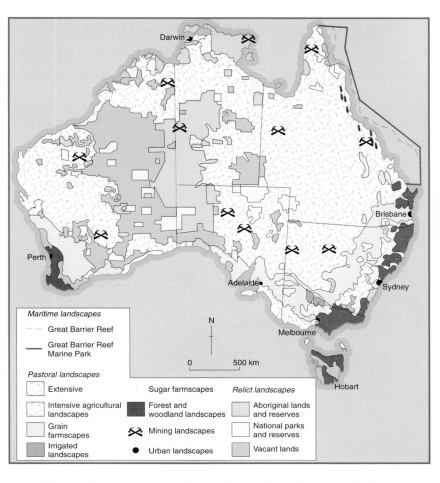

FIGURE 4.6.4 Australian landscapes in the 1990s

again, like the Simpson Desert, little has changed over 200 years. National Parks in the mulga and spinifex areas usually have wilderness zones designated, and here public access is restricted to those on foot. Certain areas, such as parts of the Uluru National Park, are set aside as biosphere reserves under the United Nations scheme. Heathcote describes the vacant lands as the *'quiet timeless lands of the continent'*, but warns that *'their vacant character is seen only as a temporary phenomenon'*. They remain, at the moment, unmanaged wilderness ecosystems.

4.7 *The Antarctic marine ecosystem*

'And a thousand thousand slimy things
Lived on; and so did I.'
  Samuel Taylor Coleridge, *The Ancient Mariner*

Unlike the relatively simple terrestrial ecosystem of the Antarctic continent, the marine ecosystem is much richer and more diverse. Some would even consider that 'wilderness' is a misnomer for such a biologically diverse system! To find such abundant marine life in the persistently cold Southern Ocean is indeed a paradox for the lay person. However much of the early exploration of the region was as

much concerned with the possible commercial exploitation of the marine ecosystem as it was with making a landfall on the continent. This rich marine resource has now been utilised for over 200 years, and its management is still a fundamental environmental issue in the Antarctic. Both sealing and whaling took their toll during this period, and current concern over Antarctic fisheries, and the exploitation of krill in particular, has provoked much discussion over present and future management strategies.

The environment of the Southern Ocean

Figure 4.7.1 shows the main circulation features of the Southern Ocean. Surface currents close to the Antarctic Continent are easterly and are driven by the strong east winds that blow close to the continent, although more complex patterns develop in the Ross and Weddell seas. Farther away from Antarctica the strong westerly air flow drives the Antarctic Circumpolar Current. These two flows of water are separated by the Antarctic Divergence. When the pack ice freezes in the autumn, very dense, saline water is formed beneath it, and sinks and flows northwards along the continental shelf and into the deep ocean basin as Antarctic Bottom Water.

FIGURE 4.7.1 Main circulation features of the Southern Ocean

Cold Antarctic surface water flows north until it meets warmer SubAntarctic Water flowing south at the Antarctic Convergence, regarded by many as the northern limit of the Southern Ocean. The Antarctic Surface Water, being denser, sinks beneath the SubAntarctic Water, and continues its flow at depth as Antarctic Intermediate Water. Between this water, and the deep flow of Antarctic Bottom Water there is a poleward flow of warmer, nutrient rich Circumpolar Deep Water, which upwells near the Antarctic Divergence. This upwelling water releases nutrients at the surface which will encourage highly localised primary production in the summer months when there is a maximum solar energy available and ice cover is minimal.

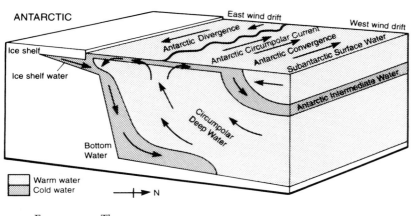

FIGURE 4.7.2 The Antarctic marine ecosystem

Structure and functioning of the Antarctic marine ecosystem

The main features of the Antarctic Marine Ecosystem are shown in Figure 4.7.2. It can be seen that the **trophic structure** exists in two different linkages. The simple chain that connects phytoplankton, with what many regard as the key element in the system, **krill**, and the **baleen whales**, exists alongside a more complex one. In the latter, krill play a fundamental role, since they are food for so many organisms at different levels in the structure.

The growth of **phytoplankton**, at the lowest level in the ecosystem, is controlled by light, nutrient supply and temperature in the ocean. Light appears to be the most important influence. In winter, the short days and the frozen sea ice, limit photosynthesis. In the Antarctic summer, however, melting of the sea ice releases algae living on the interface between ice and water. The algae flourish under the renewed sunlight and good nutrient supply, and they enable phytoplanktonic blooms to develop. Total primary production of phytoplankton is of the order of 10 000 wet tonnes per year, which, contrary to popular belief, and given the size of the area, is not particularly large.

Zooplankton, including the krill, feed on the phytoplankton blooms, which are a very concentrated food source, so that the zooplankton grow very rapidly. Krill, small shrimp-like creatures (Figure 4.7.3) live in particularly dense swarms (sometimes up to 1 million in a 1000 m³ water). Their concentrations are shown in Figure 4.7.4. In winter krill feed on algae on the underside of pack ice, although they can also feed off low concentrations of phytoplankton in locations such as the waters around South Georgia.

Between 400 to 650 million tonnes of krill are found in the Southern Ocean. Annual consumption of krill by other organisms in the food chain is as follows.

Seals	130 million tonnes
Birds (mostly penguins)	100 million tonnes
Baleen whales	60 million tonnes

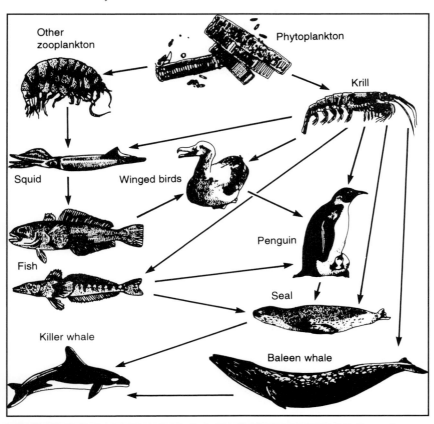

Fish and squids eat much smaller amounts.

Little is known of the ecology of the squid population, but they appear to have a short life span and be fast-growing. Up to 35 million tonnes of squid a year are eaten by mammals and birds. Fish that live in Antarctic waters show special adaptations to the cold water. Many contain special 'anti-freeze' molecules in their body fluids. In ice fishes, red blood cells are virtually eliminated, and in one variety there are none. Fishing for squid is already important commercially in the Antarctic. Fin fish, such as 'Antarctic cod', and more recently ice fish have also been caught in the Antarctic on a commercial basis.

Two groups of birds play a role in the Antarctic marine ecosystem. The albatrosses and petrels feed in the upper 2 or 3 m of the sea, whilst penguins generally feed on krill and fish in the top 100 m. The Emperor penguin feeds on both squid and fish down to depths of 300 m.

Six species of seal live in the Antarctic, of which three live in the pack ice area. Crab-eater seals live on krill, whilst the leopard seal (Figure 4.7.5), although it consumes krill, is an active predator of penguins and other seals. The Ross seal lives on squid and fish. The fish-eating Weddell seals live in the fast ice area, breeding in late winter and maintaining holes in the ice. The southern elephant seal, and the Antarctic fur seal are found in lower latitudes, on subAntarctic islands and even further north. They feed on squid and krill respectively.

The baleen whales (Figure 4.7.6) form the top of the Antarctic 'fast food' chain, and feed on krill. They take in vast quantities of water (tens of cubic metres in large animals) and then strain this through the baleen plates hanging from their upper jaws: the krill are retained and swallowed. When baleen whales migrate into the Southern Ocean, they appear to follow the retreat of the sea ice, where the krill are concentrated. The main toothed whales are the Sperm whale (now only present in relatively small numbers) and the Killer whale, which hunts fish, penguins and seals.

Student Activity 4.12

1 Why might krill be regarded as the pivotal feature of the Antarctic marine food web?
2 Discuss the ways in which the food web may become disrupted, through human intervention.

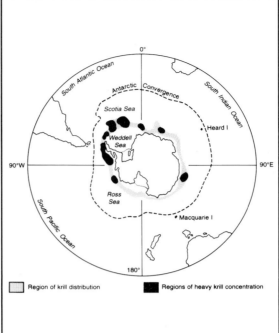

FIGURE 4.7.3 (*far left*)
Krill

FIGURE 4.7.4
Concentration of Krill

FIGURE 4.7.5 (*above*)
Leopard seal

FIGURE 4.7.6 Blue whale

Managing the ecosystem: the problem of the Antarctic fisheries

'The history of the relationship between mankind and the Southern Ocean contains a record of greed and ignorance alongside the great landmarks of exploration and discovery.'

Dr Julian Priddle

The resources of the Antarctic marine ecosystem have now been exploited for almost two centuries. In the nineteenth century, and the first half of the twentieth, sealing and whaling resulted in large-scale reduction of the stocks in the Southern Ocean, largely as a result of lack of management. In the second half of the twentieth century the emphasis has changed to fishing for krill, squid and fin fish. Krill fishing began on a large scale in the 1970s, and reached a peak in the early 1980s. It appears to have been bedevilled with the problem of finding a suitable market for krill products in countries like Russia and Japan. Fin fisheries in the 1970s were probably guilty of overexploitation. In the 1970s the Antarctic Treaty nations became increasingly concerned about the effects of overfishing on the Antarctic marine ecosystem, and in 1982 the Convention on the Conservation of Antarctic Marine Living Resources (CCAMLR) was put into operation. It adopted an ecosystem approach to resource management, with a concern not just for the target species, but also a consideration of the effect of its reduction on other trophic levels of the system.

FIGURE 4.7.8 (*far right*) Antarctic whale catches

FIGURE 4.7.7 Seal hunting

Sealing and whaling in the Antarctic

exploited for the oil in their blubber. Although the industry was under much closer scrutiny and control, this did not prevent numbers declining steadily between the 1930s and 1952. In 1952 a quota of seal catch was introduced in South Georgia, related to the relative abundance of seals in different waters around the island. In 1972 a Convention for the Conservation of Antarctic Seals (CCAS) was introduced, which stimulated the ecological research necessary for management and control should exploitation recommence.

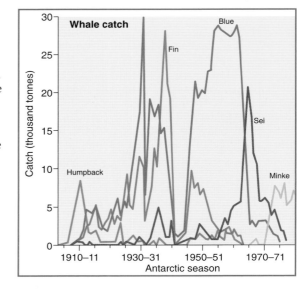

The pattern of Antarctic whale catches is shown in Figure 4.7.8. Whaling was first shore-based (Figure 4.7.9), and this imposed some sort of control on the total catch, but the advent of factory ships widened the areas available for the catching of whales, and in addition, neither licences or leases were required for this new system. Overfishing resulted in a vast decline in the number of whales. Management was inadequate because no information was available on how fishing might be continued on a sustainable basis. Furthermore, capital investment had been on such a scale that operators were anxious to realise the maximum income before the industry collapsed. A total ban on whaling was introduced in 1986 by the International Whaling Commission.

FIGURE 4.7.9 (*far right*) Whaling Station, South Georgia

Sealing for skins began in the years shortly after Captain Cook discovered South Georgia in 1775 (Figure 4.7.7). By the 1870s the fur seal population had been so seriously diminished that in three successive seasons only 1450, 600 and 110 seals were reported. A century or so later numbers were showing a rapid increase again. Elephant seals were

Student Activity 4.13

1 Discuss the reasons for the fluctuating nature of whale catches in the Antarctic as shown in Figure 4.7.8.
2 Why should the pattern of whale catch shown in Figure 4.7.8 have led to a total ban on whaling?
3 Why should the resumption of sealing be ecologically inadvisable?

Fin fishing and krill fishing in the Southern Ocean

Large-scale fin fishing began in the late 1960s around South Georgia. The first peak was reached in 1970 (see Figure 4.7.10) and a second was reached in 1978. Evidence from ecological studies showed that overfishing of Antarctic cod had resulted in a major decline in the spawning stock. Low egg production in the fish caught meant that large numbers of the spawning fish needed to be retained in order to sustain stocks. Mackerel ice fish were targeted by the Russians in the early 1970s in the South Orkneys and the South Shetland Islands once it became clear that the Antarctic cod resource was being seriously overfished.

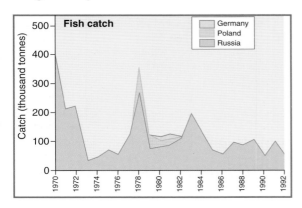

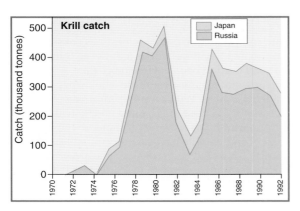

The main commercial problem with krill fishing has been finding a suitable market. Krill paste and krill cheese products were produced in the former Soviet Union, but do not seem to have been particularly popular. 'Peeled' krill has some potential, and it can be used in a variety of products such as burgers, stews, sauces and fish sticks, or marketed as 'Antarctic shrimp', a luxury food. Krill meal is another possible use, but it has certain drawbacks, such as a high fluoride content, and fishing for this purpose alone would not be viable. Despite these reservations, the krill fishery has been the largest fishery in the Southern Ocean since 1979 (Figure 4.7.11), mostly concentrated in the South Atlantic section.

The Convention for the Conservation of Antarctic Marine Living Resources (CCAMLR)

The regulations of the Convention came into force in 1982 and:
■ apply to all populations of fin fish, molluscs, crustaceans, and all other species including birds found south of the Antarctic Convergence, which form part of the Antarctic Marine ecosystem;
■ state that any harvesting of resources shall be conducted in accordance with the following principles of conservation:
  – prevent reduction of any population below a sustainable level;
  – maintain ecological relationships between harvested, dependent and related populations of living marine resources;
  – prevent changes to elements of the marine ecosystem that cannot be reversed over two or three decades;
■ conservation measures will be determined by the Commission and will be binding on all members 180 days after notification;
■ a scientific committee will advise the Commission on criteria for conservation measures, and carry out research on the status and population trends of marine living resources, and assess the direct and indirect impact of harvesting on them.

CCAMLR has attempted to set fishing limits that are sustainable. The total fin fish catch is now 100 000 tonnes annually and the amounts of krill caught are restricted to 1.5 million tonnes a year.

Student Activity 4.14

1 What are the main ecological bases on which CCAMLR operates?
2 What are the main difficulties in enforcing the regulations of CCAMLR?

Figure 4.7.10 (far left)
Fish catch: Antarctica

Figure 4.7.11 (far left)
Krill catch: Antarctica

ESSAYS

1 Explain why wilderness ecosystems are of such outstanding global importance.

2 Discuss the main threats to wilderness ecosystems, and show how management strategies may be designed to lessen these risks.

5
MANAGING CONSERVATION AND TOURISM IN WILDERNESS REGIONS

'With the wreck of human passage: sandclogged bottles,
Blown paper, ruined plastic, blackened fires,
Gifts to the land of tourists like ourselves.
Now no one lives here. Wheeltracks not footprints,
Mark the edge of this world with fading scars –'
Jack Rowland, *Towards Lake Eyre*

KEY IDEAS

■ There is a potential conflict between conservation and tourism in wilderness areas.
■ Designation of areas such as Nature Reserves and National Parks seeks to promote a balance between the twin claims of conservation and tourism.
■ Zoning in designated areas enables different priorities to be established.

■ Excessive development of tourism in wilderness areas can damage the environment and possibly exploit indigenous people.
■ Sustainable development appears to be possible where proper co-ordination is achieved between different groups and interests.

5.1 Conservation and tourism: conflict or harmony?

FIGURE 5.1.1 Tourist coaches at the Olgas, Northern Territory

Much of the writing on wilderness has stressed the need to maintain its qualities in order to fulfil a spiritual need in people. Herein lies the fundamental dilemma for those who manage wilderness areas. With growing improvements in accessibility to these areas, more people will have the opportunity to visit remote regions whose scenery and wildlife have an inherent appeal to tourists. There has been considerable growth in the market for tourist ventures in wilderness regions such as Amazonia, Alaska, the remote outback of Australia (see Figure 5.1.1) and increasingly, Antarctica. Equally there has been a parallel growth in the number of areas that are protected in some form or other (see Figure 5.1.2).

Most countries, both the more economically developed, and the less economically developed have to achieve a balance between providing adequate facilities for tourists, and at the same time

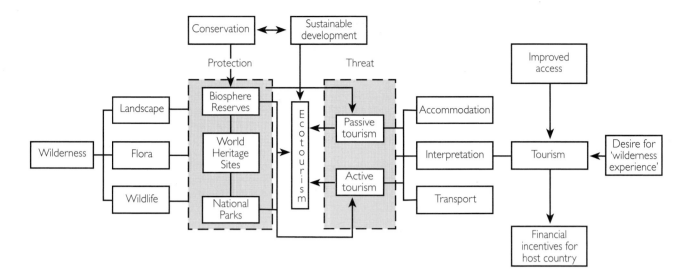

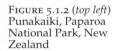

FIGURE 5.1.3 (*above*)
Relationship between
tourism and protected
areas

FIGURE 5.1.2 (*top left*)
Punakaiki, Paparoa
National Park, New
Zealand

FIGURE 5.1.4 (*top right*)
Tourist Lodge: Amboseli
National Park, Kenya

FIGURE 5.1.5 (*bottom left*)
Gokyo Valley, Khumbu
Himalayas

FIGURE 5.1.6 (*bottom
right*) Remote route in
the Australian outback

protecting both landscapes and ecosystems so that heritage is preserved for the future.

Since the designation of Yellowstone as the first National Park in the USA most countries have seen the need to establish some form of protection in their wilderness areas. The World Conservation Union recognises eight categories of protected areas. Five of these are listed as National Parks or equivalent reserves. These are areas of outstanding scenic and wildlife value which have national and global significance, and are protected for scientific, educational or recreational use. The remaining three categories are less stringently protected, and the sustainable production of timber, game and other natural resources is permitted, together with the

traditional use of the areas by indigenous peoples. In addition to these eight categories, World Heritage Sites (see Chapter 7) and Biosphere Reserves are other protected areas where conservation is a key theme in their management.

Tourism in wilderness regions clearly has to respond to the requirements of visitors, but nowadays has, in the majority of cases, also to operate within the conservation context of protected areas. The relationship is a complex one and is illustrated in Figure 5.1.3. Tourist operators offer a range of different packages to the visitor of wilderness regions. Although the visit is often advertised as a 'wilderness experience', many tourists will require the full range of facilities that they would expect in traditional resorts. These facilities are now increasingly available (see Figure 5.1.4). However, the true wilderness may only be explored by those tourists that are prepared to accept more primitive accommodation and facilities available on camping and backpacking ventures. Such areas and experiences include the Brooks Range of Northern Alaska, trekking in the high Himalayan valleys (see Figure 5.1.5) and four-wheel drive expeditions into the remote Australian outback (see Figure 5.1.6).

Management of tourism in wilderness areas has to focus on the inevitable impact that it will have on the environment and, in some cases, the indigenous people of the area. Jack Rowland's poetry summarises the all too often seen impact of four-wheel drive tourism in the Australian outback.

Similarly the trekking route up to Everest Base Camp in the high Himalayas has sadly now acquired the epithet of 'the Kleenex Trail'. Wilderness safaris in Africa are often accused of disrupting wildlife to unacceptable levels in order for tourists to experience animals in their habitats at close quarters. It is a well-worn cliché that people are inevitably destroying the very wilderness that they have come to see, and it is a goal of wilderness management to stop this from happening. Thus sustainable tourism, or ecotourism is emerging as a new theme, where a better balance is established between the apparent conflict of conservation and development values.

5.2 Case studies of managing conservation and tourism in wilderness regions

The first case studies set the theme of conservation, looking at Biosphere Reserves in Britain. Not all of these reserves can be regarded as wilderness areas, but the chosen example of the Beinn Eighe Reserve in Wester Ross, Scotland remains one of the finest wildernesses in Britain. Two National Parks in developed countries are then examined to illustrate the interplay of conservation and tourism: the

Kakadu National Park in Australia and the Fjordland National Park in South Island, New Zealand. By way of contrast National Parks and wildlife issues are examined in some less economically developed countries: Nepal (the Sagarmatha National Park and trekking in the high Himalayas) and the wilderness National Parks of Kenya, Zimbabwe and Botswana.

5.3 Biosphere Reserves

FIGURE 5.3.1 Multi-purpose role of biosphere reserves

UNESCO's Man and the Biosphere Programme was first launched in 1971 to: *'provide the knowledge, skills, and human values to support harmonious relationships between people and their environment throughout the world.'* Within the Man and the

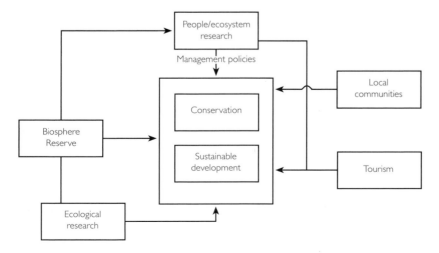

Biosphere Programme, one Task Force was set up with the responsibility of drawing up a set of guidelines for defining and designating Biosphere Reserves. Eventually these reserves would form part of an international system that had common standards, and would allow the exchange of information relevant to the conservation of natural and managed ecosystems.

Biosphere Reserves display one or more of the following characteristics.
- Protected areas of land and coastal environments.
- Representative samples of biomes.
- Unique communities with unusual natural features of international interest.
- 'Harmonious landscapes' resulting from traditional patterns of land use.
- Modified or degraded ecosystems capable of being restored to more natural conditions.

Designation of Biosphere Reserves is to envisage a multi-purpose role. They are not considered to be areas where conservation is the sole function. It is important that they provide the opportunity for local communities and other bodies to use natural and managed ecosystems without damaging and degrading them. Research into the way the ecosystem functions and the way in which it responds to people's activities enables sensible management policies to operate that will sustain the healthy future of the system. This multi-purpose role for biosphere reserves is summarised in Figure 5.3.1.

Zoning in Biosphere Reserves

Biosphere reserves should ideally have three-fold zonation.

1 One or more strictly protected core areas that includes examples of natural or minimally disturbed ecosystems. The size and shape of the core area will vary according to the type of landscape or aquatic environment within which they are located. The core area should be large enough to act as a conservation unit within which monitoring of the long-term change of the ecosystem can take place.

2 A surrounding buffer or intermediate zone. This is normally strictly delineated and can form, with the core area, part of a clearly defined administrative unit. Activities that take place within the buffer zone must be compatible with the protection of the core area: they will include such things as research, environmental education and training, and tourism and recreation.

3 The outer transition zone. Within this zone there may be research areas, areas of traditional, sustainable use, and rehabilitation areas. Its role is seen as integrating the functions of the inner zones within a much wider area, encouraging sustainable resource development, which is reconciled with the essential functions of the Biosphere Reserve.

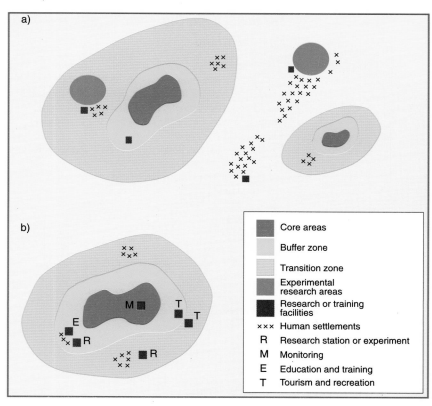

Two possible models for a Biosphere Reserve are shown in Figure 5.3.2. The simple Biosphere Reserve follows a basically concentric arrangement as outlined above. In the cluster Biosphere Reserve a wider mosaic of the three different zones is created.

FIGURE 5.3.2 Models of Biosphere Reserves

Student Activity 5.1

1 Discuss the ecological value of the two different systems of zoning in Figure 5.3.2.
2 What other spatial alternatives can you suggest to the two systems proposed above?

FIGURE 5.3.3 (*left*) Biosphere Reserves in the United Kingdom

Biosphere Reserves in Britain

Biosphere Reserves in Britain were first designated in 1976 and 1977, in response to the initiatives of UNESCO and the Man and the Biosphere programme. The sites originally selected are shown on Figure 5.3.3. It is evident from the map that a number of these sites are not true wilderness sites, particularly those in southern and eastern England. Those that best illustrate wilderness qualities are located in Scotland, particularly Merrick-Kells, Beinn Eighe and St Kilda.

Britain withdrew from UNESCO in 1985, and a Working Group set up in 1989 to review the British Biosphere Reserves suggested that this withdrawal had prevented the implementation of some of the new guidelines established in the 1980s. In particular the British Biosphere Reserves only seemed to be fulfilling the functions of the core area, with less attention being given to the buffer and transition zones.

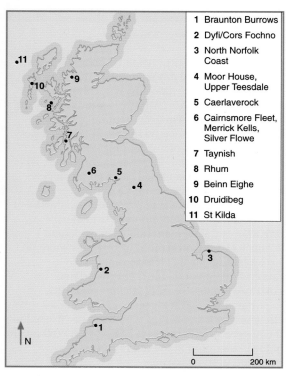

1 Braunton Burrows
2 Dyfi/Cors Fochno
3 North Norfolk Coast
4 Moor House, Upper Teesdale
5 Caerlaverock
6 Cairnsmore Fleet, Merrick Kells, Silver Flowe
7 Taynish
8 Rhum
9 Beinn Eighe
10 Druidibeg
11 St Kilda

0   200 km

N

The Beinn Eighe Biosphere Reserve, Wester Ross, Scotland

'I traversed the ridge of Beinn Eighe ... I headed westwards, when suddenly a gap appeared in the mist to reveal a glen bathed in sunlight, thousands of feet below. In a flash it disappeared. All afternoon there were tantalising glimpses of the landscape, while stag calls echoed across the slopes.'

David Bellamy, *The Wild Places of Britain*

The extent of the Beinn Eighe Biosphere Reserve is shown in Figure 5.3.4. Core, buffer/intermediate and transition zones are shown, but in practice the most active conservation work is done in the core zone (see Figure 5.3.5), although the Gairloch Conservation unit does include parts of the core, buffer and transition zones.

Much of the reserve is true wilderness country, and the transition zone includes Fisherfield Forest (see Chapter 3, Section 3.3).

FIGURE 5.3.4 The Beinn Eighe Reserve

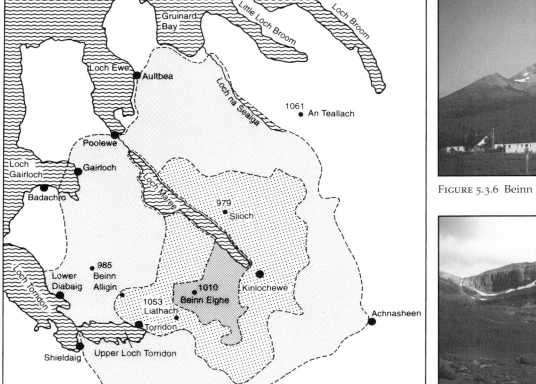

FIGURE 5.3.6 Beinn Eighe

FIGURE 5.3.7 Coire Mhic Fhearchair

The core area is dominated by Beinn Eighe (see Figure 5.3.6), a wild mountain mass that rises to 1010 m, with spectacular corries opening northwards into Glen Grudie (see Figure 5.3.7) and huge scree slopes of quartzite running down towards Glen Torridon on the south-facing slopes. Much of the core is of outstanding geological interest, underlain by Torridonian sandstone, with a cover of younger Cambrian rocks on the upper mountain slopes (see Figure 5.3.9).

Although within the reserve there is a mosaic of woodland, upland and montane habitats, the fragment of Caledonian Scots Pine woodland (Coille na Glas Leitre) on the south west shore of Loch Maree is the most important from a conservation point of view. This woodland possesses a unique genetic quality, and has important affinities with similar woodlands elsewhere in Europe. Pine woodland has existed in the reserve since 8000 years ago, and covered much of the low ground in the reserve. Now it is restricted to some 200 ha.

FIGURE 5.3.5 (*right*) The Beinn Eighe Reserve

Within the habitats of the Reserve species diversity is generally low, but because of the wide variety of communities and habitats overall diversity is quite high.

Red deer are common in both the woodland, and the upland and montane habitats. Although much of the natural woodland habitat has disappeared in the area, the red deer seem to thrive on the upland vegetation, provided good wintering areas are available. The Gairloch Conservation Unit was formed in 1967 in order to properly control the growth in deer populations (see Figure 5.3.8). This Unit consists of the core Nature Reserve, and four other estates that extend into the buffer and transition zones. It covers some 35 000 ha, with about 1000 red deer of which some 120 are culled each year to maintain balance within the ecosystem. Environmental threats to the core of the Reserve are surprisingly few (see Figure 5.3.10). Research fields and community involvement are shown in Figure 5.3.11. The Intermediate and Transition Zones have been created to protect the integrity of the core region.

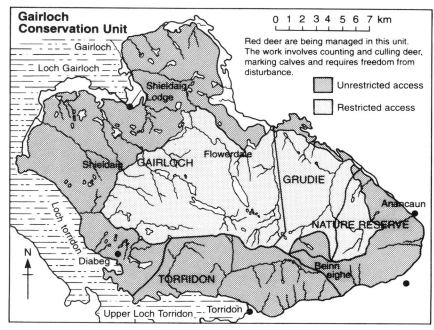

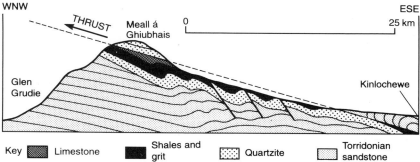

FIGURE 5.3.10 (*below*) Environmental threats to core zone of Beinn Eighe Nature Reserve

TYPE OF THREAT	NATURE OF THREAT
Ecological	Overgrazing of red deer. Pollution of mature Scots Pine gene pool by cross-pollination from adjacent stands of Scots Pine. Invasion of reserve by Scots Pine seedlings. Invasion of reserve by seedlings of rhododendron.
Recreational	Accidental fires. Localised problems of erosion on paths, trails and access routes.
Pollution	Acid rain damage to high altitude communities.

Student Activity 5.2

1 How far does the Beinn Eighe Reserve conform to the Simple Biosphere Reserve model?
2 Draw simple diagrams to compare the models in Figure 5.3.2 with the situation at Beinn Eighe.
3 What type of developments might be acceptable in the Intermediate and Transition Zones?

FIGURE 5.3.8 (*top*) The Gairloch Conservation Unit

FIGURE 5.3.9 (*above*) Geological cross-section of the core zone of the Beinn Eighe Reserve

FIGURE 5.3.11 Research fields and community involvement in the Beinn Eighe Reserve

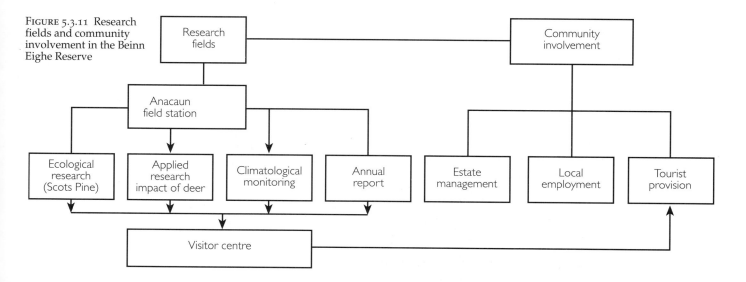

5.4 Managing conservation and tourism in National Parks

'They [National Parks] are a tangible acknowledgement, at the highest level, that the planet is more than a work place or a playground for man. A wild marsh, a stretch of heathland, or a scene of mountain grandeur, deserves as much protection as a great cathedral or a famous painting.'

Sir Peter Scott, in the foreword to *National Parks and Reserves of Western Europe*, Eric Duffey

Although National Parks are found in most countries now, there is a bewildering variety of approaches to their designation and management. A common factor might be the United Nations' definition which is as follows.

A relatively large area:

■ where one or several ecosystems are not materially altered by human use and settlement;
■ where plant and animal species, geomorphological sites and habitats are of a specific scientific, educational and recreative interest, or which contain a natural landscape of great beauty;
■ where the Government of the country has taken steps to prevent or eliminate, as soon as possible, use or settlement in the whole area and to enforce the respect of ecological, geomorphological or aesthetic features which have led to its establishment;
■ where visitors are allowed to enter under special conditions.

Most of the National Parks within the major wilderness regions would conform well to these defining guidelines. Ownership is often in the hands of Governments, which makes policy making easier than in Britain's National Parks where most of the land is privately owned. Conservation of landscapes and ecosystems, many of which are of outstanding international importance is the prime aim in the wilderness National Parks. In some, such as the North East Greenland National Park, the activities of a relatively small local population can easily be absorbed into a management plan that concentrates primarily on conservation. Such National Parks are, however, becoming increasingly scarce, as the growth of national and international tourism seeks access for its clients to the remoter wilderness National Parks. Management plans now have to cope with an increasingly wide range of demands which will include the following:

■ maintaining the essential wilderness qualities of landscape within the Park;
■ monitoring the structure and function of ecosystems within the Park;
■ deciding the level and type of tourist and other activities appropriate for wilderness country;
■ monitoring and possibly controlling the number of tourists that enter the park;
■ monitoring the impact of tourists on landscapes and ecosystems within the park;
■ adopting a policy for **interpretive presentation** of the park for visitors;
■ deciding on the balance between public and private participation in the provision of facilities within the park.

Kakadu National Park, Northern Territory Australia

'The strange and awesome beauty of this ancient land is striking.'

Masterworks of Man and Nature: Preserving World Heritage

Australian National Parks are defined in the following way. *'A National Park is a relatively large area set aside for its features of relatively unspoiled natural landscape, flora and fauna, permanently dedicated for public enjoyment, education and inspiration and protected from all interference other than the essential management practices, so that its natural attributes are preserved.'*

Kakadu National Park is approximately 120 km east of Darwin, and covers an area of 19 804 km² (see Figure 5.4.1). It extends from the coast of Van

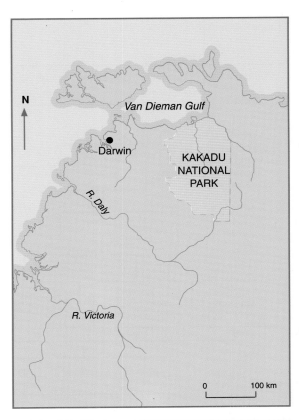

FIGURE 5.4.1 *(far right)* Kakadu National Park, Australia

Diemen Gulf south eastwards across floodplains and low-lying hills to the sandstone escarpment (see Figure 5.4.2). It possesses particularly rich and varied wildlife (see Figure 5.4.3). An incomplete list reveals 65 mammal, 275 bird, 120 reptile, 25 frog and 55 fish species recognised at present. Clearly this constitutes a major attraction for visitors.

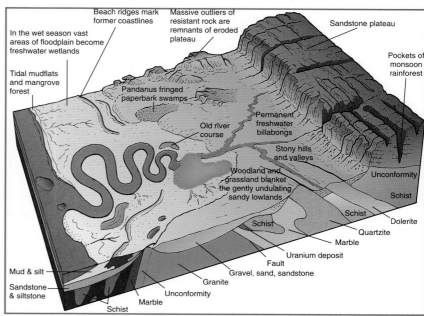

Aborigines in Kakadu

Kakadu is interesting because management of the National Park involves co-operation with the indigenous people, the Aborigines. They are the owners of the land within the National Park, and it is leased from them by the National Park Authorities. The terms of the agreement include payments for the lease, a share in revenue generated by the Park, and increased protection of Aboriginal rights within the Park. About 300

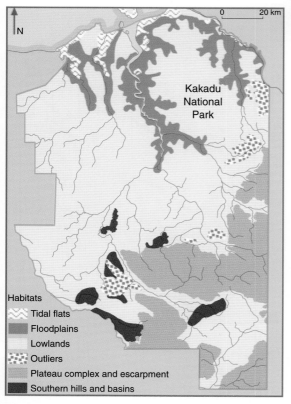

Habitats
- ≈≈ Tidal flats
- Floodplains
- Lowlands
- Outliers
- Plateau complex and escarpment
- Southern hills and basins

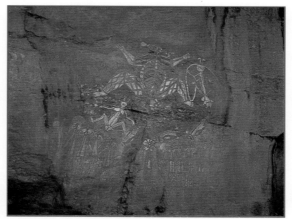

FIGURE 5.4.2 (*above*) Cross-section of Kakadu

FIGURE 5.4.3 (*above left*) Wildlife: Kakadu

FIGURE 5.4.4 (*left*) Aborigine rock art

Aboriginal people live within the Park and are concentrated for the most part in ten living areas. Traditional activities of Aboriginal peoples, such as fire management and resource harvesting, are safeguarded within the management guidelines for the Park. Provision is made on another level for Aborigines to be employed in the running of the Park, both in administration, and as rangers.

Within the Park there are a number of sacred Aboriginal sites, and Park management recognises the need for the continued well-being and integrity of these sites. Rock art (see Figure 5.4.4) and archaeological sites are of equal importance to the Aborigines, and management involves both conservation and a detailed interpretive programme for tourists.

Figure 5.4.5 shows the range of habitats in Kakadu. The Management Plan for the Park reports that the ecosystems are more or less intact. The vegetation structure almost certainly reflects the fire regimes practised by Aborigines over thousands of years. Aboriginal advice is sought for all forms of vegetation management, largely because of their unique understanding of plant regimes. Two

FIGURE 5.4.5 (*far left*) Habitats in Kakadu

What is *Mimosa pigra*?

Mimosa is a woody prickly weed which grows up to 6 metres tall. Mimosa is native to Central and South America. It was introduced to Australia in the 20 years prior to 1891 via the Botanic Gardens in Darwin, probably as a curiosity plant as its leaves close when touched.

It causes few problems for about 100 years.

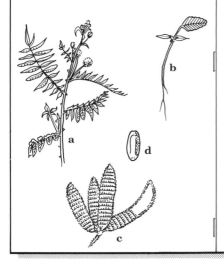

How can you help?

- Avoid entering mimosa thickets whether it be on foot or by vehicle as the seed will drop onto your vehicle. If this occurs, **remove them before leaving the area,**

- If seed drops into your boat from overhanging plants, **clean them out before leaving the area** to prevent new infestations.

- **DON'T** remove soil or sand from areas where mimosa occurs.

- Report any new infestations of mimosa or isolated plants to the Weeds Branch, DPIF, on the phone numbers listed on the back of this pamphlet.

- Remove or kill isolated plants on your property as soon as they are found. Contact the Weeds Branch for information on control methods.

Mimosa pigra
(a) part of a flowering stem
(b) seedling,
(c) pods, and
(d) seed.

FIGURE 5.4.6 Information leaflet on Mimosa pigra

FIGURE 5.4.7 (*top right*) Saltwater crocodile, Australia

FIGURE 5.4.8 (*below*) Crocodile awareness

FIGURE 5.4.9 (*far right*) Zoning in Kakadu National Park

species of weeds are currently causing concern in Kakadu, Mimosa pigra (Figure 5.4.6) and Salvinia molesta. Further introduction of Mimosa from vehicles entering the Park has to be vigorously monitored. Salvinia has been successfully managed by using biological controls.

Wildlife conservation has the expected high profile in Kakadu. Aboriginal groups respect the special status given to the fauna of Kakadu, and harvesting of animals is relatively unimportant since they depend mainly on other foods. Mammals display more species than any other area of north west Australia: one-third of all Australian bird species are found in Kakadu. Reptiles such as the two species of crocodile (Figure 5.4.7) present particular challenges for management, since they have such a high tourist profile. The threat posed by crocodiles to both the indigenous groups and visitors has led to an intensive awareness campaign for visitors (see Figure 5.4.8), and where crocodiles pose a threat to indigenous communities, individuals are caught and removed. **Feral animals** are subject to a strict control regime.

Fire management is an important tool of conservation in the Park. Traditional fire management techniques of the indigenous groups were disrupted with the arrival of white groups, but since official proclamation of the Park, there has been a serious attempt to return to the more harmonious management techniques of the Aborigines. Late dry season fires, introduced by white groups, have now been much reduced in number because of the damage to the ecosystem that resulted.

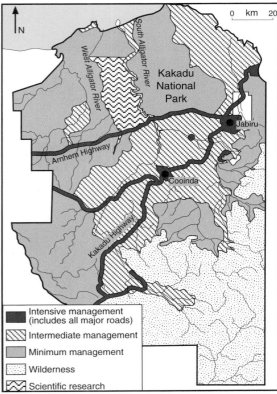

Zoning in Kakadu

Kakadu National Park authorities operate a system of zoning within the Park. Figure 5.4.9 shows the zonal arrangement in the Park and Figure 5.4.10 shows the relationship between the different zones and the appropriate type of recreational activity. It will be noted that approximately one-third of the Park, in the remote south east is classified as 'wilderness', and most recreational activities are regarded as inappropriate in this zone.

Student Activity 5.3

1 Comment on the relationship between the zones and the habitats shown in Figure 5.4.5.
2 For a Park with such a low population, why has only one-third of Kakadu been given a wilderness zoning?

Visitor management

Visitor management within the Park presents a number of challenges. Figure 5.4.11 shows the seasonal fluctuation in visitors, and the growth in visitor numbers in the period from 1982 to 1990. The obvious seasonal peak between May and October creates problems of **carrying capacity** at high profile natural and cultural sites. Management strategies have to be developed to cope with these problems of overloading of capacity.

The decrease in camping, boating and fishing is, in part, related to the high profile status of Kakadu as a World Heritage Site. Appropriate management strategies to handle increase in numbers include:
■ the provision of an increase in high order accommodation in the area, such as the Four Seasons Kakadu Hotel (see Figure 5.4.12), and the Kakadu Frontier Lodge in Jabiru;

FIGURE 5.4.10
Relationship between recreation and zoning

ACTIVITY	ZONE 1 INTENSIVE MANAGEMENT	ZONE 2 INTERMEDIATE MANAGEMENT	ZONE 3 MINIMUM MANAGEMENT	ZONE 4 WILDERNESS	ZONE 5 SCIENTIFIC RESEARCH
Driving	Scenic driving (easy on good roads)	Scenic driving (sealed roads or graded gravel roads)	Regulated 4WD touring	Inappropriate	Inappropriate
Walking	Short distance easy walking on formed or cleared tracks	Walking on formed or cleared tracks	Walking on existing tracks or bushwalking	Bushwalking	Inappropriate
Nature studies	Nature interpretation (exhibits and displays)	Nature trails (interpretive)	Nature studies (discovery or self-directed)	Nature studies (discovery or self-directed)	Intensive nature studies (research)
Camping	Camping (tent, caravan), hut or hotel accommodation in designated areas with hot and cold water, flushing toilets	Bush camping. Car-based camping in designated areas, toilets	Bush camping, permit required	Bush camping, permit required	Inappropriate (camping by research personnel only)
Picnicking	Picnicking with facilities in close proximity to vehicles	Picnicking with facilities provided in popular areas	Picnicking with minimal facilities	Bush picnicking	Inappropriate
Cycling	Cycling on existing roads	Cycling on existing roads	Cycling on existing roads	Inappropriate	Inappropriate

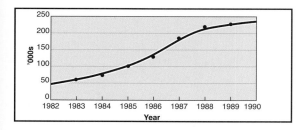

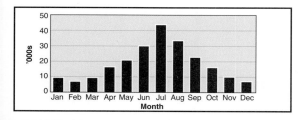

FIGURE 5.4.11 (*far left*)
Visitors to Kakadu: seasonal fluctuation and growth

FIGURE 5.4.12 Four Seasons Hotel, Jabiru

- the provision of campsites for 'safari camping' by commercial organisations;
- the upgrading of roads in the area. Sealed roads (tarmac) allow all weather access: graded roads (gravel) are often flooded or damaged during the wet season (see Figure 5.4.9). Although there are a number of airstrips and seaward approaches to the Park, few visitors arrive in this manner;
- continued improvement in the range, detail and style of interpretative facilities in the Park.

Student Activity 5.4

1 What measures could be taken to lessen the risk of key sites within Kakadu exceeding their carrying capacity during the peak season?
2 What particular difficulties are likely to arise in a National Park in Australia that has a rich Aboriginal cultural heritage, and in which small groups of Aborigines live?

Fjordland National Park, New Zealand

FIGURE 5.4.13 (*below*) Fjordland

Fjordland National Park is the largest of New Zealand's National Parks, and is part of the South West New Zealand World Heritage area (Te Wai Pounamu). It includes 1 252 297 ha of high glaciated mountains, with deeply-cut fjords extending in from the remote west coast (see Figure 5.4.13). With rainfall in many areas in excess of 5000 mm, much of Fjordland is covered with dense beech-dominated rainforest, although there are some high alpine grasslands in some of the drier areas.

FIGURE 5.4.14 (*bottom right*) Visitor facilities: Fjordland

Fjordland is part of a much wider 'tourist region' in South West New Zealand, focusing on Queenstown, which offers the largest amount of accommodation and the widest range of tourist facilities. The Park offers a range of activities to the visitor, varying from enjoyment of the scenic beauty of the fjord country, to walking along well-maintained tracks, and enjoying the 'wilderness' experience in the remoter areas.

The Park attracts some 450 000 visitors a year, with the peak season being from mid-October until May. Heavy rain and snowfall are responsible for the drop in tourist numbers in winter months. A profile of visitor nature and preferences reveals that:
- most visitors only spend one day or less in the Park;
- the major proportion of visitors in the park are in the 35–65 age bracket, and visit the Park as part of a bus tour;
- an increasing proportion of visitors is in the younger age bracket (<35), particularly from Europe and North America;
- the main visitor preference is for viewing scenery, and wildlife, with an expressed desire for undertaking one of the less demanding walks;
- younger age groups inevitably express interest in low-cost outdoor recreational pursuits such as track-walking;
- there is an increase in fly-drive holidays using camper vans.

Recreational facilities in Fjordland
- Walking tracks: 500 km of walking tracks, ranging from short nature walks to long-distance

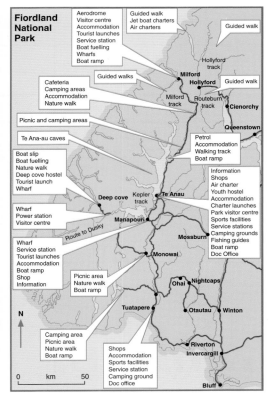

tracks (graded according to degree of difficulty and surface conditions). Milford Track is controlled by a quota system, with only 40 walkers pre-booked each day.

■ Picnicking and camping sites in the Eglington Valley are fully equipped, and at other locations shown in Figure 5.4.14. Low impact camping is permitted anywhere in the Park, except in areas adjacent to roads, and high-use tracks.

■ Boat ramps and jetties are available at popular locations on all the major lakes and at Deep Cove and Milford Sound.

■ Milford Sound (see Figures 5.4.15 and 5.4.16): reached by Highway 94, the only land route into the Park, occasionally closed in the vicinity of Homer Tunnel (owing to heavy snowfall or avalanche danger). Little room for expansion of existing facilities because of lack of flat ground, and high redevelopment costs. Hotel operations reduced to accommodation for Milford Track walkers and a limited number of other visitors. Projected figures of 2500 visitors a day in late 1990s and 4000 a day in two decades. Latter figure regarded as the environmentally sustainable limit. Minimal change to waterfront in next 20 years.

■ Te Anau Township (see Figure 5.4.17): lake-front subject to increasing pressure from both tourism and growth of the township. Lake-front itself is a significant amenity for Te Anau, with accommodation benefiting from quality views across the lake.

■ High-use tracks: four high-use tracks (see Figure 5.4.14) at Milford, Routeburn, Kepler and Hollyford.

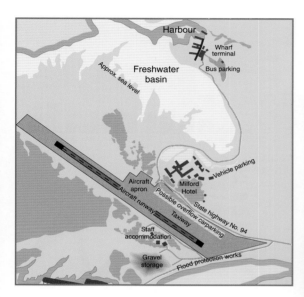

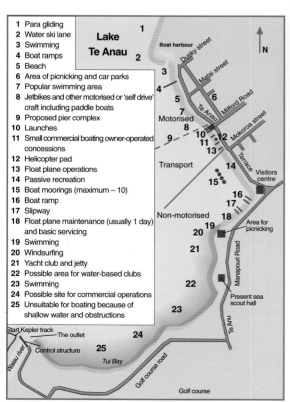

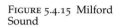
FIGURE 5.4.15 Milford Sound

FIGURE 5.4.16 (*far left*) Milford Sound: facilities

FIGURE 5.4.17 (*left*) Te Anau Township

Numbers of independent walkers for 1988–1989 season	
Milford	5600 (16 700 bed nights)
Routeburn	9000 (10 000 bed nights)
Kepler	3500 (9300 bed nights)
Hollyford	2500

Camping along the Kepler, Hollyford and Routeburn Tracks restricted to designated campsites only. Camping prohibited along the Milford Track. Mountain biking prohibited along walking tracks.

5.5 Trekking in the High Himalayas of Nepal

'Tourism's far-reaching potential to bring the world closer together, to know first hand the ways of life and attitudes of another culture, is nowhere easier realised than in Khumbu. But, if the natural environment continues to suffer, perhaps the only solution lies in closing the national park to allow plant and animal life to recuperate. Unfortunately, this solution would hurt the Sherpas, who have become economically dependent on the tourist business.'

Sir Edmund Hillary, in *Sir Edmund Hillary's Sagarmatha*

FIGURE 5.5.1 (*below*)
Cho Oyu

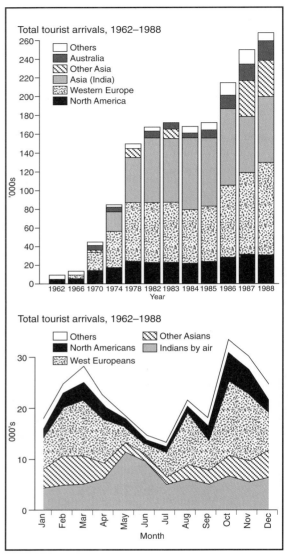

FIGURE 5.5.2 (*top right*)
Growth of tourism in Nepal

Hillary's words carry a familiar ring to them. Because of its size, Nepal does not possess the vast empty spaces of Alaska, Australia or Antarctica, but the high Himalayas (see Figure 5.5.1) along the border with Tibet still guard remote valleys and unclimbed peaks that are true wilderness. Foreign people were excluded from the secretive kingdom of Nepal until 1950. Mountaineering teams began to gain entry to the country in the 1950s in order to climb the major Himalayan peaks.

FIGURE 5.5.3 The Khumbu Himalaya

Figure 5.5.2 shows the growth of tourism in Nepal between 1962 and 1988 (although it must be remembered that of the 250 000 people that visited Nepal in 1988, only 60 000 or so were actually intending to trek in the Himalayas). The graph of tourist growth in Nepal shows two periods of rapid increase. One in the late 1960s and early 1970s was characterised by the growth of the hippy cult in Katmandu in particular, and the easy availability of drugs. This phase waned with the Nepalese ban on drug sales in 1975. The second growth period came in the early and mid-1980s, when there was a general growth in international travel. Two seasonal peaks appear to be indicated in Figure 5.5.2. The autumn peak represents the arrival of the trekking groups, since conditions then are ideal for trekking in areas like the Khumbu Himalaya (see Figure 5.5.3) before winter storms and deep snow make conditions impossible.

Figure 5.5.4 shows the major National Parks and wildlife reserves of Nepal, and the number of trekking permits issued. Annapurna is the most popular destination for trekkers, while remote Kanchenjunga is the least visited. Most trekkers come as part of a package tour, that may combine trekking in the Himalayas with a short stay in Katmandu, the capital, or a visit to the Royal Chitwan National Park in the southern part of the country.

One of the most popular trekking areas is the

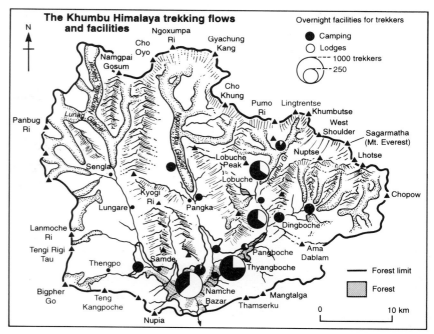

The Khumbu Himalaya trekking flows and facilities

Overnight facilities for trekkers
● Camping
○ Lodges
1000 trekkers
250

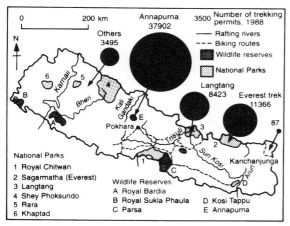

Number of trekking permits, 1988
— Rafting rivers
--- Biking routes
■ Wildlife reserves
▨ National Parks

Annapurna 37902
Others 3495
Langtang 8423
Everest trek 11366
Kanchanjunga 87

National Parks
1 Royal Chitwan
2 Sagarmatha (Everest)
3 Langtang
4 Shey Phoksundo
5 Rara
6 Khaptad

Wildlife Reserves
A Royal Bardia
B Royal Sukla Phaula
C Parsa
D Kosi Tappu
E Annapurna

Khumbu Himalaya (Figure 5.5.5), where trekkers can fly in to the airstrip at Lukla (see Figure 5.5.6) and then use the trekking route up the Dudh Khosi Valley to the Sherpa capital, at Namche Bazar. From here they continue their trek either up to the Everest Base Camp at Gorak Shep, or up the Gokyo Valley, or the less frequented valleys to the west.

Student Activity 5.5

Figure 5.5.7 is an extract from an article 'No litter please on Everest'.
1 Examine some of the environmental costs of trekking indicated in Figure 5.5.7.
2 Examine the consequence of the suggestion from Sir Edmund Hillary that Sagarmatha National Park (in which Everest is located) should be closed to visitors to allow recuperation of the environment.

FIGURE 5.5.4 (*above left*) Nepal: National Parks and wildlife areas

FIGURE 5.5.5 (*above*) The Khumbu Himalaya

FIGURE 5.5.6 (*far left*) Lukla airstrip

FIGURE 5.5.7 No Litter, please

No litter please on Everest

Man's quest to reach the highest summits is turning the mountain trails of the Himalayas into garbage dumps.

In his report to a ten-day meeting on Unesco's Man and the Biosphere Programme last November, Dr Kamal K. Shrestha of Tribhuvan University's Institute of Science, said that the trekkers and mountaineers who come in their thousands to view the majestic peaks of the Himalayas have earned an unsavoury reputation because of the cans, paper, bottles and assorted rubbish which they leave behind. He termed one of the most popular routes – a 200-kilometre stretch to the Sherpa town of Namche Bazaar – a garbage trail.

The damage is compounded by the fact that trekkers use the same sites time and again to install their tents and kitchens. As Dr Shrestha observed, 'If the present trend continues unabated, the degradation of the mountain environment may cause irreversible damage to the mountain ecosystem of Nepal, with negative consequences for the development of tourism in this country.'

Tourism has been increasing steadily since the 1960s and is now Nepal's largest source of foreign exchange. From barely 6000 in 1962, the number of tourists rose to more than 70,000 in 1974 and there were probably around 100,000 in 1975.

Trekkers and mountaineers make up 13 per cent of all tourists, numbering 14,649 in 1974, four times as many as in 1970. Mountaineering teams are also on the increase. There have been 325 expeditions since 1949 when a British team explored Lantang and Ganesh Himan. In 1975 there were twenty-three teams.

The kind of equipment these expeditions carry varies considerably. The Austrians who climbed Mt Manaslu in 1973 used only two and a half tons, whereas a Japanese team of women needed twenty-one tons to perform the same feat. The number of Sherpas also varies considerably, with some teams employing as many as 800 and others only a handful. Since the average weight carried by a porter is thirty-five kilogrammes and twenty kilogrammes at high altitude, the trail of discarded trash can be very long.

Dr Shrestha called attention to the serious deforestation and diminishing supply of firewood along the trails. He estimated that 800 tons of wood were used for camp fires and cooking in 1974. To this should be added several hundred tons used by mountaineering expeditions and the firewood burnt by pilgrims. Pastures are also being destroyed by camping sites, and this destruction of the scant vegetation in Nepal's mountain regions has led to frequent landslides and rockfalls.

To stem further pollution, trekkers must become more environment conscious. The 1975 British Mountaineering Expedition to Mt Everest took a minimum load and carried its own fuel. Research will also be needed into the impact of man's activities on the ecosystem. Nepal is establishing four national parks and five wildlife reserves as models for environmental protection.

Geographical Magazine, April 1976

5.6 Wildlife tourism and conservation in Africa

'There are no words that can tell the hidden spirit of the wilderness, that can reveal its mystery, its melancholy and its charm.'

Theodore Roosevelt, *African Game Trails*

FIGURE 5.6.1 The Great Escarpment, Tsavo West National Park, Kenya

Standing on the Great Escarpment in the Tsavo West National Park in Kenya (Figure 5.6.1), and looking southwards over thousands of square kilometres of bush, it is easy to appreciate these words of Theodore Roosevelt written in 1909. Yet Roosevelt could not have begun to appreciate the great loss in wildlife that Kenya's wilderness was to suffer. Just below the Great Escarpment at Ngulia lies one of the special sanctuaries set up for black rhinoceros. This species declined dramatically from 20 000 animals in 1970 to less than 500 animals in the early 1980s. Only ten rhinoceros live in the Ngulia sanctuary, but living under protection, their numbers are increasing now as they are elsewhere in Kenya.

Growth of wildlife tourism

Figure 5.6.2 shows the number of visitors to countries in Africa with major wildlife attractions (1985).

Tourism has become Kenya's largest single foreign exchange earner, and is the fastest-growing sector of the economy. The number of tour operators and vehicle-hire enterprises increased from 82 in 1970 to 1240 in 1990. In Botswana wildlife tourism only contributes some 4 per cent to GNP at the moment, but estimates show that it

could increase from its present level by a factor of five. Species availability and diversity in Tanzania, Malawi, and Uganda are as great if not greater in these countries as in Kenya. At the moment these countries may be foregoing substantial income through not developing a wildlife tourism industry more vigorously.

Student Activity 5.6

1 Suggest reasons why these three countries are not developing wildlife tourism at the moment.
2 What steps could be taken to encourage them to do so?

Initiatives in wildlife tourism and management

In the previous section it was suggested that some African countries could probably make more use of their wildlife resources in wilderness areas. Most of Botswana's wildlife resource tends to be concentrated in its National Parks and wildlife reserves, which are mostly wilderness land and make up some 17 per cent of the country. A further 21 per cent of the country is covered by 'wildlife management areas', where wildlife is managed as an economic resource. The four main wildlife regions are shown in Figure 5.6.3. In Botswana there are two aspects of wildlife tourism, the dominant game-viewing industry, and the safari hunting industry. Financial returns suggest that there is a considerable leakage of income out of Botswana, and that the country is failing to capture much of the value of its wildlife tourism.

FIGURE 5.6.2 Growth of wildlife tourism

Kenya	541 000
Botswana	327 000
Zimbabwe	320 000
Zambia	144 000
Cameroun	130 000
Tanzania	59 000
Malawi	44 000
Zaire	35 000
Uganda	14 000
Figures for South Africa are not available	

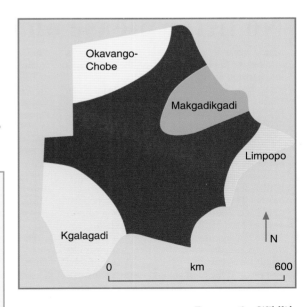

FIGURE 5.6.3 Wildlife regions of Botswana

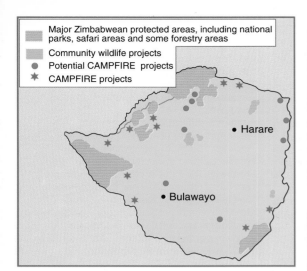

Similar schemes exist in Zambia. The Luangwa Integrated Resources Development Programme (LIRDP) and the Administrative Design for the Management of Game Management Areas (ADMADE) both grew out of the Lupande Development Project in the Luangwa Valley (see Figure 5.6.5). LIRDP is essentially a programme to encourage local communities to manage all their resources, including sustainable management of wildlife. ADMADE is a strictly wildlife utilisation programme, with the community benefiting from up to 50 per cent of the revenues.

FIGURE 5.6.4 (*far left*) Protected areas and CAMPFIRE in Zimbabwe

In Zimbabwe CAMPFIRE (Communal Area Management Programme for Indigenous Resources) is a fairly recent development in wildlife resource management. In the last 50 years there has been a considerable increase in land set aside for the protection of wildlife in National Parks and Wildlife Reserves – now about 12.5 per cent of the country. Figure 5.6.4 shows that since the 1960s a range of other types of land has been brought into wildlife management. CAMPFIRE was introduced in 1984 in order to involve communities more closely in wildlife management. Early reports on the scheme suggested partial success in most areas with such operations as impala cropping, safari operations, problem animal control and hunting and culling quotas for wildlife.

FIGURE 5.6.5 (*far left*) Luangwa Integrated Resources Development Programme (LIRDP) in Zambia

FIGURE 5.6.6 (*left*) The National Parks of Kenya

Kenya's National Parks (see Figure 5.6.6) make up nearly 8 per cent of the country. Although revised legislation for the National Parks and Reserves was put in place in the 1970s, the loss of wildlife from poaching became a serious concern in the 1980s to the extent that 85 per cent of the country's elephants and 97 per cent of its rhinoceros were lost in 15 years. In 1990 the Kenyan Wildlife Service (KWS) was created by the President. Its principal objectives are:
■ to conserve the natural environments of Kenya and their flora and fauna, for the benefit of present and future populations and as a world heritage;
■ to use the wildlife resources of Kenya sustainably for the economic development of the country and for the benefit of people living in wildlife areas;
■ to protect people and property from injury or damage from wildlife.

ELEPHANT CONSERVATION

Between 1973 and 1989 ivory poaching reduced Kenya's elephant population from some 130,000 individuals to an estimated 16,000. By 1988 the poaching of elephants had escalated to such an extent that negative international press reports began to threaten the tourism industry. The strong steps taken by Kenya since then, including its leading role in the campaign to shut down the ivory trade and the dramatic burning of confiscated ivory, have re-established its image as a country committed to the conservation and wise management of its wildlife resources. Elephants, once a symbol of the deterioration of Kenya's wildlife heritage, have the potential to symbolise its restoration over the coming years. To a large extent, KWS will be judged, both in Kenya and abroad, on its success in managing the elephants, with all the problems posed by their ivory, their wide roaming habits, their crop raiding and their fence breaking.

The elephant deserves special attention during the stage when KWS is redefining its wildlife policies, for a number of reasons. As a large charismatic mammal, the elephant is a major tourist attraction and can be used to raise financial support for many of Kenya's Parks and Reserves and the other, less charismatic species that live within them. Elephants have the potential to modify – sometimes radically – the habitats in which they live, so clear management policies for elephants are essential for the future integrity of the ecosystems they inhabit. Further, by providing protection and sound management for elephants, KWS will be able to secure the overall biodiversity of its priority wildlife areas and, in so doing, secure the country's highly profitable tourist industry. Finally, in some parts of the country elephants are the focus of severe crop damage complaints, so that protecting people and their property from elephants is an important, but difficult and costly, task for KWS. For all these reasons the elephant influences KWS policies and investment plans more than any other species. An Elephant Programme has been established:

– To ensure the long-term survival of biologically and touristically important elephant populations.
– To guide KWS's efforts to prevent any upsurge in elephant poaching or trafficking of ivory.
– To monitor the trends in numbers and status of elephant populations.
– To cooperate with other countries for the better conservation of elephants in the region and globally.
– To find solutions to the problems confronting the conservation and management of elephants within and outside Parks and Reserves.
– To reduce the amount of injury and damage caused to human life and property by elephants.
– To build up the expertise in KWS to deal with elephant conservation and management issues.
– To contribute research of high quality to the body of international scientific knowledge.

The Elephant Programme strategy will focus on the following issues: anti-poaching, the monitoring of the illegal trade in ivory, the management of elephants in enclosed Parks and Reserves, monitoring and research, the reduction of crop damage, and the contribution elephants can make towards stimulating tourism and increasing revenues for KWS.

KWS will carry out surveys to select the most appropriate populations for monitoring the effectiveness of conservation efforts. Monitoring and research will focus on reviewing the status of elephant populations; providing recommendations for conservation and management action; identifying basic research requirements; and designing better methods to assess the status of elephant populations and their habitats. In addition, if KWS is to secure viable populations of elephants for the future, it will need the support and cooperation of the people who share their land with elephants. KWS will therefore build fences in strategic areas to reduce the level of crop damage caused by elephants, and initiate revenue sharing in areas adjacent to Parks, where local communities support elephants and other wildlife on their land.

The boundaries of many of the protected areas do not encompass the full geographical range of elephant populations and in some cases migration corridors will need to be acquired if the population is to remain viable in ecological, genetic and demographic terms, e.g. between Shimba Hills National Reserve and the Maluganji Forest. KWS will be negotiating for the use of land for elephants where the viability of priority populations is threatened without it.

Kenya: Land of Opportunity, Central Bank of Kenya

FIGURE 5.6.7 Elephant Conservation

Student Activity 5.7

Read the extract on elephant conservation in Figure 5.6.7.
1 Summarise the management policy for elephants in Kenya in approximately 100 words.

2 Explain why this is a sustainable policy and show how it matches the objectives of the KWS outlined above.

5.7 Managing tourism in Antarctica

'Proper management of commercial tourism in Antarctica depends on accurate, reliable statistics, which will reveal trends to form a basis from which to consider impact assessments, and facilitate the formation of effective tourist policies within the Antarctic Treaty System.'

Debra J Enzenbacher, *Tourists in Antarctica: numbers and trends*

Antarctica, and the oceans around it have much to offer the tourist. Its coastal wilderness landscapes, distinctive wildlife, historic exploration sites and scientific bases together form a range of attractions that are different from any other tourist destination. Its appeal is to the well-informed, reasonably affluent tourist, who wishes to experience Antarctic wilderness at first hand. The majority of tourists arrive by cruise vessel, and spend most of their time sailing in Antarctic waters, with only a few hours spent ashore at different locations.

Tourist destinations in Antarctica

Most tourists originate in the Northern Hemisphere, and then join their cruise vessel in Australia or South America. As seen from Figure 5.7.1, South America has an obvious advantage over Australia because the distance to the Antarctic Peninsula is only one-third of the distance between Australia and Antarctica, and the route possesses the additional attraction of such islands as the Falklands and South Georgia. The Antarctic Peninsula, with its summer temperatures above freezing point, and its spectacular coastal scenery, abundant wildlife, and range of historic sites and scientific bases has much to offer the tourist, and this explains the current growth in cruises to this destination. The tourist potential of the various Antarctic sectors is summarised in Figure 5.7.2. The relative advantages of the Antarctic Peninsula are clear.

The growth of tourism in Antarctica

Figure 5.7.3 shows the total growth in tourism in the period between 1980 and 1991. The proportion of seaborne visitors is usually above 90 per cent, with over 30 tour vessels arriving in Antarctica each year (see Figure 5.7.4). Most cruises leave from Argentinian, Chilean or New Zealand ports. Disadvantages of seaborne tourism are the relatively long and sometimes uncomfortable lengths of time spent crossing the often stormy Southern Ocean, and the vagaries of the weather which mean that some advertised destinations are not visited. Airborne tourism is relatively unimportant, largely because of safety and logistic concerns. Overflights of Antarctica from Australia and New Zealand were popular until the crash of the Air New Zealand DC-10 on Mount Erebus in

1979, killing all 257 occupants. Chile offers flights to King George V Island with stays at the first Antarctic hotel, Estrella Polar. In 1991 seven tour operators formed the International Association of Antarctic Tour Operators, which has established a series of guidelines within which the industry should operate.

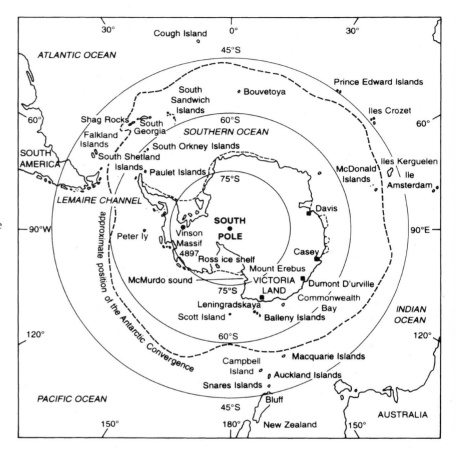

FIGURE 5.7.1 Antarctica and the Southern Continents

	SOUTH AMERICA	NEW ZEALAND	AUSTRALIA
Approximate distance from Antarctica	1000 km	3000 km	≥3000 km
Antarctic climate	Mild, cloudy	Very cold	Very cold, windy
En route islands	South Georgia South Sandwich South Orkneys South Shetlands Falklands	Snares Aucklands Campbell Macquarie Balleny	Heard Kerguelen Crozet
Summer sea access	Open	Ross Sea pack ice	Off-shore pack ice
Wildlife	Several species of penguins, birds and seals on islands and Antarctic coasts	Several species of penguins, birds and seals on islands and Antarctic coasts	Several species of penguins, birds and seals on islands and Antarctic coasts
Historic sites	Charcot, Nordenskjöld, Shackleton, Rhymill, Falklands war	Borchgrevink Scott, Amundsen, Byrd	Mawson hut Law
Scientific bases	Many	Few	Few

FIGURE 5.7.2 Tourist potential of various sectors of Antarctica

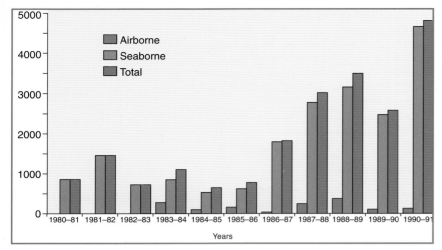

FIGURE 5.7.3 (*above*)
Growth of tourism in
Antarctica, 1980–1991

FIGURE 5.7.4 Tourist
cruise vessel in Antarctic
waters

Environmental impact of tourism in Antarctica

At present it would appear that seaborne tourism has a minimal impact on the environment in Antarctica. Most tours are self-policing, and companies emphasise the conservation ethic to all parties that go ashore. Difficulties exist, however, with the repeated use of popular sites, such as penguin rookeries and seal breeding grounds. Human footprints can damage fragile plant life, and recovery from damage is exceedingly slow in the Antarctic climate. Damage to moss mats and hummocks has been reported from the Antarctic Peninsula. No comprehensive tourist impact study has yet been undertaken in Antarctica, although Project Antarctic Conservation, set up to monitor the impact of tour parties in the South Shetland Islands, began in 1991.

Student Activity 5.8

1 Using the relevant sections of Chapters 2, 3 and 4, write a short summary of the attractions that Antarctica offers to the tourism industry.
2 Outline a programme of field work that could be used to monitor the impact of tourism on an island in the Antarctic Peninsula.

ESSAYS

1 Explain the difficulties of reconciling the twin aims of tourism and conservation in wilderness regions.

2 Discuss the importance of the concept of zoning for managing conservation and recreation in wilderness regions.

6
MANAGING RESOURCES IN WILDERNESS REGIONS

'The bottom line, however, is that adopting stable
management regimes, however imperfect, is far preferable
to creating a policy void and a return to unregulated
activity.'

Lee A Kimball, *Southern Exposure: Deciding
Antarctica's Future*

KEY IDEAS

■ Internationally important physical resources
are located in wilderness regions.
■ Uncontrolled development of these resources
could result in irretrievable damage to wilderness
landscapes and ecosystems, and to the way of life
of indigenous peoples.
■ Proposals for the development of these
resources often result in tension and conflict
between different groups.

■ Commercial companies have to show increased
awareness of environmental concern over their
activities, and modify their operations
accordingly.
■ The role of local, national and international
pressure groups is becoming increasingly
important in establishing a more sustainable
approach to the development of resources in
wilderness areas.

6.1 Some resource management issues

The opening comment on resource management in
Antarctica echoes present ideas on development in
many wilderness regions. It has been noted in
Chapter 2 that the development of resources was a
primary incentive for the acquisition of wilderness
territory through Europe-based colonisation in
Latin America and Africa and in much of the
frontier movement in North America. Much of the
former Soviet Union's interest in Siberia was based
on schemes to exploit its huge resources. With
increasing depletion of existing resources,
wilderness regions have attracted increasing
attention from companies in the more economically
developed countries (MEDCs). Often they have
sought new resources within wilderness areas in the
more developed world, such as the intensive
exploration of the North Slope of Alaska for oil and
gas (Figure 6.1.1), the development of the iron ore
resources in the wilderness lands of Western
Australia and the exploitation of water resources in
the Canadian Northlands. Parallel with the search
for and exploitation of resources in the wilderness

areas of the economically more developed world
there has been inevitable interest in the resources of
the wilderness areas of the less economically
developed countries (LEDCs). Developments such
as Carajas in Amazonia have acquired a high profile
in the last decade, whilst the exploitation of oil and
gas in the Saharan wildernesses of Algeria and
Libya extends back to the 1960s.

FIGURE 6.1.1 Oil drilling
rig at Prudhoe Bay

The development of resources in remote wilderness areas has been possible because of considerable advances in technology. Much exploration for minerals in wilderness regions is initially done by air now, using a range of sophisticated equipment, before detailed ground survey work begins. Exploitation of minerals and their transport from mining locations has required the development of new technology, particularly in the Arctic wilderness country of Alaska, Northern Canada and Siberia.

Management of resources in wilderness areas has to take into account a whole range of factors.

FIGURE 6.1.2 Open mining in Coober Pedy, South Australia

Whereas in the past the decision to develop was largely controlled by physical and economic factors (Figure 6.1.2), now environmental and political factors, and the interplay between them, play a much more important role. This is particularly important in the wilderness areas of the MEDCs, as the case studies of Alaska, and Northern Australia will show. Nevertheless the awareness of wilderness has also increased in the LEDCs, particularly in Brazil and some of the countries of South East Asia. Not only is the protection of a fragile environment much higher on the agenda, but the needs and aspirations of local indigenous groups have to be taken into account, as was shown in the case study of Weipa in Chapter 2.

A number of elements in the management of resources in wilderness regions are therefore important.

■ The concepts of wilderness and resource development appear to be diametrically opposed to one another, and are likely to be a source of conflict.
■ A range of local, national and international pressure groups are likely to be opposed to development on the grounds of the possible irrevocable damage to wilderness environments if exploitation were to go ahead.
■ Most management strategies for the development of resources now include a range of proposals to safeguard the wilderness environment.
■ Careful continuous monitoring of the wilderness environment is essential in areas where resource development is permitted to ensure that protection strategies are adequately supervised.
■ In some particularly fragile wilderness environments global concerns may make it necessary to ban resource development.

6.2 Case studies of resource management in wilderness areas

A number of case studies follow to demonstrate the different aspects of the management of resources in wilderness regions. Three main resources are considered in this section – minerals, forests and water. North Slope oil and gas in Alaska and general mineral development in Northern Territory Australia illustrate resource management in very different wilderness regions. Several contrasted studies of forest resource development in British Columbia, Siberia, Malaysia and Indonesia are used. Finally, two examples of conflict in water resource development are studied from Tasmania and South Island, New Zealand.

6.3 Oil and gas on the North Slope, Alaska

'Wild and wide are my borders, stern as death is my sway:
From my ruthless throne I have ruled alone for a million years and a day;
Hugging my mighty treasure, waiting for man to come . . .
and I wait for the men who will win me – and I will not be won in a day;'

Robert Service, *The Law of the Yukon*

The first major discoveries of oil in Alaska occurred in the south of the state, in the Kenai Peninsula National Wildlife Refuge in 1957, with subsequent discoveries in Cook Inlet. Ten years later the Prudhoe Bay field, the largest in North America, was discovered on the North Slope. Subsequently a number of other oilfields were discovered on the North Slope, with seven currently in production.

Figure 6.3.1 shows the location of the main oilfields of the North Slope, and the inset shows their relationship to the rest of Alaska. Details of past, current and future predicted production are shown in Figure 6.3.2.

Production of oil and gas on the North Slope involves a number of technical, logistic and environmental issues. Since production began vast technological advances have been made in drilling techniques. Wells were originally spaced about 35 m apart, but now they are only 3 m apart (see Figure 6.3.3). All drilling is done on gravel pads built on the tundra surface, and the reduction in size of the drilling pads has obviously reduced the disturbance of the tundra surface.

Located nearly 1300 km from the south coast of Alaska, supply problems are considerable. Personnel fly to Prudhoe Bay or Kuparak from either Anchorage or Fairbanks (Figure 6.3.4). Oilfield supplies are brought in along the Dalton Highway (see Chapter 1). Large oil production modules and other sizeable production facilities have to be brought on barges by sea from Seattle. Reduction in size of the modules means that these sea-lifts, which have to be carried out in the six week 'window' when the sea ice retreats offshore, are likely to become less frequent in the future.

Operation of the oil and gas fields takes place within a strict set of regulations administered at local (North Slope Borough), state (Alaska) and federal (USA) levels. Federal regulations cover hazardous waste, gravel construction in wetlands and discharge from waste and sea water treatment plants. The State of Alaska controls oil and gas leases, exploratory well drilling and the construction of new facilities. The North Slope Borough is responsible for overseeing land management regulations. North Slope operations have been particularly concerned with wetland legislation, since all of the area is classified as wetland. The 'no net loss' policy for wetlands was introduced in 1989, whereby if 1 ha of wetland was developed, then the equivalent hectare of wetland had to be created. In 1991 the 1 per cent rule was proposed whereby if states had developed less than 1 per cent of their wetland (which would apply to Alaska) then limited wetland development could occur without compensatory creation of wetland. The Clinton administration withdrew this proposal in 1993.

Student Activity 6.1

1 Refer to the section on the tundra ecosystem in Chapter 4. What would be the main threats to the ecosystem posed by the developments at Prudhoe Bay and neighbouring oilfields?
2 The 'wetland' lobby has become increasingly important in the United States in recent years. Why do you think the Clinton administration withdrew the 1 per cent proposal in 1993?

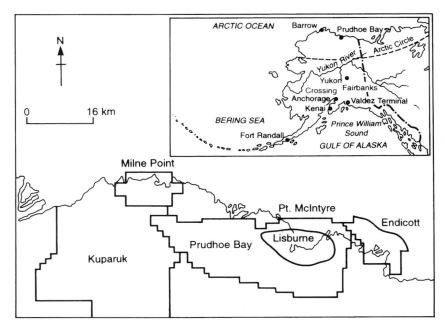

FIGURE 6.3.1 (*above*) Oilfields of the North Slope, Alaska

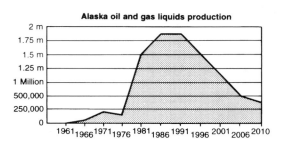

FIGURE 6.3.2 (*left*) Oil production on the North Slope

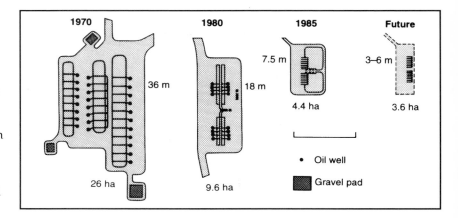

FIGURE 6.3.3 (*above*) Well spacing on the North Slope, Alaska

FIGURE 6.3.4 (*left*) Deadhorse airstrip

The TransAlaska pipeline

'We have spent many years trying to roll back the wilderness in Alaska. Don't worry about it, it doesn't roll easily.'

Ernest Wolff, President of the Alaska Miner's Association, to the Senate Interior and Insular Affairs Committee, 26 February 1971

Inevitably the discovery of oil and gas on the North Slope of Alaska posed the problem of transporting it to the 'Lower 48'. Feasibility studies were carried out to see if tankers could use the North West Passage to transport the oil to the Lower 48. After two trial runs it was decided that, although the route was feasible, it was not practical, owing to the possibility of damage to tankers and rupturing of oil tanks. The possibility was also considered of constructing a pipeline through the Yukon and Canada. However in February 1969 TAPS (TransAlaska Pipeline System) announced its preferred path, the 1300 km route from Prudhoe Bay to Valdez, the most northerly ice-free port in the USA (see Figure 6.3.5).

The building of the pipeline posed very considerable environmental and social problems.
■ Over virtually all of its route it would have to be built through permafrost country.
■ In the southern section of the route, through the Alaska Range, there was a real danger of seismic disruption to the pipeline.

FIGURE 6.3.5 The TransAlaska pipeline

■ It would cross the Denali fault in southern Alaska.
■ It would cross over 800 streams, including the Yukon, Alaska's longest river.
■ Exceptionally severe winter weather conditions prevail along all of the route.
■ It would be built through tundra and taiga ecosystems, which are both extremely sensitive environmentally.
■ It would cross considerable areas of Native lands.

Student Activity 6.2

1 Discuss why each of these points represents a problem.
2 Listed below are individuals or groups who were likely to be concerned over or involved with these problems.

United States Bureau of Land Management.
The Wilderness Society.
Harmon Hendricks (who lives with his wife at the Colville Delta some 80 km west of Prudhoe Bay). In the early stages of Prudhoe Bay operations he complained about *'bandido operations'* that *'tore up the country fantastically'*.
John E Clark, Fairbanks resident and former gold miner, who had lived in Alaska for 35 years: *'The North Slope is the most desolate place in the world. If I never see it again it's fine by me.'*
Ted Stevens (Senator for Alaska): *'I am up to here with people who tell us how to run our country. There are no living organisms on the North Slope.'*
John C Reed, Chief Scientist at the Arctic Institute of North America.
William R Wood, President of the University of Alaska quoted as saying *'Pipeline opponents were anti-God, anti-Man and anti-mind.'*
Eben Hopson, executive director of the Arctic Slope Native Association.
For each of the individuals or groups:
(a) discuss their probable views on the various problems;
(b) suggest what conflicts might develop between them and other groups and individuals.

Much discussion of the problems surrounding the construction of the pipeline continued within Alaska and at Governmental level in Washington. Many lawsuits were filed against the pipeline operation, and caused inevitable delays, while alterations to the pipeline's design and route were made. The TransAlaska Pipeline Authorization Act was passed in 1973, and oil began to flow along the pipeline in 1977. Figure 6.3.6 shows the range of measures that had to be taken to reduce the impact of the pipeline.

Alaska's worst environmental disaster was the oil spill in Prince William Sound, which occurred in March 1989, when the *Exxon Valdez*, loaded with crude oil from Valdez, ran aground on the Bligh Reef. Nearly one-fifth of the cargo of crude oil was lost. Slow reaction to the spill and bad weather caused the oil to spread some 900 km from the

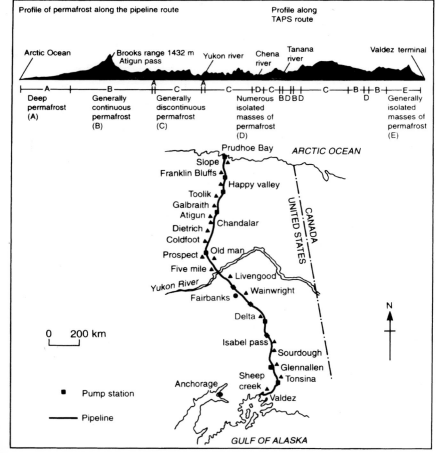

ISSUE OR PROBLEM	PIPELINE SOLUTION		
Pipeline route	Buried (608 km) to depth of 1–5 m	– in permanently thawed soils – in bedrock (frozen or thawed) – some types of permafrost	
	Elevated (672 km)	– in unstable permafrost	
Temperature fluctuations	Zig-zag design to allow for expansion and contraction		
Caribou migration routes	Buried for up to 30 m underground		
Denali fault crossing	Design allows 6 m of horizontal motion 1.5 m of vertical motion		
Stream crossing	Either buried beneath scour level, or on bridges – 700 m crossing of Yukon River		
Construction phase	Permafrost insulated under construction pads. Haul road construction halted until Dall sheep lambing period over		
Post-construction phase	Revegetation of disturbed areas with cold resistant grasses 1.4 million willow trees to screen pipeline in elevated sections		
Pump stations Spill protection	Where unstable permafrost, fully insulated Specially designed valves at stream crossing, environmentally sensitive areas and population centres		

FIGURE 6.3.6 Measures taken to reduce environmental impact of the TransAlaska pipeline

FIGURE 6.3.7 Arctic National Wildlife Refuge

wreck. Enormous loss of wildlife occurred, and the far-reaching effects of the spill are probably still not fully understood.

The Arctic National Wildlife Refuge

The so-called D2 lands in Alaska were referred to in Chapter 3. Amongst the largest of these National Interest lands is the Arctic National Wildlife Refuge (see Figure 6.3.7). In the Act the ANWR was enlarged from 3.56 million ha to 7.6 million ha, of which 3.2 million ha were designated as wilderness. In the coastal plain section of the refuge, known as the 1002 area, estimates of reserves of 29 billion barrels of oil have been tabled (three times the size of the Prudhoe Bay field) although this estimate is now regarded as excessive, with 9.2 billion barrels being more realistic. It would appear that the battle that was fought over TAPS is likely to be repeated over the ANWR. Further damage to the fragile tundra ecosystem would be likely to occur (see Figure 6.3.8), although, as Figure 6.3.9 indicates a measure of recovery is possible). Opponents of the exploitation of ANWR for oil will no doubt refer to the report on the ecological impact of the oil development at Prudhoe Bay, and the TAPS north of the Brooks Range, which was highly critical. It found that:

■ the environmental damage in the oil development area around Prudhoe Bay, and TAPS was much greater than that forecast in the environmental impact statement for TAPS in 1972;

■ the area devoted to oil development was 2000 km² instead of 1375 km²;

■ there had been considerable fresh water pollution on the North Slope as a result of oil spills and erosion;

■ the quality of off-shore water had deteriorated considerably as a result of off-shore production;

■ there had been considerable decline in bird

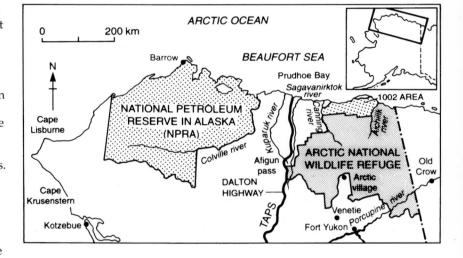

FIGURE 6.3.8 Geophysical prospecting vehicles

habitat and that most bird species had declined in population;

■ loss of vegetation had been twice as large as forecast in the impact statement;

■ revegetation measures had been more or less a complete failure;

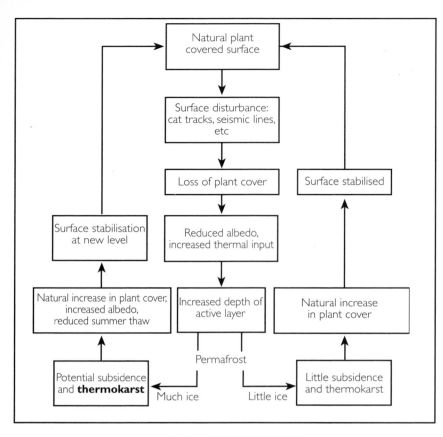

FIGURE 6.3.9 Recovery of tundra vegetation from damage

■ normal movements of the Central Arctic caribou herd have been interfered with. (Interestingly, the oil companies point to the increase in numbers in the herd as evidence that oil field operation is not having any serious effect on caribou numbers. The increase is however due to the fact that wolves, the main predators of the caribou have themselves suffered a dramatic decrease in numbers as a result of illegal killings by truck drivers.)

The extract in Figure 6.3.10 from a leaflet from Arctic Power, a strong lobby group for the development of the 1002 lands in the ANWR is a statement from Walter Hickel, Governor in Alaska in 1993.

Student activity 6.3

1 Analyse the nature of the values in Figure 6.3.10.
2 Discuss the ways in which the article expresses prejudice.
3 How would you expect Governor Andrus of Idaho to reply to this statement?

FIGURE 6.3.10 Extract from Arctic Power

Hickel issues call to Alaskans to rally against Outside interests
By Walter J. Hickel, Governor, State of Alaska

The newly formed Alaska Wilderness League should be a call to arms to every Alaskan. This new organization – primarily made up of Outsiders – has been established for the sole purpose of lobbying Congress to create more Alaska Wilderness.

Main proponents of this group are Robert J. Mrazek, a former U.S. Representative from New York and Idaho Governor, Cecil Andrus, who as Interior Secretary, under President Carter, left us the legacy of the Alaska National Interest Lands Conservation Act (ANILCA).

In a prepared statement, Mrazek stated, 'We're not just a bunch of guys trying to lock up Alaska.'

Did I miss something? Which one has Alaska's driver's license?

I believe most Alaskans would take exception to his organization for the following reasons:

* ANILCA, championed by Andrus, has a section in the bill which is dubbed the 'No more cause'. It clearly states that conservation system units, new national conservation areas, or new national recreation area, has been obviated (made unnecessary) thereby.'

This is clearly in direct conflict with Governor Andrus' newfound intention of creating more Wilderness in Alaska.

* Our statehood compact was written to give us equal footing with all other states and to provide our new state with a solid economic foundation, partially through royalties from mineral development on federal lands. This group attacks the very foundation that we were guaranteed at statehood.

* The group is made up of Outsiders who won't have to live with the results of the actions they are promoting, the loss of jobs and opportunities for our young people and the degradation of our basic government services because we will have no way to pay for them.

* Alaska is proud of our Wilderness. But we have enough. We already have 70 per cent of all national parks acreage, and 90 per cent of all federal wildlife acreage – and 62 per cent of all federally designated Wilderness here.

* Land in Alaska designated by law as Wilderness, allowing no economic activity, is 57 million acres (larger than either New York or Idaho). Much of this land contains resources of great value. In comparison, Cecil Andrus' state has only 4.5 million acres, and not surprisingly, Bob Mrazek's state has no federal Wilderness. None.

* Less than one-half of 1 per cent of Alaska has been developed. And that has been done carefully, with strict environmental protections.

* In our lifetime, we will probably never see one per cent of Alaska developed. Contrast that with any other state!

Obviously, this group is in a 'league of their own'. I think Robert Mrazek of New York or Cecil Andrus of Idaho would be offended if I started a group whose primary focus was to create more Wilderness designations in their state. The recent developments of Outsiders focusing on creating more Wilderness in Alaska is a sure sign of things to come. We must fight back with education, and we must do it now.

It's time for Alaskans to get involved at the grass roots level, to help educate the rest of America and the world, that we too, are environmentalists. However, we understand there must be a balance – and that balance must include people and people's needs – as well as nature.

6.4 Minerals in Northern Territory, Australia

'Mining companies, oil companies and the many related service and supply organisations are major contributors to the economic prosperity of the Northern Territory. We acknowledge that fact with our enlightened approach to resource development policies. Australia's Northern Territory has a big ground floor: you should get in on it.'

> Barry Coulter, Minister for Mines and Energy, Northern Territory, 1991

Figure 3.7.2 on page 45 shows the extent of the areas that have high wilderness value in Northern Territory, probably between a half and one-third of the Territory. Figure 6.4.1 shows the main mineral resources, both worked and potential.

Student Activity 6.4

1 Comment on the two distributions (areas having high wilderness values, and main mineral resources).

2 From an examination of Figures 3.7.2 and 6.4.1, discuss the extent to which wilderness areas may be threatened by the development of mineral resources in Northern Territory.

The varied geology of Northern Territory (see Figure 6.4.2) offers much in resources for the mining industry. Much of the Territory is underlain by Pre-Cambrian rocks, which include not only igneous and metamorphic groups, but also a wide range of sedimentary rocks, all of which contain metalliferous resources. The younger sedimentary rocks of Palaeozoic Age yield important supplies of oil and natural gas, and similar hydrocarbon resources appear to be important in Mesozoic and **Tertiary** Basins.

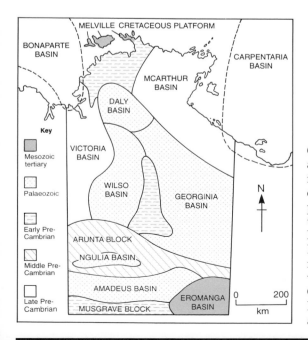

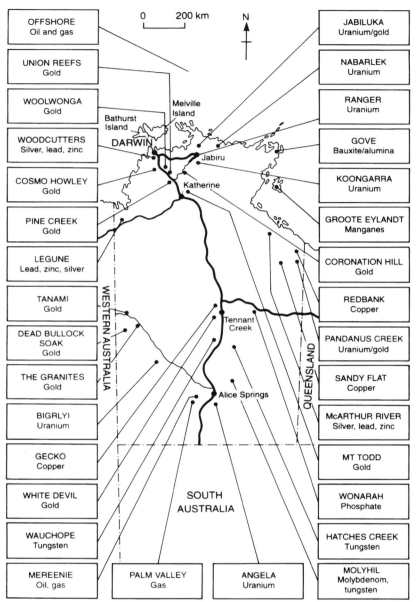

Production figures for 1993 are shown in Figure 6.4.3. Bauxite is produced on the Gove Peninsula, and the project is the largest mineral development in the Northern Territory. Total reserves are estimated at 250 million tonnes, with annual open-pit production currently running at 5 million tonnes. Workers are housed in the township of Nhulunby. Manganese is produced on Groote Eylandt, where reserves of 200 million tonnes remain after 25 years of mining. Groote Eylandt is a wilderness island, sharing the remoteness of the Gove Peninsula, on the eastern side of the Arnhem Peninsula, which is one of the largest wilderness areas on the north coast of Australia. Gold has been

FIGURE 6.4.1 Mineral resources of Northern Territory

FIGURE 6.4.2 (*left*) Geology of Northern Territory

FIGURE 6.4.3 Mineral production, Northern Territory

ENERGY PRODUCTS	OUTPUT	$(000's)
Crude oil (mill litres)	2478	435 446
Uranium oxide (tonnes)	1342	76 515
Natural gas (mill litres)	337 168	23 043
Energy products		535 004
Mineral products	(tonnes)	
Gold	18	326 408
Manganese	1 478 503	139 301
Bauxite	5 846 687	132 956
Zinc concentrate	62 159	16 755
Copper concentrate	5 656	5027
Lead concentrate	23 650	1981
Silver	1.8	320
Extractive minerals	1 941 643	16 008
Limestone	13 661	1901
Gemstones	5	48
Mining products		640 705
Processed products	(tonnes)	
Alumina	1 653 247	404 942
(less bauxite converted)	4 094 557	(93 089)
Processed products		311 853
Energy products		535 004
Mining products		640 705
Processed products		311 853
TOTAL		1 487 562

FIGURE 6.4.3 Mineral production, Northern Territory

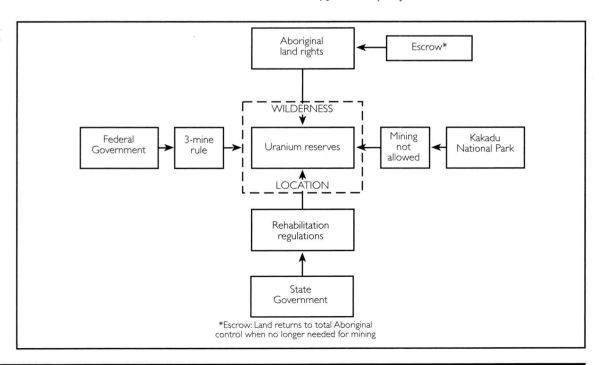

FIGURE 6.4.4 (*far right*) Uranium mining in East Alligator country

Uranium mining in Northern Territory

produced in Northern Territory since the middle of the nineteenth century, but production today has been concentrated in two locations: Pine Creek and Tennant Creek. Neither of these mining communities have the remoteness of Gove or Groote Eylandt, since both are on the Stuart Highway, and the original wilderness has long since disappeared.

Although the amount of uranium oxide produced in Northern Territory is relatively small, compared to the amounts of bauxite and manganese, the location of the resource in wilderness locations has raised a number of interesting political, environmental and social issues, as shown in Figure 6.4.5. The majority of the uranium resources in

FIGURE 6.4.5 Uranium mining issues

*Escrow: Land returns to total Aboriginal control when no longer needed for mining

Northern Territory are in the country on either side of the East Alligator River, with four main locations at Ranger, Nabarlek, Koongarra and Jabiluka. Nabarlek was mined in the years from 1979, and stockpiled ore treated over the next ten years. Ranger (see Figure 6.4.6) is the only producing mine in Northern Territory at the moment. Both Jabiluka (now known as North Ranger 2) and Koongarra are on hold at the moment due to the three-mine policy.

All of the uranium deposits in the East Alligator River area are in Aboriginal lands. Negotiations with Aboriginal leaders have to take place before the mining lease can be granted, and Aboriginal groups can have considerable influence on the terms under which mining can take place. When mining has ceased the land will be returned to total Aboriginal control. The Australian Labour Party, until recently in Government, operated the three-mine policy, which, put simply, only allows three uranium mines to produce at any one time. The policy reflects a whole series of conflicting attitudes towards uranium mining in Australia. In the mid-1970s the Fox Commission, required to report on the future of the uranium industry in Australia could only come to ambivalent conclusions: '*The hazards of mining and milling uranium, if those activities are properly regulated and controlled, are not such as to justify a decision not to develop Australian uranium mines.*' The Liberal and National Party Government allowed some mining to go ahead, but some projects, such as Jabiluka, found considerable difficulty in negotiating with the Aboriginal groups over the terms of mining.

When the Labour Party was returned to power in 1983, the Government's attitude reflected a compromise between two opposing strands of thought. The unions wished to protect jobs in the uranium mining industry, but the Government was also under pressure from the anti-uranium lobby. Ranger and Nabarlek in Northern Territory were to be allowed to continue in production, and Roxby Downs in Southern Australia would be allowed to develop. Resources such as Jabiluka (North Ranger 2), despite the enormous cost of its Environmental Impact Statement (EIA), and the protracted negotiations with Aboriginal Groups, would not be developed in the immediate future. In 1991 it was sold to North's, the company that operates the Ranger mine.

Environmental controls

The Government of Northern Territory operates a series of strict environmental controls on mining operations. All new mines are required to have Environmental Management Plans (EMPs), and 75 per cent of the mines in Northern Territory now have EMPs. These encompass such topics as soil displacement, disturbance of native species, waste disposal and related pollution problems in both drilling and mining operations. All plans for mines have to include a comprehensive rehabilitation programme, which can cost as much as $10 000 per hectare. Old uranium mines such as the Rum Jungle

site, some 85 km south of Darwin, which was developed in wilderness country before strict environmental laws came into force, have now been completely rehabilitated (see Figure 6.4.7). Within the Kakadu National Park (which excludes the existing mineral leases of Ranger, Jabiluka and Koongarra) no new mining was allowed from 1987.

FIGURE 6.4.6 (*top*) Ranger Uranium mine

FIGURE 6.4.7 Rehabilitation: Rum Jungle uranium mine, south of Darwin

Student Activity 6.5

1 Rehearse the main arguments for and against uranium mining in Northern Territory, Australia.
2 What would be the main concerns of Aboriginal groups when approached by mining companies who wished to obtain a mining licence on their land?
3 In wilderness areas, such as that of the former Rum Jungle mine in Northern Territory, what special rehabilitation requirements would a Mines Inspector insist upon?

6.5 Coastal forest management on Vancouver Island, British Columbia

'At Macmillan Bloedel we are proud of our history of forest management in British Columbia – we believe that we are among the best in the world when it comes to forestry practices and integrated resource management.'
Ray Smith, President, Macmillan Bloedel

*'The fact that Macmillan Bloedel propose to log Carmanah at a slow rate is irrelevant. Any **clear cut logging** will inevitably release Carmanah Valley's "hydrological brakes". Catastrophic floods typically occur when the mantle of old grown forest is removed from shallow-soiled, steep-sloped west coast rainforest watersheds.*
Western Canada Wilderness Committee Education Report, Spring 1989

FIGURE 6.5.1 Logging operations: Macmillan Bloedel

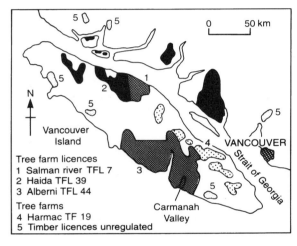

FIGURE 6.5.2 Settlement: Vancouver Island

FIGURE 6.5.3 (*far right*) Stand of Douglas Fir, Vancouver Island

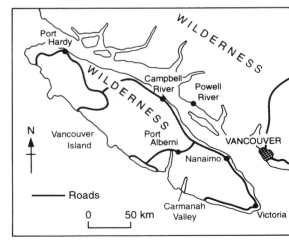

Vancouver Island is one example of wilderness areas in middle latitudes where forestry management is a key issue. Figure 6.5.1 shows the range of locations where current logging is practised, and where potential threats to wilderness country exist.

Logging poses the major threat to wilderness conservation in the mid-latitude rainforests. Currently, logging is in a transitional phase between cutting from **old growth** forests and cutting from plantations or intensively managed forests. Clearly, in this phase, considerable, and possibly irrevocable damage could be done to indigenous forests. The main threats appear to be as follows.

■ Continued demand for timber products: in the last 40 years there has been a 16-fold increase in demand for timber products.

■ The belief that continued timber production from indigenous forests is necessary to avoid a shortfall in wood products before the main plantations come on stream.

■ The need to gain access to new areas for establishing plantations.

■ Lack of new policy-making amongst forestry companies and the continuation of operations that are often economically unviable.

■ Pressure from local and national Governments, concerned to maintain employment levels, and to sustain income from logging.

■ The desire to exploit as much of the indigenous forest as possible before the industry has to conform to strict forestry conservation policies.

Much of Vancouver Island's 32 000 km² is wilderness country. Most of the populated areas are along the east coast, where the settled coastal fringe faces the mainland of British Columbia (Figure 6.5.2). Roads only penetrate to the west coast across the central mountains at four points, so the true wilderness country lies in the interior and along the west coast. Mid-latitude rainforest covers most of the wilderness country. Stands of Sitka Spruce occur along the west coast, and are replaced further inland by the Western Red Cedar and the Western Hemlock. In the drier areas farther to the east Douglas Fir dominates (Figure 6.5.3).

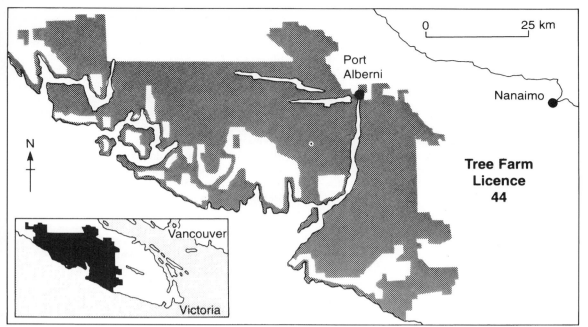

FIGURE 6.5.4 Tree Farm Licence 44

In British Columbia, 94 per cent of the forests are owned by the province; they are made available to the forest industry under various licensing agreements. Macmillan Bloedel, one of the leading forestry companies in British Columbia, does own 20 per cent of the forest land that it is currently working. Tree farm licences are the commonest form of tenure for forestry companies in British Columbia. These combine Crown land with private land owned by timber companies such as Macmillan Bloedel. The main condition of the licence is that the forestry company carries out a programme of forest protection and management. The company is responsible for all reforestation and **silviculture** costs that are incurred on both province land and private land. Timber licences confer ownership of the standing timber on the licensee but the ownership of the land, and all succeeding crops is retained by the British Columbia Government. All forest renewal is the responsibility of the licensee.

Tree Farm Licence 44: successful forest management?

Figure 6.5.4 shows the location of Tree Farm Licence 44. It occupies a position in the south west of Vancouver Island and extends over an area of 450 000 ha, of which 375 000 ha are productive forest land. British Columbia Province owns 84 per cent of the land, and 63 per cent of the timber. The record of the Forestry Company (Macmillan Bloedel) to date, since operations began in 1955, is shown below.

Total hectares logged	88 400
Total volume harvested	71 890 000 m³
Total hectares to reforest	111 500
Hectares being restocked	8500
Hectares planted and reseeded	66 900
Naturally reforested	36 100
Hectares weeded	13 100
Hectares spaced	11 500
Hectares fertilised	200
Hectares commercially thinned	500

FIGURE 6.5.5 Macmillan Bloedel records

FIGURE 6.5.6 (*far left*) The Carmanah Valley Forest

Student Activity 6.6

1 Examine Figure 6.5.5 which shows forest management progress in TFL44 from 1955–1990.
 (a) Comment on the nature of the regeneration programme evident in the statistics.
 (b) How might you expect the programme to change over the next 30 years?
 Before an area can be cleared for logging the following points have to be checked.
■ Is the area a watershed supplying community water?
■ Are there any fish spawning or rearing streams near the area to be logged?

- What wildlife lives in the area? Will it be endangered by logging?
- Are the soils stable, or sensitive to erosion?
- Is this an area of unique beauty?
- Are there any archaeological sites present?

Student Activity 6.7

1 Explain why each of the above points has to be investigated before logging can begin.
2 Suggest what modifications to the logging programme would have to be made if the investigating team found there was a problem.

Decision making exercise: The Carmanah Valley

The position of the Carmanah Valley is shown in Figure 6.5.1. Considerable concern has been expressed as to the advisability of approval being given to plans for logging stands of Sitka Spruce in this watershed area. Conservationists wish to see the whole of the valley preserved (at the moment the forestry company proposes to create two reserves, covering 1.4 per cent of the entire valley). You are an official of the British Columbia Forestry Service, and require clear answers to a number of questions from the forestry company before you write a report to the forestry service on whether the logging proposals should go ahead.

1 Draw up a list of questions that you would wish to put to the forestry company (consider clear felling, waste management, environmental safeguards, multi-purpose forestry and so on).
2 Outline the responses that you would need in order to write a report which supported the proposal of the mining company.
3 Outline the responses that would encourage you to write a negative report.

6.6 Forest destruction in the Siberian wilderness

FIGURE 6.6.1 Wasted effort

Wasted effort

Four days by train southeast of Moscow lies the Siberian city of Krasnoyarsk. It is the last staging post for travellers heading into the vast wilderness beyond. During the 74 years of Soviet rule, the only regular 'travellers' going that way were criminals sentenced to terms of hard labour in one of the region's penal camps for crimes against communism. Today, with the end of the Soviet regime, a new type of traveller is becoming more common – entrepreneurs, both from Russia and abroad, seeking lucrative mineral or logging concessions in the region.

However, Russian judges are still handing out sentences of hard labour, even if they are not for political crimes. The helicopter shuttle, or light plane link between Krasnoyarsk and the outlying communities of Boguchany and Kodinskij, frequently takes off with a contingent of sentenced criminals on board. Their punishment: to fell trees in Siberia's seemingly endless forests.

Siberia is home to the world's largest forests. They lie in a belt of 8.8 million square kilometres, an area twice as large as the Amazon. They make up 57 per cent of the world's coniferous forests and a quarter of the world's inventoried forest volume.

Some 20,000 prisoners are currently doing logging work in Siberia, under the control of the Ministry of Internal Affairs. And it is in the Krasnoyarsk region, as well as in the northern Ural areas around Perm and Yekaterinburg, that they are most concentrated.

Surprisingly, this gargantuan forced logging effort reaps little reward for the Russian economy. Because the priority is punishment and not profit, the felled trees are not collected efficiently. Each prisoner is assigned a daily quota to cut down, which they are strongly encouraged to achieve. But most of each man's quota is left to rot on the ground. As a result, an estimated 60 million cubic metres of wood is left to decay every year in Siberia – three times the size of the official harvest. The camp near Kodinskij, in the Kezhma or K-100 region, contains 300 high-security prisoners. Thirty other camps are dotted around the Kezhma region.

The impact of this prison logging operation on the local environment is plain to see. Large areas of land have been stripped bare. And once the protective cover of the trees has gone, many plant and animal species perish. Local residents complain that the mushrooms and berries which form a staple part of their diet are becoming almost impossible to find, because so much forest has gone. Moreover, they gain no material benefit from the felled wood.

'Because they cut it down completely there are no animals in the forest and no new trees,' says a member of the Kezhma nature protection group, 'they cut a lot of trees from the region and yet there is real poverty here and the villagers don't gain anything from it. We can't see a future for our grandchildren.'

Geographical, October 1994

The extract in Figure 6.6.1 by Steve Morgan reveals the lack of concern for wilderness ecosystems in Siberia.

FIGURE 6.6.2 Siberian coniferous forest

6.7 Some concerns over forest management in Malaysia

Reference has already been made to deforestation in Amazonia in Section 4.4 (page 61). The main causes of the loss of wilderness tropical rainforest appear to be as follows.

■ Development of unsustainable forest policies by less economically developed countries in order to reduce their foreign debt levels.
■ Continued high demands for timber and timber products from the more economically developed countries.
■ Damaging policies of timber exploitation by transnational corporations.
■ Continued high growth rates of population in less economically developed countries.
■ Use of wilderness forest for firewood collection.

Changing management of wilderness forest in Malaysia

'The West has already become rich by destroying most of its forests. They have adopted hypocritical principles which they did not apply themselves and which they now insist on imposing on us. Yet we are doing a better job of looking after our forests than ever they did.'
Dr Lim Keng Yaik, Malaysian Minister for Primary Resources

'It is growing increasingly obvious to all and sundry that people in the rural areas affected by the logging activities have been very badly done by and have simply not been afforded a fair deal.'
Editorial, *Sarawak Tribune*, 13 June 1987

In Chapter 4, the section on the Belalong Forest in Sabah stressed the great value of its biodiversity. Yet it is such ecologically fragile and sensitive forests as the Belalong that are increasingly coming under threat by logging in Malaysia.

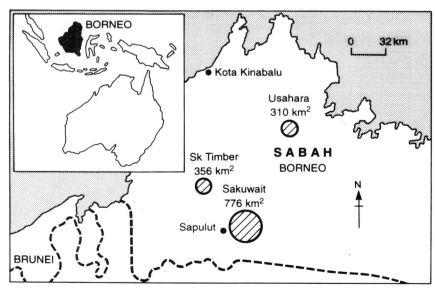

Figure 6.7.1 shows three areas currently being worked in Sabah, Malaysia. A *Sunday Times* Insight investigation team in 1989 found that:
'Dense verdant rainforest which, ten years ago supported the densest, most impenetrable foliage in the world, has been thinned dramatically by workers with chainsaws, who follow the paint signals to those trees that are to be felled next.

FIGURE 6.7.1 Three logging areas in Sabah

FIGURE 6.7.2 Traditional logging techniques, with their reliance on heavy machinery, do extensive damage to the roots of other trees and the forest floor ecosystem.

■ helilogging, where trees are lifted out of the forest, rather than being dragged out (it is, however, four to eight times more expensive than traditional logging techniques).

Nevertheless concern is still being expressed about the logging industry in Malaysia's wilderness forests. In 1990 the International Tropical Timber Organisation's report made a number of recommendations, most of which have been ignored by the Malaysian Government. The report recommended that the annual timber cut (40 million m³) be reduced, but the Government was only prepared to promise a cut in several years' time. The Government pointed out that raw logs were now only exported from Sarawak, and that such export had been stopped from the peninsula states and Sabah. Processing the wood in Malaysia increases the value of exports and requires less timber to be cut.

A range of problems still remains and include:
■ Government officials own many of the timber concessions, and land claims by indigenous groups are largely ignored;
■ land and timber affairs are controlled by the semi-autonomous states that make up the Malaysian Federation, and thus central policies are difficult to enforce;
■ logging companies appear to ignore Government regulations in order to maximise profits;
■ corruption in the distribution of licences for logging concessions appears to be widespread, although it is inevitably denied by the Government.

Student Activity 6.8

1 Explain how the forests of Malaysia illustrate the basic dilemma that exists in so many wilderness areas – the conflict between development, and sustainable use of resources.
2 Why is the sustainable use of wilderness forests so difficult to implement?

They slice into the rainforests, cutting through the trunks that have stood undisturbed for hundreds of years, the crashing timber crushing smaller trees and foliage lying in their path.

The landscape is scarred by tractors dragging the broad trunks out to loading areas, flattening yet more forest (see Figure 6.7.2). Moving the fallen timber has eroded large tracts of topsoil, creating less fertile ground. No attempt has been made to replant the forest: instead it is being abandoned to scrub and weeds.'

Insight Team, *Sunday Times*, 25 June 1989

In the 1990s it would appear that Malaysia has adopted some more enlightened policies of forest management:
■ reduced impact logging (RIL), which restricts the use of bulldozers, and other heavy machinery in the forest, and ensures that skid trails are kept at least 1 km apart;

6.8 Managing water resources in the Tasmanian forest wilderness and in South Island, New Zealand

'Enough was enough. There would be no more nonsense on the dams issue. The Tasmanian Wilderness Society would be silenced or ignored and outside interference in Tasmania's affairs would not be tolerated.'

'I could not see the point of treating the symptoms of stress-related diseases if the last places on earth where people could find tranquillity were to be destroyed for political expediency.'

Dr Bob Brown, Director of the Tasmanian Wilderness Society

South West Tasmania is a World Heritage Area (see Figure 6.8.1). It occupies some 20 per cent of Tasmania, includes tracts of wild glaciated upland, and parts of it carry a cover of virgin temperate rainforest (Figure 6.8.2). Many species of plants and animals are either unique to the area or rare in Australia. Twenty per cent of the 185 plant species endemic to Tasmania are unique to the South West, and two-thirds of the 32 Tasmanian mammal species are also found within the World Heritage Area.

Conflict between conservationists and developers has been an important theme in the last 25 years in Tasmania's South West. Its forests are obviously a major resource, but the schemes that have excited most controversy are those that have involved the development of the hydro-electric resources of the region.

In the 1960s, Lake Pedder in the South West National Park, was at the centre of the first major controversy. The Tasmanian Hydro-Electric Commission examined ways of developing power on the Gordon River and its tributaries. The proposed scheme involved the diversion of two rivers, the Upper Huon, and the Serpentine into the Gordon, and the flooding of Lake Pedder. Opposition to the scheme was widespread, particularly from groups such as the Save Lake Pedder National Park Committee, and the South West Committee. After the flooding in 1972, Edward St John, the QC on the National Lake Pedder Court of Enquiry commented on the attempts to return the lake to its original state: 'Our children will undo what we so foolishly have done.'

The controversy caused by the Lake Pedder Scheme was far less than that resulting from the next proposal from the Tasmanian Hydro-Electric Commission in 1979. It involved the possible damming of three rivers in the Wild Rivers National Park, the Lower Gordon, the Franklin and the King (Figure 6.8.3). The Gordon-below-Franklin Dam was to dominate Tasmanian politics for the next four years. After a year of lobbying by pro- and anti-dam groups the Tasmanian Government passed legislation, for an alternative dam site, the Gordon-above-Olga site. This was essentially a compromise that pleased nobody. In 1981 the creation of the Wild Rivers National Park was announced, together with a proposal for the new National Park to form a part of a World Heritage Area, with the existing National Parks in South West Tasmania.

Although the Tasmanian people were promised a referendum on the two dam sites, events moved swiftly, and an election resulted in the Liberal Party being elected to office on a pro-dam platform. The construction of the dam site at Gordon-below-Franklin began, amidst a welter of protests from conservationists, led by the Tasmanian Wilderness Society.

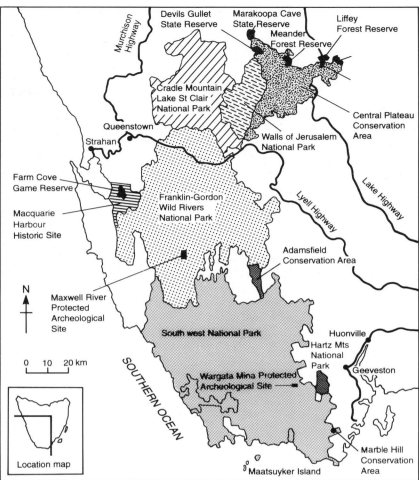

FIGURE 6.8.1 (*above*) World Heritage Area, South West Tasmania

FIGURE 6.8.2 (*top left*) Temperate rainforest in Tasmania

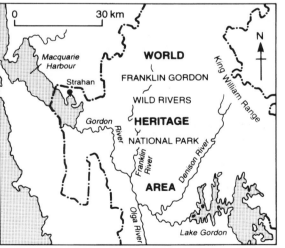

FIGURE 6.8.3 Wild Rivers National Park

The dam site was blockaded by conservationists of whom over 1400 were arrested. In 1983 the Gordon Dam controversy was an important issue in the General Election campaign in Australia, with the opposition Labour Party committed to the stopping of dam construction. The Labour Party won the election, and a major conflict between the Federal Labour Government of Australia and the Liberal Government of Tasmania was unavoidable.

After several compromise approaches to the Tasmanian State Government, all of which failed, the Australian Government passed legislation forbidding Hydro-Electric Commission works in the World Heritage area. This was challenged in the High Court by the Tasmanian Government, but the challenge was defeated by a majority of 4–3. Work on the dam immediately ceased, and Tasmania received grants for alternative projects.

Student Activity 6.9

---

1 Hold a class debate on whether the Gordon-below-Franklin Dam should have been built. Some of the roles that could be taken are indicated below.
■ Bob Brown, Chairman of the Tasmanian Wilderness Society.
■ Eric Reece, former west coast miner and trades union organiser, who rose to be Prime Minister of Tasmania, and steam-rollered all opposition to the original Lake Pedder proposals.
■ Kelvin McCoy, Chairman of the Organisation for Tasmanian Development.
■ Chairman of the Queenstown Chamber of Commerce. Queenstown is a town of 3700 population, and it stood to gain financially from its service function during the construction period of the dam.
■ Harry McDermott, councillor at Strahan, who saw road access to the lower Gordon as a threat to the Gordon River launch cruises and maintained that the period of dam-filling and dry summers would lower water levels in the Lower Gordon.

■ Representative of the World Heritage Unit, UNESCO.
■ David Bellamy, internationally renowned botanist, who manned the blockade lines at the dam site.
■ Chairman of the company supplying all earth-moving equipment to the dam site.
2 When the debate has been concluded, draw up a table to show all the arguments for and against the Gordon-under-Franklin site.
3 In early 1982 Tasmania suffered from quite high unemployment levels, and claimed that it had a power shortage (hence the need for the Gordon-under-Franklin site). Suggest a range of measures that could have been adopted by the Tasmanian Government, using the considerable sum of $276 million compensation from the Federal Government of Australia.

The Lake Manapouri controversy, South Island, New Zealand

'Manapouri was the first major environmental issue when New Zealanders indicated that they cared about and were willing to fight for the retention of a pristine natural area, whether or not they had, or intended to visit it.'

Alan Mark, public lecture 1992

Lake Manapouri and Lake Te Anau are located on the eastern side of Fiordland National Park in South Island, New Zealand (see Figure 6.8.4). Both are deep glacial lakes, bordered on the west by high forested mountains, and to the east by a strip of gently rolling sheep farming country. On the eastern side of the two lakes lie the two small rural service centres that have developed a tourist function, Manapouri and Te Anau.

In 1956 the idea of utilising the Manapouri–Te Anau water resource was put forward by the manager of the New Zealand Electricity Department. Hydro-electric power would be generated at an underground power station at West Arm, and a tailrace tunnel built to discharge the water into Deep Cove at the head of Doubtful Sound on the west coast (Figure 6.8.5). The power would be used in an aluminium smelter located at the deep water port of Bluff, on the south coast of South Island, New Zealand. The project involved the raising of the level of Lake Manapouri to the level of Lake Te Anau if the developers decided to create a single storage lake.

The level of Lake Manapouri would be raised by 8 m. Around the shores of both Lake Manapouri and Lake Te Anau a clear zonation of vegetation occurs (Figure 6.8.6). Raising of the lake level would cause serious ecological damage along about 105 km of the Te Anau shoreline. Seventeen out of 22 wooded islands would be lost in Lake Manapouri. Up to 1600 ha of lake fringe vegetation would be flooded around Lake Manapouri. Landslides and tree avalanches were more likely to occur if lake levels were raised. New beaches created at the

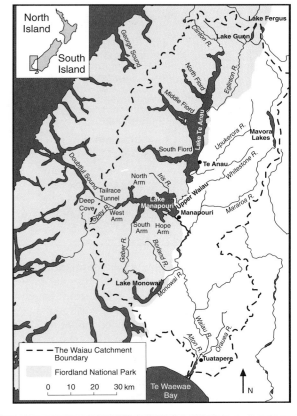

FIGURE 6.8.4 Lake Manapouri and Lake Te Anau

North Island

South Island

The Waiau Catchment Boundary

Fiordland National Park

0   10   20   30 km

N

higher level would almost certainly be unstable. Habitats for the rich bird life around the lake would be lost, and spawning areas for trout would disappear. Radical changes would occur in the regime of the Waiau River.

Local opposition to the raising of the level of Lake Manapouri resulted in the formation of the Save Manapouri Committee, as well as the Scenery Preservation Society, both of which acted as foci for the lobbying of the New Zealand Government. Save Manapouri Committees sprang up all over New Zealand, even in places as far away as Auckland. Cartoonists were quick to seize the opportunity to comment on the wave of protest over Manapouri (Figure 6.8.7).

Construction of the power station was completed in 1967, and the generators were commissioned in 1969. COMALCO, the company operating the aluminium smelter, began to operate the plant in 1971. At this stage no attempt had been made to raise the levels of the two lakes to assist power generation. A Commission of Inquiry was set up by the Government in 1970.

This Commission reported that the Crown was contractually bound to raise Lake Manapouri to 186 m and possibly by an extra 3 m. It commented unfavourably on plans to give cosmetic treatment to the new shoreline, and acknowledged the environmental impact of the scheme. In 1972 Lake Manapouri became an election issue, and it was a clear contributory factor in the defeat of the ruling National Party. The new Labour Party Minister of Electricity sent the following memo to the general Manager of the New Zealand Electricity Department: '*Lakes Manapouri and Te Anau must be held at their natural levels.*'

In the period since 1972 a body known as the Guardians of Lakes Manapouri and Te Anau has had the responsibility of devising guidelines for the lakes' management, reporting directly to the Government. The Guardians appointed were academics and prominent local people who had played an important part in the campaign.

"The view stinks but it's worth millions!"

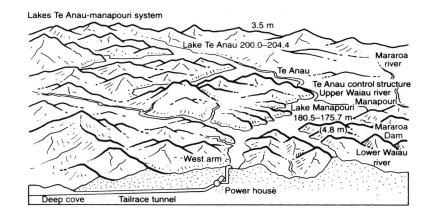

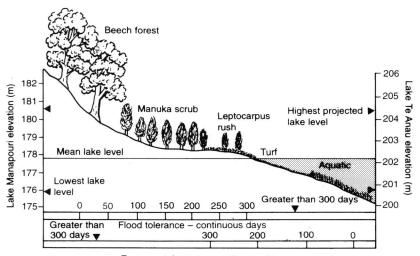

The role of the Guardians in the period between 1992 and the mid-1990s appears to have been a successful one. During this period they have advised the Government on a whole range of issues, including both high and low water levels on the lakes and pollution.

Student Activity 6.10

1 Both the Gordon-under-Franklin and Manapouri issues became heavily politicised. Discuss the reasons why environmental issues in wilderness regions have now moved into the political arena.
2 Although there are some obvious similarities between the two cases, there are some important differences. Identify what these differences are, and explain their environmental and political significance.

FIGURE 6.8.5 (*top*) Schematic view of the Te Anau-Manapouri catchment hydro-electric development

FIGURE 6.8.6 (*above*) Zonation of vegetation on Lakes Te Anau and Manapouri

FIGURE 6.8.7 (*left*) Lake Manapouri

ESSAYS

1 Environmental considerations now seem to outweigh all others in the development of resources in wilderness regions. To what extent do you agree with this statement?

2 Discuss the increasingly influential role of protest groups in decision making in wilderness resource development.

7
MANAGEMENT STRATEGIES AND THE FUTURE IN WILDERNESS REGIONS

'We are on the brink of the greatest battle mankind has ever faced, which is the battle to save our planet. In spite of some success in setting aside protected areas and saving some species and increasing public awareness of the dangers, we have not managed to get through to the place where the battle must be won, and that is in the minds and spirits and hearts of individual human beings.'

Sir Laurens van der Post, at the launch of the Wilderness Trust at the Royal Geographical Society, December 1994

KEY IDEAS

■ Wilderness awareness is increasing throughout the world, but has a particularly high profile in some countries, such as the United States and Australia.
■ International programmes of conservation are improving prospects for wilderness areas.

■ International initiatives on biodiversity have important implications for wilderness management.
■ International co-operation in wilderness management can be remarkably successful as in Antarctica.

FIGURE 7.1.1 High levels of protest in the Manapouri–Te Anau Controversy in South Island, New Zealand

Introduction

Evidence from all of the preceding chapters in this book points to the overwhelming need for well-planned and sensitive management of the world's wilderness regions. The pristine landscapes and rich ecosystems of wilderness regions are threatened in many countries by different forms of development. Examples from Alaska and Australia, from Malaysia and Kenya show that the conflict between conservation and development in wilderness regions has acquired a high profile of awareness at all levels from local to national. The conservation lobby now possesses sufficient resources and influence for it to be able to intervene when unwanted development threatens in wilderness areas (Figure 7.1.1).

Ideas, however, are changing. Increasingly conservation thinking is turning towards the concept of sustainable development in appropriate wilderness locations, as has been seen in parts of Amazonia, and in wildlife management in various African countries. There are encouraging signs too in large-scale resource development: rehabilitation of mining sites such as Rum Jungle in Northern Australia is almost complete; in New Zealand informed local bodies have shown that they can work with engineers in determining how water levels in hydro-electric developments can best be managed; ecotourism is becoming increasingly popular and even fashionable (Figure 7.1.2). However, such enlightened attitudes are not universal. Hardened attitudes still exist in the more economically developed world as the study of North Slope oil in Alaska revealed, and corruption and development still go hand-in-hand in some less economically developed countries.

The awareness of wilderness has had a high profile in countries such as the United States and Australia. In the United States the idea of wilderness ran parallel with the concept of the frontier in the developing West of the nineteenth century, and the two are interwoven in current attitudes in Alaska. In Australia, wilderness awareness is high not only because so much of the interior is still empty, but also because of the threat to relatively small areas of 'wilderness' in the heavily populated South East. It is not surprising therefore that both countries have important legislation embodied in Wilderness Acts (in Australia at State Level), which provide a framework for management. Where appropriate, as in the case of Alaska, these Wilderness Acts are amended to suit conditions within the state (Figure 7.1.3) and there special provision had to be made for the so-called (D)2 lands. In most of western Europe little true wilderness remains, and thus legislation is uncommon: here wilderness is used in a rather loose way to describe areas of high scenic value or areas with threatened ecosystems that are often protected and managed in other ways. In the less economically developed countries wilderness is

usually recognised through the existence of National Parks and Biosphere Reserves.

At the international level several bodies are involved in wilderness affairs. Prominent amongst these are the World Conservation Monitoring Centre (WCMC), and the World Conservation Union (IUCN), although their concern is not just for wilderness areas in the strictest sense. Important conventions organised by these groups allow the sharing of management issues, and commissions such as the IUCN Commission on National Parks and Protected Areas produce useful reports that attempt to set universal standards. The recently launched Wilderness Trust aims at raising levels of wilderness awareness through wilderness experience opportunities, particularly for the young. Other important initiatives include the UNESCO Man and Biosphere Programme (see Chapter 5, Section 5.3) and the World Heritage Site

FIGURE 7.1.2 Ecotourism

FIGURE 7.1.3 Moist tundra: Denali

FIGURE 7.1.4 Ecotourism or ecological imperialism?

Ecotourism or ecological imperialism?

'Ecotourism' is the buzz word in tourism. Exciting industry, government and conservationists alike, it has come to embrace 'environment-friendly', 'community-friendly' and 'market-friendly' tourism. But despite its value in raising awareness of the relationship between tourism and the environment, the term has become so abused and misused that it is little more than a worthless cliché which is probably at least as harmful as conventional forms of tourism.

Ecotourism products have become a major selling point of tourism destinations and specific tourist packages. It has a lot going for it: tourists are made to feel that they are contributing to saving the planet while having a good time in the process. And who can argue with a concept that simultaneously promotes economic development and helps to preserve the environment?

The problem, however, is that the concept of ecotourism reflects Western ideas about environmental conservation which tend to separate humankind from nature. In traditional societies, there is no division between the natural and cultural components of the landscape – the physical environment is an everyday lived-in experience. However, many advocates of tourism either ignore or fail to understand the relationship of indigenous people to their environment.

Tourism is an environmentally-dependent industry. And ecotourism is only the latest expression of this relationship. In many developing countries, Western supporters of ecotourism have focused on species preservation at the expense of indigenous peoples. Since the natural environment is a cultural resource, we should be talking of 'sustainable' tourism with its emphasis on the interrelationship between ecology, society and economy, and the role of local people in making decisions which affect their land. Any form of tourism development needs to be based not on the culture of tourists, but on the values and culture of the host community.

In his book *Ecological Imperialism: The Biological Expansion of Europe, 900–1900*, Alfred Crosby describes the sometimes forced Europeanisation of the global environment through the spread of the plant and animal species most-desired by Europeans. Today, many Europeans are seeking ways to restrain gene, species and ecosystem loss and preserve biodiversity. Ecotourism is one way of doing it.

Undoubtedly, the maintenance of biodiversity is a critical component of sustainability. But sustainable development also teaches us that the environment and the economy are integrated with society and culture. Many promoters of ecotourism have either forgotten or ignored this lesson. Perhaps, therefore, we are facing a new form of ecological imperialism in which Western cultural values are being impressed on indigenous cultures through ecotourism. To neglect the socio-cultural dimensions of development, is to completely oppose the principles of sustainability which ecotourism claims to support.

Geographical Magazine, February 1995

---

programme, which also includes important sites of outstanding cultural importance, such as the Pyramids in Egypt and the Acropolis in Athens, in addition to such locations as Kakadu, and South Western New Zealand. Important biodiversity initiatives, such as Agenda 21 at the Earth Summit in Rio in 1992 clearly have relevance to wilderness issues.

International co-operation on wilderness issues is both indirect and direct. Commissions on climatic change such as the IPCC (Intergovernmental Panel on Climatic Change) consider carbon dioxide emissions, global warming, and other forms of atmospheric pollution. Inevitably discussions cover such topics as the effect of sea level rise on wilderness wetland areas (which have their own **Ramsar** convention), and the effect of acid rain on wilderness forests. More direct co-operation is obvious in the eight nation Arctic Environmental Protection Strategy. International co-operation is seen at its most effective in the signing of the Antarctic Treaties, and the establishment of the Environmental Protocol for the Antarctic.

It is not easy to predict how environmental strategies for wilderness regions may develop in the future. Awareness of the threats to wilderness regions, and the need for management have clearly increased, and environmental pressure groups and informed public opinion have no doubt been partly responsible for this improvement. Within individual countries conservation policies will continue to be promoted at various levels from Nature and Biosphere Reserves to National Parks, with increasing emphasis on sustainable development. Wilderness-specific strategies in countries such as Australia and the United States will be further developed, with the creation and monitoring of wilderness inventories being an important feature. At the international level signs of realistic co-operation are beginning to emerge at various levels.

Student Activity 7.1

1 Study Figure 7.1.4. Comment on the views expressed in the article.

2 To what extent does the article suggest that there is a conflict between different cultures over conservation issues? How might such conflicts be resolved?

7.2 Wilderness strategy in Australia

Figure 3.7.1 on page 45 shows the major wilderness regions of Australia. Figure 7.2.1. shows the wilderness areas of South Eastern Australia.

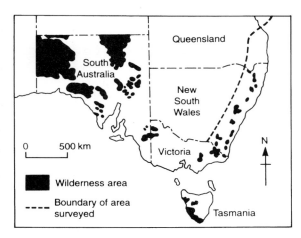

Figure 3.7.1 on page 45

Student Activity 7.2

1 Compare the methods used for showing wilderness areas.
2 Which do you consider to be the more effective? Give reasons for your answer.

The Australian Conservation Foundation considers that all wildernesses should be zoned, with a core area of at least 25 000 ha, and a buffer zone that should be roughly similar in size. Size is expected to vary: in the flat, semi-arid areas that make up much of Australia, wilderness areas would be much larger than in remote, inaccessible mountain and coastal areas. A suitable comparison might be between the vast dry expanses of the Great Victoria Desert, and the much smaller wilderness of South West Tasmania.

In 1986, the Australian Heritage Commission authorised work on the National Wilderness Inventory (NWI). This should be completed by the late 1990s. The NWI fulfils a number of roles:
■ the identification and evaluation of wilderness quality across the Australian landscape;
■ delineating wilderness areas;
■ monitoring wilderness loss;
■ defining management options;
■ predicting the effects of development on wilderness values.

It is seen as an important tool in the development of linkages between wilderness quality, biodiversity and conservation objectives. The National Red Index, a separate concern, acts as a database for all wilderness areas in Australia. A Red Index was first established in New South

FIGURE 7.2.1 (*far left*) Wilderness areas in South East Australia

FIGURE 7.2.2 Blue Mountains, South East Australia

FIGURE 7.2.3 Models of wilderness legislation in Australia

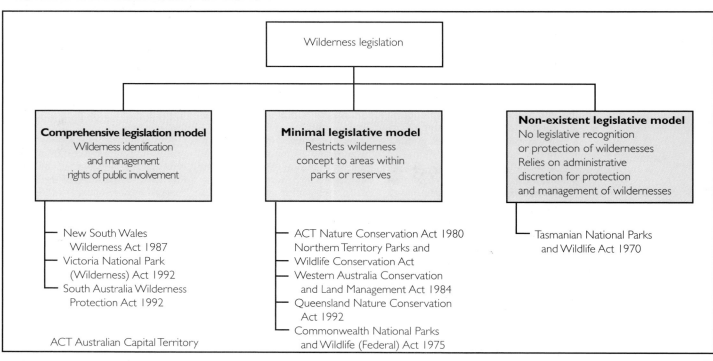

Wilderness legislation

Comprehensive legislation model
Wilderness identification and management rights of public involvement

Minimal legislative model
Restricts wilderness concept to areas within parks or reserves

Non-existent legislative model
No legislative recognition or protection of wildernesses Relies on administrative discretion for protection and management of wildernesses

— New South Wales Wilderness Act 1987
— Victoria National Park (Wilderness) Act 1992
— South Australia Wilderness Protection Act 1992

— ACT Nature Conservation Act 1980
— Northern Territory Parks and Wildlife Conservation Act
— Western Australia Conservation and Land Management Act 1984
— Queensland Nature Conservation Act 1992
— Commonwealth National Parks and Wildlife (Federal) Act 1975

— Tasmanian National Parks and Wildlife Act 1970

ACT Australian Capital Territory

Wales, but in 1993 it was decided to extend it to the whole of Australia.

Legislation to protect wilderness in Australia has been largely at the state, rather than at the national level. This is partly due to the fact that the original wilderness concept in Australia was largely focused on the recreational use of forested country in South East Australia (Figure 7.2.2). It was thus a regional, rather than a national concept. Now the concept has evolved to fully embrace the principles of ecosystem management and the protection of biodiversity. Different models of wilderness legislation exist, ranging from the comprehensive treatment of wilderness management to purely discretionary provision (see Figure 7.2.3). The legislation which provides for the most effective management strategies appears to be in place in

New South Wales (Wilderness Act, 1987), Victoria (National Parks (Wilderness) Act, 1992) and South Australia (Wilderness Protection Act, 1992).

In Western Australia and Northern Territory, where the largest areas of wilderness exist, legislation exists but belongs to the Minimal Legislative Model.

Future management strategy for wildernesses in Australia would appear to be embodied in the further development of the National Wilderness Inventory and the National Red Index. Further legislation along the lines of the New South Wales, and South Australia Acts is probably needed, particularly at the national level, although development lobbies would obviously be strongly opposed to this.

7.3 Some international initiatives

FIGURE 7.3.1 Growth of a green network

Growth of a green network

In its two decades of existence and development, the biosphere reserve concept has become widely recognised as one of the most innovative and viable means of long term biodiversity conservation.

The conservation protected areas known as biosphere reserve provide scientific knowledge, skills and human values to support the sustainable management of natural resources both within biosphere reserves themselves and in the larger regions of which they are a part. There are now 324 biosphere reserves in 82 countries. The most recent additions to the network include sites as diverse as the Cerrado Biosphere Reserve, a 226,000 hectare reserve near the Brazilian capital Brasilia encompassing a spectrum of campos-cerrados communities, and Wadi Allaqi, a 2.57 million hectare reserve in Egypt. Wadi Allaqi is a 275 kilometre-long valley running northwestwards from the Red Sea hills to the Nile Valley. A multi-disciplinary research project on sustainable development, piloted by the Faculty of Science at the University of Assiut, Aswan, includes research on fauna, flora, water, soil fertility, mineral and energy resources in this area.

The first phase of the Cerrado Biosphere Reserve includes 44 endangered or threatened animal species and 41 endangered or threatened plant species. Reserve management and a considerable research

capability are provided by the Brazilian Department of Environment, Science and Technology. An existing Brazilian biosphere reserve, the Atlantic Forest Cluster, has been extended to cover the span of the Sierra do Mar forests, with the addition of the green belt areas around São Paulo, and forests in the southeastern and northern part of the country.

Other recently designated reserves include the 420,000 hectare Archipelago Sea Area, which lies in and around southwest Finland; the island of Lanzarote in the Canaries and the 70,000-hectare Balearic island of Menorca. The latter, which had a resident population of 60,000 and accommodates between 300,000 and 500,000 tourists a year, is using the biosphere reserve concept to develop a management plan for sustainable development.

Like Menorca, Lanzarote is an 'entire island' biosphere reserve. The total land area of 73,500 hectares comprises a heavily-eroded volcanic massif rising to an altitude of 670 metres above the Atlantic Ocean. Its biosphere reserve also includes 38,000 hectares of contiguous marine systems.

The Finnish Archipelago Sea Area Biosphere Reserve incorporates a number of habitats, from coniferous forests to heaths, sandy and rocky islets, shorelines and open sea. It includes 65 endangered or threatened plant species and 29 endangered or

threatened species of animal. The Finnish National Board of Forestry, part of the Ministry of the Environment, is responsible for reserve management, and most research is carried out at the University of Turku's Archipelago Research Institute on Seili Island.

The forthcoming International Conference on Biosphere Reserves, to be held next month in Seville, will herald a significant step for the biosphere reserves network. The 300 to 400 participants will be able to take stock of progress and shortcomings in putting the biosphere reserve concept into practice. And a new phase will open for biosphere reserves, in line with the priorities identified at UNCED (United Nations Conference on Environment and Development) in Rio de Janeiro in 1992, when participants draft a new plan of action and statutes.

Narrowing the gap between the reality and potential of biosphere reserves calls for improvement of both individual reserves and of the links between them at national and international levels. A number of activities are already being undertaken to improve these links, including twinning (eg Cevennes in France and Montseny in Spain) and the development of comparative studies at a subregional level, such as those established between the biosphere reserves in five east Asian countries.

Geographical, February 1995

Biosphere Reserves

UNESCO's Man and the Biosphere Programme was referred to in Chapter 5, Section 3, with a specific examination of a wilderness Biosphere Reserve in Scotland. The programme is now nearly 25 years old.

Student Activity 7.3

The extract in Figure 7.3.1 from *Growth of a Green Network* by Dr Alison Semple indicates recent progress with the programme.
1 How far will the Biosphere programme aid future management strategies for wildernesses?
2 Which of the examples mentioned could be recognised as having a wilderness status?
3 Why do the examples chosen suggest the new emphasis on sustainable development is gaining ground?

Biodiversity initiatives

'The one process ongoing in the 1990s that will take millions of years to correct is the loss of genetic and species diversity by the destruction of natural habitats. This is the folly that our descendants are least likely to forgive us.'

E O Wilson, Harvard University, USA

International strategy for action on biodiversity involves a number of different organisations. In 1992, three of these organisations (the World Resources Institute (WRI), the World Conservation Union (IUCN), and the United Nations Environment Programme (UNEP)), in consultation with the Food and Agriculture Organisation (FAO) and UNESCO published an important document, *Global Biodiversity Strategy*. The world 'wilderness' is not mentioned in the report, but it is clear that many of the recommendations are appropriate to wilderness management.

The report proposed a seven-fold strategy for action.
1 Establishing a national policy framework for biodiversity conservation;
2 creating an international policy environment that supports national biodiversity conservation;
3 creating conditions and incentives for local biodiversity conservation;
4 managing biodiversity through the human environment;
5 strengthening protected areas;
6 conserving species, populations and genetic diversity;
7 expanding human capacity to conserve biodiversity.

The primary aim in the first instance would be the formation of an International Panel on Biodiversity Conservation. Its mode of operation is shown in the diagram Figure 7.3.4.

Countries with greatest 'species richness'
A listing of the countries with the greatest number of species reveals several patterns. Many of these countries share common characteristics: they are typically tropical, forested, less economically developed countries and several have important wilderness areas.

Mammals	Birds	Reptiles
Indonesia (515)	Colombia (1721)	Mexico (717)
Mexico (449)	Peru (1701)	Australia (686)
Brazil (428)	Brazil (1622)	Indonesia (600)
Zaire (409)	Indonesia (1519)	India (383)
China (394)	Ecuador (1447)	Colombia (383)
Peru (362)	Venezuela (1275)	Ecuador (345)
Colombia (359)	Bolivia (1250)	Peru (297)
India (350)	India (1200)	Malaysia (294)
Uganda (311)	Malaysia (1200)	Thailand (282)
Tanzania (310)	China (1195)	Papua New Guinea (282)

FIGURE 7.3.2 Species richness

FIGURE 7.3.3 Loss of habitat in selected countries

The elements of biodiversity in the Belalong Forest of Brunei were fully discussed in Chapter 4, Section 4.3. It is now important to set biodiversity in a wider global context. Figure 7.3.2 shows the countries with the greatest species richness. It will be noted that the majority of these countries are less economically developed, and most still contain a significant amount of tropical rainforest. Figure 7.3.3 shows the loss of habitat in selected countries. Although there are only two countries common to these lists, Indonesia and Malaysia both contain considerable wilderness areas, and the threat to their biodiversity is clear.

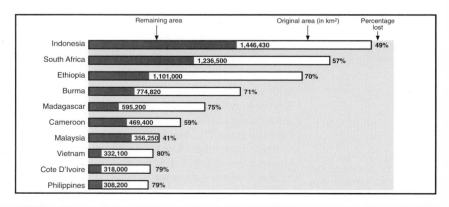

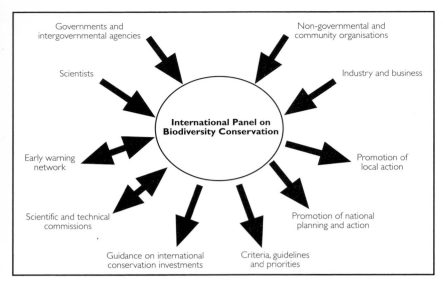

FIGURE 7.3.4 Mode of operation of international panel on biodiversity conservation

the summit seemed to polarise some important differences between the MEDCs and the LEDCs. The latter seemed to regard the conservation-minded North as forcing its system of conservation values on them, and of wanting to interfere too much in the way that the LEDCs managed their forest resources.

One recent programme, known as the debt-for-nature swap has had some effect on the maintenance of biodiversity in tropical rainforests. In such arrangements the debt-holder (the country to whom money is owed) forgives the indebted country (the one that owes the money) in exchange for the debtor country's commitment to invest in conservation projects in its own regions. Some 20 such arrangements had taken place by 1993. Such swaps may benefit countries with poor economic and environmental records. However, reservations have been expressed.

	IUCN CATEGORY I–III		IUCN CATEGORY IV–V		TOTAL	
	NUMBER	AREA (HA)	NUMBER	AREA (HA)	NUMBER	AREA (HA)
Africa	260	88 722 877	381	35 918 296	641	124 641 173
North and Central America	610	170 344 290	1073	91 415 737	1683	261 760 027
South America	289	58 190 622	291	56 182 497	580	114 373 119
Asia	410	35 397 425	1762	66 025 886	2172	101 423 311
Europe	289	8 056 879	1635	32 031 759	1924	40 088 638
Soviet Union	175	23 908 331	38	465 995	213	24 374 326
Australia and South Pacific	443	67 872 385	494	16 481 489	937	84 353 874
Antarctica	12	220 649	1	36 700	13	257 349
Total	2488	452 713 458	5675	298 558 359	8163	751 271 817

FIGURE 7.3.5 Distribution of protected areas

Figure 7.3.5 shows the distribution of protected areas under the World Conservation Union's categories I–III (Strictly Protected Areas) and IV–V (Extra-active Protected Areas, i.e. where some form of development is allowed).

Student Activity 7.4

1 Comment on the distribution of the different categories in the different continental areas shown in Figure 7.3.5.
2 What is the significance of the data in Figure 7.3.5 in terms of biodiversity conservation in wilderness areas?

Figure 7.3.6 shows the distribution of vegetation and protected areas in Madagascar.
3 Comment on the distribution of protected areas shown in Figure 7.3.6.
4 What information would you need in order to find out how effective these protected areas were?

Most of the recommendations in the Global Biodiversity Strategy document were embodied in the Biodiversity Statement in Agenda 21 at the Earth Summit in Rio de Janeiro in 1992. The estimated cost of putting all the recommendations into practice was $3.5 million, of which half would be available from the international community on grant and concession terms. Negotiations during

FIGURE 7.3.6 (far right) Distribution of protected areas and vegetation in Madagascar

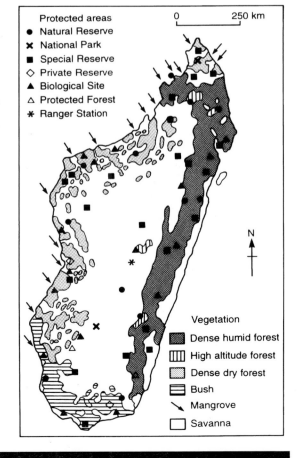

World Heritage Areas

'Over the last three million years, and more especially within the last ten thousand, our own species have increasingly set its mark on nature . . .

Wilderness and natural beauty have been in retreat before this onslaught. The retreat has accelerated within recent decades, and there is now no place on earth that has wholly escaped the mark of humanity. Conservationists everywhere have been increasingly alarmed at these transformations and are concerned to save the best of nature that remains to us.'

Martin W Holdgate, Director General, The World Conservation Union (IUCN)

UNESCO's World Heritage Convention was first discussed in the USA in 1965, and received very strong support at the ninth General Assembly of the IUCN in Lucerne in 1966. The Convention concerned with the protection of World Cultural and Natural Heritage was adopted by the General Conference of UNESCO in 1972. In 1972 there were 20 states party to the Convention: there are now well over 100. The World Heritage Committee acts on proposals from all of the state parties and is responsible for establishing the list of natural and cultural sites of outstanding value.

Although once again, 'wilderness' receives no specific mention in the criteria on which natural sites are assessed for recognition by the World Heritage Committee, many wilderness areas readily qualify for inclusion. Natural sites must fulfil the following criteria.

They should:

■ represent a major stage of the earth's evolutionary history;
■ represent an area of significant ongoing geological processes and biological evolution;
■ contain remarkable formations or areas of exceptional natural beauty;
■ contain the natural habitats of endangered species.

Once a site has been inscribed on the list, the state within which it is located must ensure that the site is protected and has to take responsibility for it on behalf of the international community.

Where the state's obligations are not being fulfilled the World Heritage Committee will remind the country of its responsibilities, and this pressure has had the required effect in the cancellation of a range of projects. The importance of the existence of World Heritage status in South West Tasmania, and in South West New Zealand have been referred to in the case studies of water resource development in these two wilderness areas.

Many important wilderness locations are listed as World Heritage Sites (see Figures 7.3.7 and 7.3.8). Most of the really extensive wilderness areas can claim World Heritage Sites, such as Alaska (the Wrangell-St Elias Mountains), the Sahara (Air-Tenere in Niger), several sites in the Zaire rainforest, and the Australian Outback (Uluru). However, there are, to date, no World Heritage Sites in northern Canada, Greenland, northern Siberia, Amazonia or the Antarctic. Future management of these wildernesses may well see important sites added to the list, although in many cases the detailed research needed for a submission still remains to be carried out in extremely remote sites.

FIGURE 7.3.7 (*far left*) Mount Cook (Aoraki)

Student Activity 7.5

1 Return to Chapters 3, 4 and 5. Explain why Uluru (Section 3.7), the Queensland rainforests (Section 4.4) and Sagarmatha (Section 5.5) are all listed as World Heritage Sites.

FIGURE 7.3.8 The Olgas (Kata Tjuta)

7.4 Antarctica: environmental protection and management

'There are those who say that Antarctica should essentially be left entirely alone, while others believe in the importance of control and constructive conservation through acquiring knowledge and understanding.'
British Antarctic Survey, A Continent for Science

Introduction

The Antarctic wilderness presents unique problems and challenges both at the present time and, more importantly, for the future. The global value of the pristine continent is unquestioned, yet serious questions remain on the forms of management most appropriate to Antarctica. The extent of the physical resources of the continent is still largely unknown, but their development raises important environmental and political questions. Territorial claims have been made by seven countries (see Figure 7.4.1), but no other country recognises these claims. Military use of the continent is banned by the Antarctic Treaty of 1959. The role of tourism has been discussed in Chapter 5, Section 5.7, and the need for studies of its environmental impact emphasised. At present though, Antarctica is still properly regarded, as the quotation implies, as a continent for science. The value of scientific research on the continent is quite unchallenged, although the issue of its possible environmental impact remains.

FIGURE 7.4.1 (*below*) Territorial claims in Antarctica

FIGURE 7.4.2 (*far right*) Temperature cycles in Antarctica

The value of Antarctica

Since it was part of the supercontinent Gondwanaland, Antarctica carries in its rocks and ice valuable evidence of 160 million years of earth history. Rock specimens from Antarctica yield valuable evidence concerning the rifting apart of Gondwanaland, and its subsequent movements. Ice cores drilled at United States and Russian scientific bases have yielded invaluable data on 150 000 years of climatic and atmospheric change. Temperature cycles of the earth have been revealed (see Figure 7.4.2): particulate matter reveals the onset of the industrial age, the use of insecticides, and nuclear testing. Recorded historic carbon dioxide and methane levels act as controls on present levels as global warming is monitored.

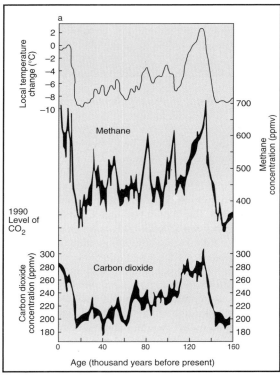

Antarctica plays a fundamental role in the heat balance of the globe. Heat flows from the equatorial 'source' to the polar 'sinks', where it is radiated into space. This flow establishes the global circulation in both the atmosphere, and the oceans. Meteorological recordings in the Antarctic first yielded the data that led to the discovery of the ozone hole over the continent. In the early 1970s scientists at Halley Bay base were recording substantial losses in ozone, and by 1993 levels had dropped to 70 per cent of the 1960s level. Ozone

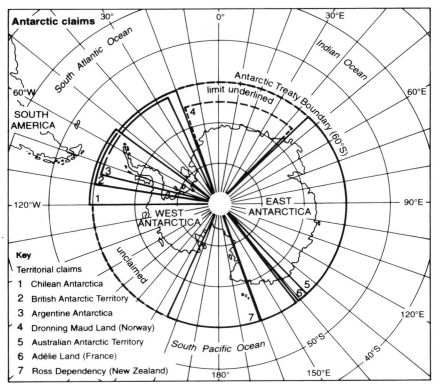

Antarctic claims

Key
Territorial claims
1 Chilean Antarctica
2 British Antarctic Territory
3 Argentine Antarctica
4 Dronning Maud Land (Norway)
5 Australian Antarctic Territory
6 Adélie Land (France)
7 Ross Dependency (New Zealand)

level recordings from the Antarctic provided crucial evidence, which led to the signing of the Montreal Protocol in 1987, when signatories agreed to a progressive elimination of **CFCs** by the year 2000. The Antarctic thus becomes the earth's 'early warning system' for any atmospheric climatic and temperature anomalies.

The importance of the Antarctic marine ecosystem has been fully discussed in Chapter 4 (Section 4.7) and BIOMASS (Biological Investigations of Marine Antarctic Systems and Stocks) has focused scientific research into the ecosystem over a period of 15 years from 1976 to 1991. As a result of this research, the BIOMASS Data Centre was established.

Antarctica has been described as a 'Laboratory for Diplomacy'. Although the seven territorial claims in the Antarctic have never been recognised, the continent has promoted a considerable degree of international co-operation. International Polar Years were held in 1882–3 and 1932–3, and a third proposal was expanded into the International Geophysical Year (1957) which attracted 12 countries to the Antarctic and led to the setting up of 48 new observation stations. Its most important spin-off was probably political in that it convinced participating countries that co-operation was both desirable and possible. Two years later the Antarctic Treaty was signed.

Student Activity 7.6

1 A 'continent for science', and 'a laboratory for diplomacy'.

Write a short summary showing how both of these positions on Antarctica have been justified.
2 On what grounds might these justifications be challenged?

Threats to Antarctica

Antarctica is threatened from two sources, those resulting from activities outside of the continent, and those from within. Briefly, external threats seem to be on two levels. Insecticides, such as DDT, were recorded in Antarctic penguins in 1966: the compounds have entered the Antarctic food chain from aerial routes. **Radionuclides** have been identified in snow samples, and are derived from nuclear explosions many thousands of kilometres from the Antarctic. Neither of these contaminants appear to pose a serious threat to the Antarctic. Much more serious are the effects of global warming, and the appearance of the ozone hole over the Antarctic. Global warming could upset the stability of the ice shelves, and the increased ultra-violet light entering the atmosphere as a result of ozone depletion may damage Antarctic flora and fauna.

Perhaps the two most obvious internal threats to Antarctica are those from the development of its physical resources, and from tourism.

Relatively little is known about the mineral resources of Antarctica. Geologists have only accurately mapped about 10 per cent of the ice-free area, and only 1 per cent has been surveyed for minerals. It is reasonable to assume the existence of commercial mineral resources in Antarctica, on the basis of current geological knowledge of deposits (see Figure 7.4.3), and on the assumption that, since other parts of Gondwanaland such as Australia and South Africa have considerable mineral wealth, Antarctica must be similarly well-endowed. For instance, the Dufek complex in Antarctica appears to be very similar geologically to the Bushveld complex in South Africa, which is internationally important for a wide range of minerals. So far geological research has failed to justify the original overoptimistic view of Antarctica's mineral wealth. It would appear that physical, technological and conservation factors will, in the short term make developments unlikely. Hydrocarbons might prove attractive, if the resource proved to be large enough. The 50-year ban on mining in the Antarctic is discussed in the next section.

FIGURE 7.4.3 Mineral resources in Antarctica

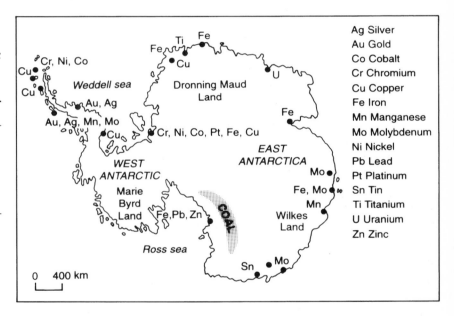

Tourism has been fully treated in Section 5.7, and it has been noted that, until proper environmental impact studies have been carried out, it is unlikely that a full assessment of its likely effect will be available.

Some discussion has arisen over the extent to which scientific research poses a threat to the Antarctic environment. It is probably true that some of the early research stations did not show as much concern for the environment as they might have done. Penguin eggs were collected for food, seal meat was fed to the dogs, and rubbish disposal was undisciplined and haphazard. However, such lack of awareness has now been eliminated and newer stations are models of environmental responsibility. Environmental Protocol (see the following section) now enforces a strict code of conduct on all scientific bases.

Managing Antarctica: the Treaty System

FIGURE 7.4.4 The Antarctic Treaty

The Antarctic Treaty – a summary

ARTICLE I: Antarctica shall be used for peaceful purposes only. All military activities, including weapons testing, are prohibited. However military personnel and equipment may be used for scientific purposes.

ARTICLE II: Freedom of scientific research and cooperation shall continue.

ARTICLE III: Scientific information, personnel, results and research plans shall be freely exchanged and international cooperation encouraged.

ARTICLE IV: The Treaty and any activities carried out under it do not endorse, support or deny any territorial claim. No new claims shall be made while the Treaty is in force. No member state is required to recognise any other's territorial claim.

ARTICLE V: Nuclear explosions and the disposal of radioactive waste are prohibited.

ARTICLE VI: The Treaty applies to all land and ice shelves below 60°S, but not the high seas, which are subject to international law.

ARTICLE VII: Any member state may send observers, with due notice, to inspect any station, installation or equipment. All members shall give notice of expeditions, stations and military personnel and equipment active in Antarctica.

ARTICLE VIII: Observers and scientists shall be under the jurisdiction of their own states.

ARTICLE IX: Member states shall meet periodically to exchange information and take measures to further Treaty objectives, including the conservation of living resources. Meetings shall be open to member states that conduct substantial scientific research in Antarctica.

ARTICLE X: Member states will discourage any activity by any nation which is contrary to the Treaty.

ARTICLE XI: Disputes are to be settled by negotiation, or ultimately by the International Court of Justice.

ARTICLE XII: After 30 years, any member state may request a review of the operation of the Treaty.

ARTICLE XIII: The Treaty is open to any member of the United Nations, or by invitation of all the member states.

ARTICLE XIV: The United States is the repository of the Treaty and is responsible for providing copies to all member states.

The Antarctic Treaty was signed in 1959 by 12 nations. Its 14 articles (see Figure 7.4.4) lay down a series of guidelines for the present and future management of Antarctica. Article 1 sets the scene: *'Antarctica shall be used for peaceful purposes only. There shall be prohibited any measure of a military nature, such as the establishment of military bases or fortifications, the carrying out of military manoeuvres, as well as the testing of any type of weapon.'* It further states that: *'it is in the interest of all mankind that Antarctica shall be used for ever for peaceful purposes and shall not become the scene or object of international discord'.* Article IV makes this possible by freezing all existing territorial claims, without commenting on their validity, and prohibits any future claims. By 1994 there were 42 signatories to the Treaty.

Attempts were made to introduce guidelines for the management of mineral resources in Antarctica, and in 1988, 19 countries signed CRAMRA (Convention on the Regulation of Antarctic Mineral Resources Activity). Organisations such as Greenpeace fought hard to ban all mining activities in the continent, and establish a World Park, with full protection for wildlife, and restriction of activities to peaceful scientific research. Greenpeace established its own World Park base in 1987, devoted exclusively to Antarctic Research and preservation. In the event, Australia and France decided not to sign the CRAMRA documents, largely on the grounds of unsatisfactory arrangements for royalty payments, and inadequate environmental controls.

Australia and France then proposed a comprehensive conservation convention. In 1991 the Protocol to the Antarctic Treaty on Environmental Protection was signed in Madrid. It declares Antarctica to be a natural reserve devoted to peace and scientific research, and bans all mineral activity except research. It is worth recording the details of the agreement.

The Protocol:
■ designates Antarctica as a natural reserve, devoted to peace and science;
■ sets out the principles for environmental protection;
■ elaborates mandatory rules in five annexes:
  i) Environmental Impact Assessment;
  ii) Conservation of Wildlife;
  iii) Waste disposal and Management;
  iv) Prevention of marine pollution;
  v) Protected areas system within Antarctica.
With regard to minerals the Protocol provides for:
■ a ban on mineral resource activity (other than scientific research);
■ mechanisms for the review of the ban after 50 years or before if all Treaty Parties agree;
■ continuation of the ban unless or until there are

rules in place under which a decision can be taken as to whether mining is environmentally acceptable.

In summary the Antarctic Treaty is underwritten by five international agreements.

1 Agreed measures for the Conservation of Antarctic Flora and Fauna (1964).

2 Convention for the Conservation of Antarctic Seals (1972).

3 Convention on the Conservation of Antarctic Marine Living Resources (CCAMLR) (1980).

4 Convention on the regulation of Antarctic Mineral Resources Activities (CRAMRA) (1988).

5 Protocol on Environmental Protection to the Antarctic Treaty (1991).

ESSAYS

1 Discuss the effectiveness of current management strategies in wilderness regions.

2 'Problems of management in wilderness regions become more difficult as the scale increases.' How far do you agree with this statement?

Glossary

Albedo the ratio between the amount of radiation falling on a surface, and the amount reflected, the average albedo of the earth is 0.34.

Arkose feldspar-rich sandstone.

Autonomy a degree of self-government.

Autonomous Okrug region with a degree of self-government within the Russian Federation.

Baleen whale group of whales that feed on **zooplankton** by straining sea water through baleen plates attached to their jaws.

Basal metabolic rate rate at which calories are consumed in basic body functions.

Bauxite the principal ore of aluminium.

Biodiversity the variety of species within biological communities.

Biome a major climatic climax community of plants and animals, usually a climatic region.

Bornhardt a steep-sided erosion remnant (**inselberg**).

Caldera enlarged crater in volcano that has lost much of its superstructure through a catastrophic explosion.

Carrying capacity maximum intensity of use that resource can sustain without unacceptable damage to that resource.

CFC chlorofluorocarbon, or chlorine-based compounds that have long residence times in the lower atmosphere.

Clear cut logging method of felling where all trees are removed.

Conglomerate sedimentary rock containing rounded fragments of other rocks.

Conduit passage that leads from the underground reservoir of water to the surface (in a geyser).

Continuum structure with a continuous pattern.

Corrie glacier small glacier that occupies corrie (large hollow) in glacial upland.

Cordilheiras patches of higher ground, above flood level, in the Pantanal.

Degree day measure of total daily amount by which the main daily temperature departs from a critical temperature (e.g. minimum temperature for plant growth).

Dipterocarp important species of giant tree in tropical rainforest.

Dolerite medium-grained basic igneous rock.

Feral animals wild or untamed animals.

Firn line uppermost line on glacier to which previous winter snowfall melts during summer.

Frost blister small upthrust of surface layer caused by frost heave.

Gene pool the sum of all genes and hereditary information that a species population possesses.

Gneiss banded high grade metamorphic rock.

Gondwanaland ancient continent that rifted apart to form the present southern Continents.

Hummock small surface mounds developed under a periglacial climate, with a core of mineral soil or stones.

Hypoxia deficiency of oxygen reaching the tissues, the result of living and working at high altitudes, where there is a shortage of oxygen.

Inlier area of older rocks completely surrounded by younger rocks.

Inselberg see **bornhardt**.

Interpretive presentation information concerning a locality presented in a manner that can be understood by the lay person.

Inter-Tropical Convergence Zone (ITCZ) zone of converging air masses in the tropics, normally associated with rainfall.

Krill small Antarctic crustaceans.

Mesozoic major era in geological time from 230 million years before present to 65 million years before present.

Micro-continental plate small tectonic plates resulting from excessive fracturing of the earth's crust (lithosphere).

Mutations genetic change which gives rise to heritable variations.

Niche the role of a species in its habitat.

Nunatak isolated rocky peak that protrudes above ice sheet.

Old growth original trees in a forest zone.

Palaeozoic major era of geological time from 600 million years before present to 230 million years before present.

Particulate matter dust and similar sized material in the atmosphere.

Patterned ground approximately symmetrical forms found in that part of periglacial zone which is subjected to intense frost action.

Periglacial climate, processes and features in zone bordering ice-sheets.

Permafrost area of permanently frozen ground.

Photosynthesis process by which plants combine carbon dioxide and water to form organic compounds, using the energy from sunlight.

Phytoplankton microscopic marine plant organisms that float on water.

Pleistocene geological period, regarded as being loosely equivalent to the Ice Age.

Polycyclic showing evidence of more than one cycle in its evolution.

Pre-Cambrian the oldest period of geological time, including all rocks formed before 600 million years ago. It is thought to have lasted up to 4000 million years.

Quartzite sedimentary or metamorphic rock rich in quartz.

Radionuclide nucleus of atom derived from radioactive decay.

Ramsar Convention convention on wetlands of international importance.

Sastrugi surface irregularities in Arctic and Antarctic snowfields created by wind scour.

Schist medium-grained rock resulting from regional metamorphism.

Sieving technique the use of a series of transparent maps superimposed on one another in order to clarify distributions.

Silviculture branch of forestry involved in the growing and tending of trees.

Skidoo small motorised vehicle used on snow-covered surfaces.

Solifluction slow downward movement of waste material saturated with water in periglacial regions.

Stomata pores in the surface of a leaf.

Stripes a type of patterned ground found in periglacial regions, where stripes of stones are found running down the steepest slopes, separated by finer materials.

Taiga coniferous forest zone that lies between the temperate grasslands and the tundra.

Tertiary era of geological time that lasted from 65 million years before present to 2 million years before present.

Thermokarst ground surface depressions that result from thawing of ground-ice in periglacial regions.

Trophic structure series of levels at which energy is transferred from one organism to another in an ecosystem.

Wadi deeply cut valley in desert region.

Zooplankton minute marine animal organisms floating in the sea.

Index